TREKKING IN THE HIMALAYA

Descending from Manidingma to the Dudh Kosi, the trail winds below terraces with Kusum Kangguru ahead (Trek 14)

TREKKING IN THE HIMALAYA

edited by Kev Reynolds

Contributors

Steve Berry, Bob Gibbons, Stephen Goodwin,

Bart Jordans, Siân Pritchard-Jones, Steve Razzetti,

Kev Reynolds and Chris Townsend

2 POLICE SQUARE, MILNTHORPE, CUMBRIA LA7 7PY
www.cicerone.co.uk

First edition 2013
ISBN: 978 1 85284 605 3

Photographs are by the authors of the chapters in which they appear, unless otherwise credited.

Maps © OpenStreetMap contributors, CC-BY-SA.
NASA terrain courtesy of Esri. ASTER GDEM is a product of METI and NASA.

 Cartography by Lovell Johns www.lovelljohns.com.

Printed by KHL Printing, Singapore.
A catalogue record for this book is available from the British Library.

Acknowledgements

I am immensely grateful to my fellow authors whose words and photographs reflect the joy of trekking and the glories of the Himalaya; their enthusiasm for this project made it a pleasure and a privilege to work with them. For additional help with photographs I am indebted to Meikel Beek, John Earle and Barbara Roberts. Publisher and fellow trekker Jonathan Williams shares our love of the Himalaya, which was an added bonus when planning this book; my thanks to him and to his talented team in Milnthorpe for producing the attractive volume before you, especially my editor, Sue Viccars, and designer, Clare Crooke. For his company and practical support on numerous treks, thanks to my good friend Kirken Sherpa in Kathmandu, and to the countless unnamed Sherpas and porters without whom many of my more remote travels would never have succeeded. To my wife, and the many friends who have trekked with me and shared both sunshine and storm in the mountains, my thanks for your patience and good humour. Limited space restricts my naming everyone – but you'll know who you are. Danyabaat!

Kev Reynolds

Thanks to Andrew Bailey, Meikel Beek, Jackie Fitzpatrick, Kenneth Hanson, Malcolm McDonald and Susan Passoni.

Bart Jordans

Thanks to Ravi Chandra Hamal, Pasang Dawa Sherpa, Mingma Sherpa and Christine Miqueu-Baz.

Siân Pritchard-Jones and Bob Gibbons

Front cover: Having crossed the Larkya La on the Manaslu Circuit, trekkers descend to Bimtang (Trek 12) (photo: Kev Reynolds)

Back cover: The Hispar Pass in the heart of the Karakoram (Trek 2) (photo: Steve Razzetti)

Map Key

━━━━━━	Major road
══════	Minor road
═══════	Track
··············	Route
●●●●●●●●	Alternative route
─ ─ ─ ─	National boundary
────────	River
⬭	Lake
	Woodland

	Glacier
⊕	Airport/airstrip
○	Village/camp
●	Bridge
⚪	Large town
▲	Peak
⋈	Pass
⏏	Gompa
⟶	Direction arrow

Advice to Readers

While every effort is made by our authors to ensure the accuracy of guidebooks as they go to print, changes can occur during the lifetime of an edition. If we know of any, there will be an Updates tab on this book's page on the Cicerone website (www.cicerone.co.uk), so please check before planning your trip. Be aware that the political situation in the country you intend to visit can change at any time, and have a major impact on your plans. It is therefore prudent to keep abreast of developments and check government websites for your own safety. The Foreign and Commonwealth Office (FCO) provides regularly updated travel guidance (www.fco.gov.uk/travel). Should they advise against visiting an area and you choose to ignore that advice, your travel insurance is likely to become invalid. We also advise that you check information about such things as transport, accommodation and local facilities. We are always grateful for information about any discrepancies between a guidebook and the facts on the ground, sent by email to info@cicerone.co.uk or by post to Cicerone, 2 Police Square, Milnthorpe LA7 7PY, United Kingdom.

Directly above Samdo, the highest village on the Manaslu Circuit, a steep acclimatisation hike gives stunning views downvalley (Trek 12) (photo: Kev Reynolds)

CONTENTS

ABOUT THE AUTHORS

Steve Berry was born in Shillong, India just south of the Bhutanese border, and has returned to the Himalaya many times as a leader of remote treks and expeditions. These include the first British ascent of Nun (7135m) in Kashmir, and attempts on the sixth-highest mountain in the world, Cho Oyu (8201m) in Nepal, and also Gangkar Punsum in Bhutan (at 7550m still the world's highest unclimbed peak). He is the owner of Mountain Kingdoms Ltd (formerly Himalayan Kingdoms), a company offering walking holidays worldwide, and is a co-founder of Wilderness Lectures in Bristol. He has written two books previously: *Kingdom of the Thunder Dragon*, published by Crowood Press, and *Straight Up* published by Himalayan Kingdoms in 2012. The former tells the story of the first, and only, British expedition to attempt Bhutan's highest mountain. The latter is a collection of stories from some of Steve's expeditions.

Stephen Goodwin is a freelance journalist and editor of the prestigious *Alpine Journal*, the oldest mountaineering journal in the world. In 1999, after 25 years as a staff journalist on *The Times* and then *The Independent*, he exchanged the turbulence of Fleet Street and politics in 'the Westminster village' for the subtler currents of Cumbria's Eden Valley. When not tempted from his desk by the crags of the nearby Lake District, most days are devoted to the *AJ*, which he has edited since 2004, and writing about mountain matters, the environment and just a dash of politics. A climber and ski-mountaineer, he got his first taste of the Himalaya in 1998, on a dream assignment, and reached the south summit of Everest, filing an award-winning diary to *The Independent*. Since then he has returned to the Himalaya most years as well as climbing, trekking and ski-touring in the Alps, Andes and Turkey. Happy sharing his enthusiasms with others, he enjoys leading trekking and climbing groups for Mountain Kingdoms. In 2009 he published a guide to *Day Walks in the Lake District* (Vertebrate), and has recently edited books by climbers Ron Fawcett and Simon Yates.

Bart Jordans has been guiding and exploring treks and trekking peaks in the Himalaya, Karakoram, Hindu Kush, European Alps and on Kilimajaro since 1984. Originally from Holland, he lived for four-and-a-half years in the Himalayan kingdom of Bhutan, and for two years in Vietnam, but is now settled in Copenhagen. He caught the bug for mountain activities early in life when his parents took the family to either the Swiss or Austrian Alps each year, and with his brother he later trekked and climbed throughout the Alpine range. From Amsterdam he would regularly visit Belgium for rock climbing, as well as the UK. Having travelled widely throughout the world, Bart is the author of the acclaimed *Bhutan: A Trekker's Guide* (Cicerone Press) – a finalist at Canada's 2006 Banff Mountain Book Festival – and he also recently contributed the section on the Kangshung Face trek for Kev Reynolds' trekking guide to Everest. Bart is a freelance guide for several well-known trekking companies. When not in the mountains he works in the outdoor gear business and writes articles mainly on the mountains of Bhutan, of which he is a noted expert. Visit www.bhutantreks.com.

Siân Pritchard-Jones and **Bob Gibbons** met in 1983 on a trek from Kashmir to Ladakh. By then, Bob had already driven overland trucks across Asia, Africa and South America. He also worked with trekking groups in Kathmandu. Siân worked in computer programming but was drawn back to the Himalaya after her first trek, the Annapurna Circuit, en route from working in New Zealand. Since then they have been leading and organising treks in the Alps, Himalaya and the Sahara, and overland trips to Nepal. Journeys in their Land Rover from England to South Africa provided the basis for several editions of the Bradt guide, *Africa Overland*. Each winter they work for various publishers in Kathmandu, where they have written

guides on the Kathmandu Valley, Ladakh and Tibet. For Cicerone they wrote the guide to Mount Kailash and Western Tibet, as well as updating the Grand Canyon guide. During 2011 they revisited Tibet, this time driving the same old Land Rover back from Kathmandu to the UK overland via Lhasa, Kazakhstan, Russia and across Europe. It was with great relish that they returned to one of their former trekking haunts in Nepal – the Annapurna region – for the new Cicerone guide.

Steve Razzetti has wide-ranging experience of the Himalayan regions and a special affinity with the mountains of Pakistan. In May 1986 he joined Simon Yates and several other friends on a mountaineering expedition to the Hushe Valley in the Karakoram. The following year he led his first trekking group in the area, taking a group to K2 Base Camp and Concordia with mountaineer Doug Scott. The people and mountains of Pakistan's wild northern areas made such an impression on him that he spent the next 16 summers there, only taking a break when the tragic events of 9/11 temporarily ended mountain travel in the country. He played an instrumental role in developing new and exciting routes for commercial trekking in Pakistan, exploring and leading reconnaissance trips throughout the Karakoram and Hindu Kush. Steve is the author of *Trekking & Climbing in Nepal* and *Top Treks of the World* (New Holland) and *Pakistan Zindabad!* (available through his page on the Blurb online bookstore: www.blurb.com). His articles have appeared widely in the geographical and mountaineering press, and his photographic images are distributed by agencies such as Getty Images and the RGS Picture Library. He lives with his family in Cumbria.

Kev Reynolds, the contributing editor of this book, has enjoyed a lifetime's passion for mountains, which has taken him to some of the world's most exciting places. He first trekked in the Himalaya as a journalist in the late 1980s, and has since made numerous visits to Nepal, Sikkim, Bhutan and Ladakh, often leading treks for both private groups and the well-known UK-based Mountain Kingdoms, or making exploratory journeys with Sherpa friends. A member of the Alpine Club, Austrian Alpine Club and the Outdoor Writers' and Photographers' Guild, Kev has written 50 books, including guides to five major trekking regions of Nepal, and to numerous routes in the European Alps and Pyrenees, all of which have been published by Cicerone Press. His latest book, *A Walk in the Clouds*, is a collection of autobiographical short stories recording 50 years of mountain travels and adventures. When not trekking or writing about mountains, he can be found travelling around the British Isles sharing his enthusiasm for the world's wild places through his lectures.

Chris Townsend is an outdoor writer and photographer whose 19 books include *Scotland* in Cicerone's World Mountain Ranges series, the award-winning *The Backpacker's Handbook*; *Grizzly Bears and Razor Clams*, the story of his hike along the Pacific Northwest Trail; *A Year in the Life of the Cairngorms*, a photographic study, and *The Munros and Tops*, an account of his continuous round of all the 3000ft summits in Scotland – the first time this walk had been done. A passionate long-distance walker, Chris's other epic walks include the 2600-mile Pacific Crest Trail, 1600 miles along the whole length of the Canadian Rockies (another first), 1000 miles south–north through the Yukon Territory, and 1300 miles south–north through Norway and Sweden. He has also led ski tours in Norway, Spitsbergen, Greenland, Lapland and other areas, as well as treks in Nepal. Chris is involved with several outdoor and conservation organisations and served as President of the Mountaineering Council of Scotland. He writes on outdoor subjects every month for *TGO* magazine, and has a blog at www.christownsendoutdoors.com. He lives in Strathspey in the Cairngorms National Park.

In the Langtang Valley, Gangchempo makes an impressive backdrop to the kharka of Jatang (Trek 13) (photo: Kev Reynolds)

OVERVIEW OF ROUTES

Each trek has been rated according to difficulty within the following guidelines:
- gentle: 5–9 days on well-made paths at a modest altitude; suitable for first-time trekkers
- moderate: 10–15 days at a modest altitude, but with a pass crossing as a highlight
- demanding: 15–21 days of strenuous trekking with some exposure and one or more passes of 4000–5000m to cross; suitable for experienced trekkers
- expedition: these routes lead the experienced trekker into another dimension; long, hard days in remote country and with the chance of glacier crossings that may require the use of ice axe, crampons and ropes.

Where a trek's classification falls between these categories either a + sign is given to indicate a higher level of difficulty, or two grades have been amalgamated. The table below lists all 20 treks in order of increasing difficulty, showing their approximate total distances, maximum altitude reached and estimated length in days.

Trek	Distance	Max Altitude	Duration	Grade
Nanga Parbat	Various	5377m	4–16 days	Gentle/Moderate/Demanding
Kangchenjunga: Singalila Ridge and Goecha La	90km and 80km	3636 and 4940m	6 and 7 days	Gentle and Moderate+
Langtang and Helambu	160km	4610m	14+ days	Moderate
Everest Base Camp	195km	5623m	14–28 days	Moderate/Demanding
Annapurna Sanctuary	84–100km	4130m	10–12 days	Moderate/Demanding
Mount Kailash Kora	55–60km	5660m	4 days	Demanding
Annapurna Circuit	200km	5416m	21 days	Demanding
Manaslu Circuit	200km	5135m	21 days	Demanding
Makalu Base Camp	200km	4870m	18 days	Demanding
Everest: Kangshung Face	80km	5350m	10–11 days	Demanding
Kangchenjunga: North and South Base Camps	210–250km	5140m	20–23 days	Demanding
Zanskar Dream Trek	275km	5216m	22 days	Demanding
Inner Dolpo: Shey Gompa	220km	5300m	21 days	Demanding
Lower Dolpo: from Juphal to Jumla	190km	5320m	20 days	Demanding
Dhaulagiri Circuit	95km	5334m	14–16 days	Demanding
Gangkar Punsum Base Camp	160km	5200m	16 days	Demanding
Lunana Snowman Trek	350km	5345m	28 days	Demanding
Nanda Devi Sanctuary	80km	4724m	7–11 days	Expedition
K2 and Concordia	180km	4700m	18 days	Expedition
Snow Lake	180km	5151m	16–20 days	Expedition

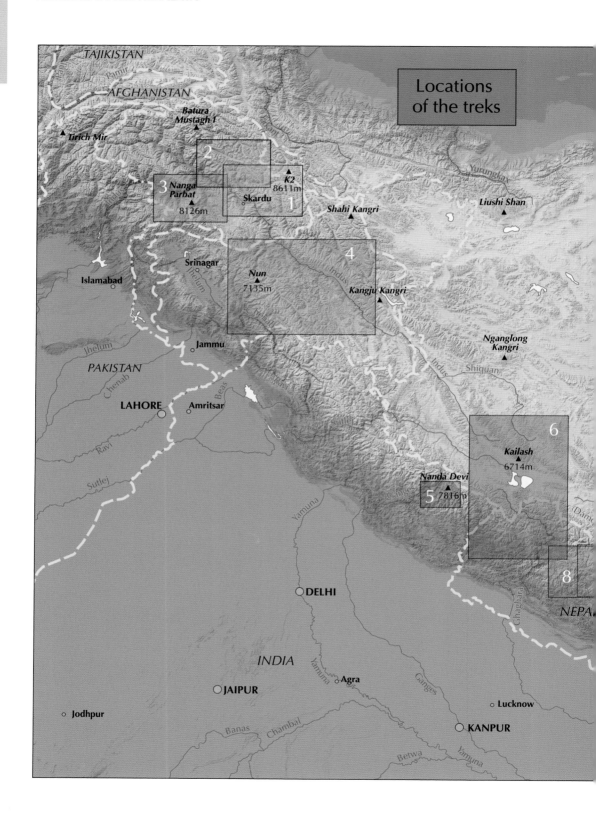

Locations of the treks

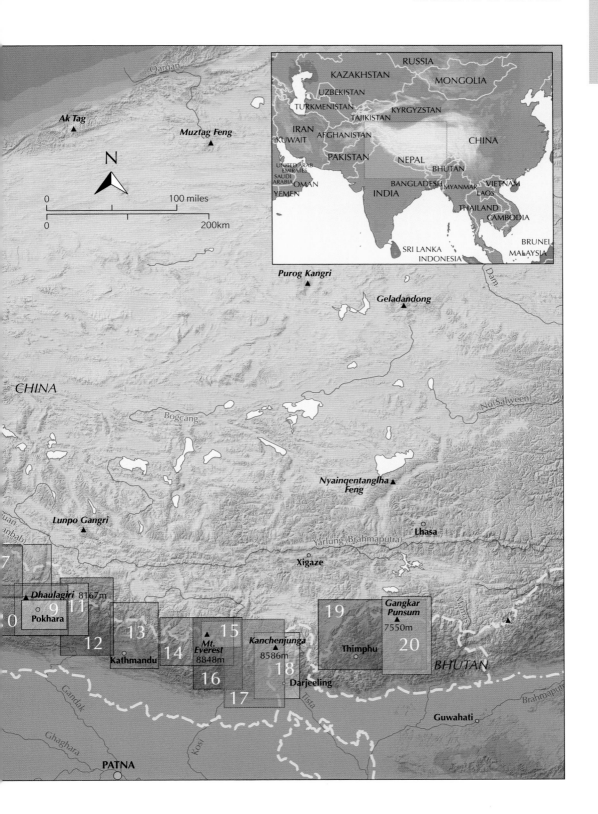

INTRODUCTION

*Crossing a temporary bridge over a Himalayan river is one way to experience
the 'now' of living in the moment (photo: Kev Reynolds)*

Trekking is addictive. Ask anyone who has been to the Himalaya on the 'trek of a lifetime' and it's odds on they'll be planning a return. Dreamers are what we become; eyes have a distant glaze and the pulse quickens as memories are drawn into focus with a host of experiences crowding the dreams of day and night to demand a repeat visit. One trip is clearly not enough; that trek of a lifetime is just the first of many. Ask the authors of this book, each one having been drawn back time and again; their accumulated experience is staggering.

So be warned. This book will feed your unrest.

The simplest things in life often spawn the greatest pleasures, and of all physical activities, trekking is surely one of the simplest. After all, it consists of the basic act that most of us master during childhood; that of putting one foot in front of the other – going for a walk. A long walk, it's true, but a walk nonetheless.

But it's what happens during that walk that elevates the experience to what one of our authors refers to as a 'meditation'. Put that down to environment, the country through which the journey leads – its challenge, its beauty, the sense of wonder it inspires; and the people of that country with their culture, hospitable nature, and their other-worldliness – all these impact on the sensitive trekker. We seek experience to take us out of our everyday lives, and each day on trek produces abundant opportunities to do just that. Life is instantaneous, there is neither past nor future, only the NOW of living in the present.

In 1949 Bill Tilman, one of the greatest of Himalayan explorers, summarised its appeal when he wrote: 'I felt I could go on like this for ever, that life had little better to offer than to march day after day in an unknown country to an unattainable goal'.

Much of the Himalaya is no longer unknown. Uninhabited valleys have been explored, passes crossed, summits reached. Maps of varying quality have been drawn, guidebooks published, and the boom in adventure travel has made accessible many places that only a generation ago would have been beyond the means and dreams of all but a select few adventurers. Accessible, yes: but they're still remote and it takes effort and determination to reach them. Therein lies some of the appeal and much of the reward of trekking.

ABOUT THIS BOOK

The Himalaya stretches for approximately 2400 kilometres between the Indian subcontinent and the Tibetan plateau. No matter how many treks you cram into your active years, one lifetime will never be enough to experience it all. So we've selected 20 routes of varying lengths and degrees of difficulty to provide a sample of what's possible or, in certain cases, what's currently not possible but will hopefully one day receive the green light of bureaucratic approval. But be aware that at any time – and with little prior warning – political decisions can limit or deny access to any of the treks in this book.

Beginning in the stark yet beguiling mountains of Pakistan where the Karakoram overlaps the western end of the Himalaya, we visit the base camp of K2 and tread glacial highways leading to Snow Lake, before taking a handful of approach routes to Nanga Parbat above the Indus River. We then move into India where the high-altitude, trans-Himalayan desert lands of Ladakh and Zanskar claim a romantic backdrop to a dream trek, contrasting the lush

highlands and glaciers of Garwhal and Kumaon where a hint may be gained of the (currently forbidden) Nanda Devi Sanctuary.

North of the border, in Tibet, Mount Kailash is revered as the centre of the universe, a sacred mountain to Hindu and Buddhist alike. Making a kora (or circuit) of this 6714m monolith is both a challenging trek and a route towards spiritual cleansing.

Not surprisingly, Nepal has the lion's share of treks in this collection. These begin with two routes in the hidden land of Dolpo; the first to Shey Gompa, made famous in Peter Matthiessen's classic book, *The Snow Leopard*; the second being a traverse of Lower Dolpo via a series of high passes. Dolpo is largely protected by Dhaulagiri, the most westerly of Nepal's 8000m peaks, which boasts a tough yet rewarding circuit for trekkers to consider.

Dhaulagiri overlooks the Kali Gandaki's valley, whose eastern side is dominated by the Annapurna massif. The ever-popular Annapurna Circuit, and the shorter yet equally dramatic trek into the Annapurna Sanctuary are both described. But then we look at the exquisite Manaslu Circuit located a short distance to the east, which sees far fewer trekkers than its illustrious neighbour, but is every bit as exciting.

Langtang and Helambu are the nearest mountain districts to Kathmandu. Totally different from one another, they're linked by a splendid route that includes the holy lakes of Gosainkund and the crossing of the Laurebina La.

It would be impossible to ignore the highest of all the high mountains, and Mount Everest receives attention here from both the Nepalese side and from Tibet. The first concentrates on the long walk in from Jiri in the foothills, and

The view from Kala Pattar is incomparably better than that from Everest Base Camp. Here the southwest face of Everest is revealed (Trek 14) (photo: Kev Reynolds) ▶

A row of chortens at Upper Pangboche directs the way towards Everest (Trek 14) (photo: Kev Reynolds)

includes several high route variations; the second approaches the eastern, or Kangshung Face of the mountain, where several outstanding peaks vie for attention.

Two other 8000ers dominate eastern Nepal: Makalu and Kangchenjunga. The strenuous trek to Makalu's base camp begins in the steamy lowlands of the Arun's valley, a valley partly contained by a foothill ridge along which the approach to Kangchenjunga's North and South base camps begins. A verdant landscape of woods and terraced fields is later exchanged for the raw beauty of glaciers, glacial lakes and old moraines.

So dominant is it of eastern Nepal and neighbouring Sikkim, that Kangchenjunga was once thought to be the world's highest mountain. With Darjeeling the springboard to adventure, it is admired on two other short treks described in a single chapter covering the Singalila Ridge and the trek to Dzongri and the Goecha La.

Finally, our geographic reach embraces Bhutan, perhaps the least known of all Himalayan countries, but one with a rich cultural heritage and a beauty all its own. Edging its western and northern borders, the Lunana Snowman Trek is the longest in this book, while the trek to the base camp of Gangkar Punsum (Bhutan's highest peak and the world's highest unclimbed summit) is described by the man who led one of the very few attempts to climb it.

So, 20 treks spread across the Himalayan range should provide plenty of dream fodder. It is not our intention, nor would it be practical, to give precise route directions for each one. Where they exist, guidebooks containing such directions for individual treks are named in the introductory panel of specific chapters, along with a basic summary of route information, which, together with a map and profile of each one, is designed to whet your appetite.

Although drawn to scale and based on satellite imagery, maps that accompany each chapter are intended for general orientation only. More detailed mapping may or may not be available for use on trek. A few regions, such as the Khumbu in Nepal, have been the subject of some very fine cartographic work, while others have only the most rudimentary representation on sheets that contain numerous errors and omissions. Having been on expedition with one such map that had somehow 'lost' a 6000m peak and a complete river valley, I consider such cartographic dyslexia as one of the delights of the Himalayan trekking experience, for it opens the door to serendipity. And serendipity is the prize for all travellers with an open mind and a zest for adventure.

TREKKING IN THE HIMALAYA: A BACKGROUND

The Himalaya captured the imagination of travellers long before the present trekking boom began, and in the late 19th and early years of the 20th century local agents in Kashmir, Simla and Darjeeling were already equipping parties eager to get close to the highest mountains and to cross some of their passes.

One of the first to be drawn to the mountains of what was then British India was Alpine Club stalwart Douglas Freshfield who, in 1899, made a seven-week tour of the Kangchenjunga massif in very difficult conditions. Freshfield had long experience of the Alps and saw the potential for mountain holidays in certain parts of the Himalaya, prophesying that Dzongri could become the Riffel Alp of Sikkim, and reporting that the Indian government had taken steps towards creating a 'mountain playground' in the Teesta Valley.

At the western end of the Himalaya in the 1920s, the American couple Robert and Katherine Barrett spent a year wandering through Baltistan and Ladakh with Rasul Galwan from Leh as their *sirdar*. Galwan, who had once been with Younghusband, spoke pidgin English and described the Barretts' journey: 'No, not shooting; not rocks-collecting, not flowers keeping; not

Makalu (left) comes into view on the approach to the 4970m Shao La (Trek 15) (photo: Bart Jordans)

heads measuring, not mountains measuring; not pictures taking. This my Sahib and Mem-Sahib travelling where their felt are liked, camping always high place to look the country.'

Decipher that, and you'll find another definition of trekking.

The Barretts travelled in style, their outfit luxurious. They slept in handsome embroidered tents, travelled with eight servants to look after their needs, and had no fewer than 20 ponies and a team of porters to carry their supplies. They lacked nothing. Not for them the light touch pioneered by Tom Longstaff who made some remarkable journeys in the first half of the 20th century, and who once advised: 'Just travel is the thing. Number your red-letter days by camps, not by summits…'

Longstaff may have been an early advocate of travelling light, but it was Bill Tilman and Eric Shipton who were the real masters of lightweight travel; for a five-month expedition Shipton decided that two shirts would suffice. Tilman thought this excessive and took only one. Together they climbed and explored the most remote regions, and in 1934 pioneered a route through the Rishi Ganga's gorge to enter the longed-for Nanda Devi Sanctuary. In

Mountains of Tartary, Shipton admitted that 'there is much to be said for a simple mountain journey, whose object, unencumbered with the burden of detailed map-making or scientific observation, is just to get from one place to another'. That surely is another definition of trekking.

Despite his penchant for exploration, Shipton's name will forever be associated with attempts to climb Mount Everest, and in 1951 he led the reconnaissance expedition that discovered the route through the Western Cwm that would lead to the South Col and the summit itself. Accompanying Shipton on that occasion was Angtharkay, a Sherpa who had been with him on no fewer than eight expeditions before the war. Since they had last met, Angtharkay had set up a business in Darjeeling organising treks in Sikkim.

The transport officer for the successful 1953 expedition that put Ed Hillary and Tenzing Norgay on Everest's summit was Jimmy Roberts, then a major in a Gurkha regiment and an experienced Himalayan climber. When he retired in the 1960s, he remained in Nepal in the shadow of Annapurna. Knowing that high-altitude mountaineering could be a masochistic pursuit with

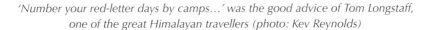

'Number your red-letter days by camps…' was the good advice of Tom Longstaff, one of the great Himalayan travellers (photo: Kev Reynolds)

The ancient gompa at Dho in the Tarap Valley (Trek 8) (photo: Kev Reynolds)

all its dangers and discomforts, the long walk to reach the foot of the mountains was one of stress-free enjoyment likely to appeal to adventurous travellers. In 1964 he registered Mountain Travel as Nepal's first trekking agency, and the following year accompanied three American ladies on a springtime trek in the Khumbu. Trekking, as we know it today, was born.

Since then the once-hidden kingdoms of the Himalaya have undergone accelerated change. Where not so long ago their highways were the bare-earth paths that snaked up, down and across the hills and mountain passes, roads are now being bulldozed to carry motor vehicles into the most unexpected places, at times more than 5000m above sea level. The isolated appeal of remote valleys is being steadily eroded by the so-called march of modernity, but while we who trek there may mourn the loss of a seemingly romantic past, if you ask locals for their opinion, many will say they welcome the change.

Thankfully the Himalaya covers a huge area, the vast majority of which has little or no access by motorised transport, and where walking is the only way to get from A to B.

TREKKING STYLES

How you trek is largely a matter of choice based on personal experience, constraints of time and finance, and the region you wish to travel in. Rules and regulations vary from country to country, as do facilities, so unless you plan to trek with a commercial organisation, background research is essential. In Nepal several routes are so well developed that an independent trekker can travel light and stay in simple lodges throughout. On some treks in Zanskar and Ladakh homestay accommodation is available; in parts of Sikkim a few 'lodges' have been built that offer shelter only. Elsewhere, and in less-travelled regions, camping with a fully equipped outfit and an army of porters

The shared experience of trekking with a group of friends can add much to a Himalayan journey (photo: Kev Reynolds)

or a string of mules or yaks to carry the baggage is normal. In Bhutan all treks must be accompanied by a qualified Bhutanese guide and entry to the country arranged through a recognised agent.

Fully supported group treks

With no shortage of adventure travel companies, and a range of exotic destinations to choose from, trekking with an organised group is the choice of those with more disposable income than time or experience. In the past this automatically meant sleeping in tents, but with more comfortable lodge accommodation being built along the popular routes, this is no longer the case in Nepal. Outside the Everest, Annapurna and Langtang regions, however, camping remains the only option.

Trekking with a group can be a very sociable experience, although there's a tendency to live within your own culture and miss the opportunity to interact with locals unless you make a conscious effort to do so. Spending several weeks in a foreign environment with complete strangers sometimes leads to a clash of personalities, so patience and a degree of diplomacy can be as important as fitness. On the other hand a trek that begins among strangers can often lead to lifelong friendships.

Each of the Himalayan countries has its own trekking culture, and without taking landscape or climate into consideration, the traveller's experience in Nepal will be very different from that in Bhutan, Tibet, India or Pakistan, but the best commercial operators employ experienced leaders and local agents and crews whose aim is to make their clients' adventures as hassle-free and enjoyable as possible.

Do-it-yourself group trekking

Inevitably a commercial, pre-organised trek will follow a set itinerary and maintain a fairly rigid schedule, which can be frustrating when passing a side valley you'd like to explore, or feel the need for an extra rest day. Travelling with a group of like-minded friends on a trek you've arranged yourselves allows greater flexibility, so if you and your friends can agree a rough outline of a route, either discuss it with a reputable company at home and let them make all pre-trek arrangements, or approach a trekking agent in Kathmandu, Darjeeling or Leh (or wherever you plan to travel) and ask them to supply a fully-serviced trek for you. Such arrangements can work admirably and lead to many rewarding days. But you'll need to remain vigilant to ensure that the equipment and staff supplied match your needs and are what you've paid for.

With a porter-guide

If you have the confidence, trekking alone with a local porter-guide can be truly rewarding if you pick the right man (or woman, if female trekkers prefer) for the job. These can be hired through a reputable agent in the country you wish to travel in, but make sure you interview the prospective candidate before agreeing a contract. A porter-guide will carry some of your baggage, help with route-finding and educate you to the ways of their country by suggesting visits to off-the-beaten track villages, and opening doors in both the literal and metaphorical sense. Choose one who can speak a little English, and learn some of their language too. Treat the porter-guide as a companion, not as a servant, and you'll have a great time.

Teahouse trekking

In the Everest, Annapurna and Langtang regions of Nepal many of the simple *bhattis* (teahouses) used by independent trekkers in the 1970s and '80s developed into rather more sophisticated lodges to meet a growing demand for Western-style accommodation. 'Luxury' lodges have become established too, so it's now possible to trek for several weeks and stay in reasonable

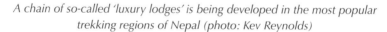

A chain of so-called 'luxury lodges' is being developed in the most popular trekking regions of Nepal (photo: Kev Reynolds)

comfort each night. Although pizza and apple pie first appeared on lodge menus decades ago to suit trekkers reluctant to immerse themselves in the culture of the country, if you're determined to add that culture to your trekking experience, teahouse trekking still gives ample opportunities.

Lodges are now being built elsewhere in Nepal, so it's possible that in the near future independent trekkers will be able to experience more of this beautiful country without tents and porters, and carrying little on their backs. Since regulations change with some frequency, check permit requirements before setting out.

WHEN TO GO

Conditions throughout the Himalaya vary from season to season and from year to year, with climate change making any long-range predictions unreliable. Two major factors dictate the

Without snow, the trail to the Thorong La is a dusty one. Here you can see the teahouse built between Phedi and the pass (Trek 10) (photo: Siân Pritchard-Jones and Bob Gibbons)

Clockwise from top left: In springtime rhododendrons brighten forests in the eastern Himalaya; in the foothills of Nepal, hibiscus blossoms hang over some of the trails; gentians grow in many of the higher valleys; primula denticulata *can often be found on pre-monsoon treks (all photos: Kev Reynolds)*

practicalities of successful trekking: the presence and quantity of snow on high passes, and the arrival and extent of the monsoon that sweeps up from the southeast to reach Bhutan and Sikkim in late May before spreading westward, often lasting until early October. Not all areas are affected though, for some lie in the rain-shadow of the mountains, where summer is the ideal trekking season.

From May to September is perhaps the best time to visit the high mountains of northern Pakistan; in the dry, trans-Himalayan regions of Zanskar and Ladakh the season begins in June and continues until October. As Garwhal and Kumaon are affected by the monsoon (which brings an abundance of flowers), trekking takes place in both the pre-monsoon (May–June) and post-monsoon (September–November) periods.

Tibet is largely shielded from rain-bearing clouds, and the southwest of the country, which includes Mount Kailash, is best visited between May and November, although the approach to Kailash via Simikot in Nepal should be avoided in July–August during the monsoon season, when flighs to Simikot are regularly abandoned due to bad weather. The north side of Everest can be trekked from summer until late October, snow on the high passes permitting.

The post-monsoon period of October to early December is the recommended season for most routes in Nepal. The weather is generally settled then, with views of the high mountains having a clarity unmatched at any other time of the year. The pre-monsoon months of March and April are also good, although views are often obscured by haze.

Sikkim and Bhutan are noted for their varieties of rhododendrons and abundant forests that benefit from a large amount of rainfall; the monsoon is heaviest here, and even outside the monsoon season rain often features in spring and autumn – the main trekking periods.

SAFETY IN THE MOUNTAINS

Trekking should be a safe and life-enhancing pursuit, and for the vast majority of those who go trekking in the Himalaya, that is indeed the case. But the mountain environment is both enriching and challenging, with a variety of objective dangers that need to be recognised. Narrow, exposed and unstable paths, precarious bridges, landslides, rockfall and hazardous river crossings may all be encountered at some time or other. A good level of physical and mental fitness will be needed to tackle these, and the countless steep ascents and descents that occur on practically every route, where a lack of concentration could have serious consequences. There may also be glacier crossings with crevasses to avoid, high and rarely trod passes to negotiate – and the sharp horns of a wayward yak of which to be extra wary.

And of course, there's the additional concern of Acute Mountain Sickness (AMS), a potentially fatal condition that can afflict those who go to altitude and disregard the rules of acclimatisation.

In the 'hidden land' of Dolpo, the remote village of Saldang hosts a trekking group's camp (Trek 7) (photo: Stephen Goodwin)

SAFETY DOS AND DON'TS

- Undergo a medical and dental check before committing to a trek in the Himalaya, and make sure you have any recommended inoculations.
- Ensure you are both physically and mentally prepared for the challenges of your chosen route.
- Before going on trek register your personal details and route plan with your embassy.
- Carry a first-aid kit and know how to use it. Make sure you have any medications you are likely to need.
- Watch where you are walking and remain alert for hazards throughout the trekking day.
- Protect yourself from the effects of the sun and dry air.
- Drink plenty of safe purified water to remain hydrated and to help with acclimatisation.
- Carry energy food with you as a boost.
- Watch for early signs of AMS among your group and crew, and act upon them when shown.
- Choose camping sites with care, and away from any danger of rockfall, avalanche or flood.
- Do not trek alone. If you have no companion, hire a guide.

These may be roughly summarised as 'climb high, sleep low and keep hydrated'. It is, however, essential to learn to recognise the symptoms of AMS, and know how to react to them.

A number of health hazards may be avoided (or at least limited) by common-sense precautions such as maintaining a high standard of personal hygiene and purifying all drinking water, by having a thorough medical and dental check-up before travelling to the Himalaya, and receiving the various inoculations advised by the health authorities.

Trekkers' Aid Posts have been set up in popular trekking regions of Nepal, and a scattering of small health clinics or hospitals appear elsewhere, but on the majority of Himalayan trekking routes there is no reliable health care available. Should you fall sick or be injured, self-help will be your only solution. An understanding of basic mountain first aid is therefore essential, and a comprehensive first-aid kit should be carried by each group. While on trek it is advisable to carry a copy of the pocket-sized handbook *First Aid and Wilderness Medicine* by Drs Jim Duff and Peter

Gormly (Cicerone). It is also prudent to be adequately insured with a specialist broker who deals with expedition cover – standard travel insurance is rarely sufficient. Read the small print with care, especially in regard to emergency evacuation, and make sure you have sufficient funds that will guarantee helicopter call-out (where possible) if the need arises.

MINIMUM IMPACT TREKKING

Each trekker has an impact on the country through which he or she travels. On its own that impact may be minimal, but the Himalaya annually attracts hundreds of thousands of back-country trekkers whose presence can affect both the environment and the lives of the people who live there. Whether that impact be positive or negative is in the hands of each one of us.

It defies comprehension that anyone drawn to the mountains by their wild beauty would do anything to detract from that beauty. But visiting trekkers, as well as locals, drop litter without apparent thought to the consequences. Yet it's so

With sorrowful eyes a young lad on the Manaslu trail is drawn by the smells of a trekking group's lunch. Moments like this enhance the trekking experience (photo: Kev Reynolds)

easy to pack out what you carry in. Remove excess packaging from items before leaving home, and carry a number of biodegradable bags with you in which to place rubbish – yours and other people's found on the trail – and take them back to the town or city where you began your journey for proper disposal. Since most developing countries have no facilities to deal with used batteries, take these home.

Ensure every campsite is left in a pristine condition, with toilet pits filled and covered properly. At lodges and homestays use the toilets provided, no matter how unsavoury they may be. If you need to defecate during the day where there are no facilities, choose a site at least 50m from any water source, bury faeces in a hole dug with a penknife or trowel, and carry a cigarette lighter to burn used toilet paper, taking care not to set fire to vegetation.

On a camping trek preserve trees and shrubs by ensuring that kerosene stoves are used for cooking. If you're on a teahouse trek opt to stay in lodges that use solar power to provide electricity and hot water for showers, and kerosene for cooking. In some above-the-treeline communities dried animal dung is the preferred eco-friendly fuel.

While internet facilities are now available in a number of seemingly out-of-the-way places, and mobile phone coverage is expanding rapidly, don't rely on daily access to technology. Leave your own culture behind and immerse yourself in that of the country you're visting, and your experience will be greatly enhanced.

Be sensitive to the local culture. Before you go, learn as much as you can about appropriate clothing, and the basic points of etiquette for those occasions when you are invited into someone's home, or when visiting a temple or monastery. This way you can avoid causing embarrassment to yourself and your hosts.

Finally, resist the temptation to hand out sweets, balloons or money to children, for this will turn them into beggars. If you wish to make a gift, consider a donation to a school, healthcare or other worthwhile community project. As for photographing local people, remember that aiming a camera at a complete stranger is an arrogant intrusion. Treat each one you meet with respect, and honour them with your time and friendship before asking permission to take their picture.

From Goro, the Gasherbrum group draws you onward to Concordia ▶

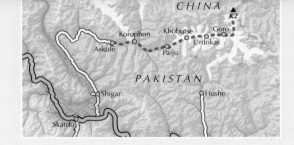

Trek 1

K2 and Concordia

by Steve Razzetti

At the northwestern end of the great arc of the Himalaya, beyond the mighty Indus River and its tributaries the Shyok and Gilgit, lies what many consider to be the most spectacular and challenging range of mountains on earth. The Karakoram takes its name from the infamous Karakoram Pass, high point on the ancient caravan route between Leh in Ladakh and Yarkhand in the Tarim Basin. Upon this 500-kilometre chain many superlatives can be laid. Here is the greatest concentration of 8000m peaks on earth, and the longest glaciers outside the Polar regions. Fifty per cent of the range is glaciated, compared with 12 per cent of the Himalaya and just 2.2 per cent of the Alps. Early exploration was carried out by a maverick rabble of men capable of enduring almost unimaginable hardships. In 1835, Godfrey Thomas 'Ramrod' Vigne was almost certainly the first European to behold the Central Karakoram, and his sentiments perfectly capture their magnificence: 'Mountain seemed piled upon mountain, to sustain the most stupendous confusion of mist and glacier, glistening with the dazzling and reciprocated brightness of snow and sunbeam…'

Route summary

Location	Central Karakoram, Pakistan
Start/Finish	Askole, Baltistan
Distance	about 180km
Duration	18 days (16 days' trekking, two acclimatisation days)
Maximum altitude	Concordia 4700m
Trek style	Camping
Restrictions	Special permits required
Grade	Expedition

The true stature and extent of the range were only properly realised when Lieutenant Montgomerie of the Great Trigonometrical Survey arrived, followed by a pair of 'coolies' bearing his theodolite, at a station atop the peak of Haramukh in Kashmir on 10 September 1856. The ascent had taken them a gruelling four days, but the view must have quickened his pulse as much as the slog up there: 'There was nothing remarkable in the first six or seven ridges... Beyond came the snowy points of the Karakoram range and behind them I saw two fine peaks standing very high above the general range...' At a distance of over 225 kilometres, he was thus the first man to take a bearing on the peak we still refer to by the designation he gave it – K2. When his observations were finally computed in 1858, K2 was proved to be the second-highest mountain in the world with a summit 8611m above sea level.

Five years later, on an expedition that confirmed him as the greatest mountaineer of his day, Captain Henry Haversham Godwin-Austen succeeded in exploring and mapping all the glaciers draining into the Braldu River, including the Biafo, Panmah and Baltoro. Determined to see K2 he made a final push up the Baltoro at the end of the expedition and, ascending a ridge above the camp we now know as Urdokas, was finally able to sketch the summit of that monstrous pyramid over the intervening ridges.

The frisson of excitement felt by Godwin-Austen as he reached a position from which he could see

K2 is still felt by all those determined and lucky enough to make the journey to this foreboding place. K2 remains hidden until the final approach to Concordia, where the Baltoro and Godwin-Austen glaciers meet in what has become known as the Throne Room of the Mountain Gods – there is a savage, elemental beauty to the Karakoram that no other range can touch.

My first encounter with the behemoths of the Baltoro came in 1987, when I accompanied Doug Scott and his international K2 expedition to Advanced Base Camp. I'd travelled for three days by road up the notorious Karakoram Highway (KKH) from Rawalpindi to Skardu, sleeping and travelling atop a truckload of our expedition and trek equipment. Today, if you have reservations and are very lucky with the weather, Pakistan International Airlines may take you to Skardu in under an hour from Islamabad in a Boeing 737. If not, then it's a tad under 700 kilometres and anything from 18 hours to a week by road, depending on your driver, the condition of the vehicle and the state of the road – not a journey for the faint-hearted.

Pakistan's attempts to make travel in these northern areas easier have only met with limited success. Depending on the clemency of the weather, there may or may not be flights to Gilgit or Skardu. The KKH may, or may not, be open. There may, or may not, be a road to the village of Askole, from where the trek theoretically begins. In 1987 that final, tenuous jeep road had not been built, and by the time we reached Askole we had already completed a hair-raising trek through the awesome Braldu gorge from the roadhead at Dassu. By today's standards of convenience, this is truly an epic journey. A hundred years ago you would have had to walk from Srinagar in Kashmir!

To Askole

Pakistan has never been an easy place to travel, but for 25 years it has certainly been my favourite. Before 9/11 and the ensuing descent into mayhem, it was challenging, rewarding and completely

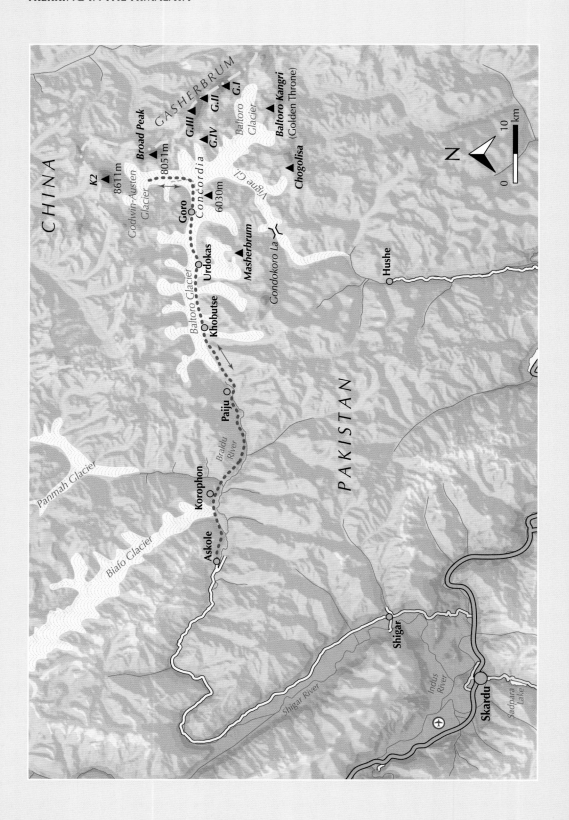

safe. Those who had been would come alive at the mention of Gilgit, Chitral, Skardu, the Karakoram Highway. From Hassanabdal, near Rawalpindi, this incredible testament to the tenacity, bravery and skill of Chinese and Pakistani roadbuilders snakes its way right through the range, eventually crossing the Khunjerab Pass to Kashgar in Chinese Xinjiang.

After Hassanabdal the road climbs through rolling green hills dotted with tea-plantations and farms, to the sleepy garrison town of Abbottabad, then on into the Indus Valley just south of Besham. There is a PTDC motel here, where groups of perspiring tourists may be spotted wilting in the welcome shade. From here the only road into the Karakoram follows the course of the river north, hugging increasingly arid and precipitous mountainsides above the torrent as it winds its way through Indus Kohistan, deeper and deeper into the range.

Just beyond Chilas, where summer temperatures frequently push the mercury above the 40°C mark and the valley floor is a shimmering furnace of boulders and scree, a miracle is revealed. Crane your neck steeply enough, and soaring in the sky at an unfeasible height are the vast snows and glaciers of Nanga Parbat. To behold such startling evidence of perpetual arctic winter from the sweat and dust of the KKH is but one of the strange incongruities of the Karakoram. A few kilometres further, just before the village of Juglote, the Skardu link-road turns off for the final 180-kilometre journey eastwards along the Indus to the capital of Baltistan, while the KKH continues to Gilgit, Hunza and China.

Coming down from the mountains Skardu can seem the epitome of a hot and dusty mountain town, but waking there on your first morning after the rigours of the KKH, or stepping onto the tarmac after an early morning flight from sweltering Islamabad, the air seems deliciously cool and clear. Poplars line the lanes, golden orioles and hoopoes flit about in the shade, and burbling irrigation channels carry the silty water of the Indus to fields of swaying wheat and barley. In the bazaar chaos reigns, with tractors, donkeys, jeeps, chickens and men all clamouring about their business; among the ramshackle shops sometimes the essentials for kitting out a trek or expedition can be found, but don't count on it.

There are many hotels and inns of varying standards in Skardu today, but stay at the fabulously situated K2 Motel for a completely authentic expedition vibe. From the elevated and carefully watered terrace out front, the vast Indus Valley is spread out before you, with the silent grey waters of the Lion River sliding imperceptibly by on its journey from Tibet to the Arabian Sea. The motel corridors are lined with posters and expedition memorabilia going back over 40 years, signed by mountaineering legends that have made their names here – Reinhold Messner, Doug Scott, Chris Bonington, Kurt Diemberger, Walter Bonatti, James Whittaker, Alan Rouse…

Back in 1987 the 'road' from Skardu up the Shigar Valley and into the Braldu towards Askole was more a statement of intent than what we generally understand the term to mean. Expeditions would load their kit into decrepit trailers behind borrowed farm tractors, which would set off from the K2 Motel at 4am in order to beat the rising snowmelt waters of the many side-streams to be forded en route to Dassu. Today, bridges have been built (and swept away again, and rebuilt!), obstacles blasted and embankments strengthened, so that given perfect conditions and a reliable Land Cruiser, it is possible to reach Askole in under 10 very bumpy hours.

Askole to Paiju

Trekking in Pakistan is not like trekking in Nepal. Gateway towns like Skardu still have few Western-standard amenities outside of the better hotels. Even the most popular trekking routes retain a real expedition quality, and the service provided by Pakistani agencies is not as slick and professional as their Nepalese counterparts. However, the hospitality and camaraderie shown to visitors

The hard life of the mountain man is etched in the features of Ishmail, a Balti porter

by the mountain folk is legendary, and though you will not be as cosseted during a trek here as

you would be in Nepal, the rewards gained are arguably much richer. This is certainly not a place for mountain novices. Expeditions and trekking groups have been passing through **Askole** for over four decades, yet there is not a single teashop, hotel or provision store. The only visible recent change to the village derives from the fact that Haji Mehdi's old campground is now used as a car park for the fleets of vintage Land Cruisers that ferry people to and from Skardu.

Altitude is rarely a problem on treks here, as most routes follow the floors of gently ascending valleys. That is not to say that it can be ignored – the altitude at Skardu is 2500m, and Askole is 3000m – but there are other equally important environmental considerations. Most importantly, the power of the sun. Another of the Karakoram's incongruities is the fact that a thermometer, placed in full sun on a boulder in the middle of a glacier at 4000m, will quickly soar to over 75°C. Concomitantly, in the dry and rarified air dehydration is a real danger, and can quickly and completely debilitate the unprepared. If you've driven to Askole and set off on your first morning's walk from your shady camping spot after 8am, you will enjoy the first kilometre or so to the end of the village fields. There you will emerge from a

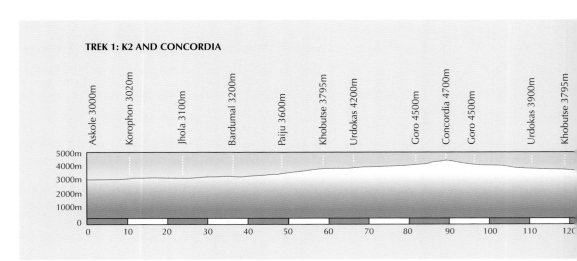

TREK 1: K2 AND CONCORDIA

| | Askole 3000m | Korophon 3020m | Jhola 3100m | Bardumal 3200m | Paiju 3600m | Khobutse 3795m | Urdokas 4200m | Goro 4500m | Concordia 4700m | Goro 4500m | Urdokas 3900m | Khobutse 3795m |

shady lane and step out into a searing, shimmering desert. Early – very early – starts are essential here, especially for those unacclimatised to both altitude and heat. Appropriate clothing is also

Murky with glacial silt, the Braldu River squeezes the trail against the mountainside

vital. In my experience it's best to copy the locals and buy a loose-fitting Pakistani *shalwar-kameez* before setting off. Then you will be comfortable and avoid offending local sensibilities about dress. Trekking in skimpy shorts and vest is definitely not on in Muslim Pakistan.

The first two or three days' trekking bring you to **Paiju**, a heavily over-used but fabulously situated spot just short of the snout of the Baltoro Glacier. This is four porter-stages, but most trekking companies schedule just two days for the walk, which is pushing it a little at the beginning. Pollution was becoming a serious problem at all the camp-sites on this route, but this has been mitigated to a large extent by the construction in 2003 of proper facilities at Jhola, Paiju and Urdokas. These small oases were suffering badly from deforestation, litter and a complete lack of sanitation, but

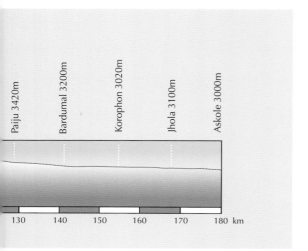

Paiju 3420m

Bardumal 3200m

Korophon 3020m

Jhola 3100m

Askole 3000m

130   140   150   160   170   180 km

today you will find latrines, washing facilities, permanent accommodation for porters, terraces for tents and even solar lighting. This project was completed just ahead of the 50th anniversary of the first ascent of K2 by an Italian expedition in July 1954, which saw a huge influx of trekkers and mountaineers from all over the world.

Shortly after leaving Askole, having crossed a large plain where villagers play polo, and surmounted a steep rocky spur above the **Braldu River**, the valley ahead seems blocked by an enormous expanse of rubble and debris. This is actually the snout and terminal moraine of the **Biafo Glacier**, and it pushes the Braldu River hard

up against the southern flanks. The first possible camp-spot is immediately beyond this three-kilometre-wide moraine, at the once idyllic and green oasis of **Korophon**, reached in four to five hours. Most commercial treks take lunch here and go on to Jhola to camp, but this makes for a 10-hour first day out, which is too much in these conditions. The trail onwards to Jhola passes one of the most difficult sections on the entire route as it enters the valley of the Dumordo River, flowing down from the Panmah Glacier. It traverses a steep and very exposed section of rock immediately above seething waters of the river, before following the river north to the first possible spot where a bridge

could be built. The campsite is immediately beyond this bridge.

Jhola is the Balti word for the type of flying-fox bridge that used to be a feature of all these crossings before the advent of jeep-roads and suspension bridges. The one here was particularly famous for both its rickety construction and the hours it would take to get a group of climbers or trekkers and all their porters and luggage across. It has now been replaced by a footbridge, but this will surely be washed away in time by a spring flood.

If you come early in the season, and reach the valley early enough in the day, it may be possible to ford the Dumordo River below these cliffs and save yourself much time and effort, but this should only be attempted by experienced folk and with great caution. The next possible camp is four or five hours on at Bardumal, which means 'troublesome place' in Balti, from where it is another five hours across a rising series of alluvial fans to Paiju. From the first of these a tantalising hint of the scenery ahead is revealed, with the Cathedral Spires, Mustagh Tower and...could that just be the tip of K2?

Ice formations on the Baltoro Glacier. Masherbrum, 'the mountain of light', is a towering presence behind

The vertical granite of the Trango Towers holds an irresistible allure to rock climbers

Paiju to Urdokas

Most treks and expeditions take a rest day at **Paiju** (3600m), to allow acclimatisation and their porters to make a supply of bread to carry onto the glacier ahead. Shade is at a premium and space may also be if there is more than one group or expedition staying over. Below camp a tiny stream descends from the spring through gnarled and much-hacked-about willow and tamarisk trees to the wide, stony flats of the riverbed. The Braldu here is a braided stream, criss-crossing the valley floor in a latticework of rivulets. Having just emerged from beneath the snout of the glacier, the water is freezing cold and full of sediment, but if you can find a still pool in the sun you may be treated to a warm, clear bath with stunning views.

Less than two hours out of Paiju the trail forks, with the way left going up to the Trango Towers and Sarpo Laggo Pass. The right fork goes straight onto the **Baltoro Glacier**, ascending steeply up the loose, dusty pile of rocks that make up the terminal moraine – there's nothing pretty about this aspect of Karakoram glaciers! Eventually the gradient eases, and ahead the glacier is nothing but a twisted sea of gravel and rocks, almost three kilometres wide and over 60 kilometres long. In bad weather this can seem a very daunting, foreboding place, but under clear skies you will struggle to keep an eye on the trail ahead, so spectacular are the peaks now revealed.

Like all things to do with trekking in the Karakoram, progress up the Baltoro will be determined by your stamina, trail conditions, the presence – or absence – of simple log bridges, and whether or not a particular spring or campsite is actually there that year. Most people do this section in two days, camping at either Liligo or **Khobutse**, approximately 10–12 hours' walk in total. Both these campsites are on the southern edge of the glacier and are marginal, with minimum space, zero shade, and only a small source of spring water. The Pakistan army maintains a series of hidden bases all the way up the Baltoro as part of its on-going dispute with India over the Siachen Glacier, and their contractors bring up a lot of equipment on donkeys and horses. To this end they maintain something of a trail up the glacier, but great care is required nevertheless; an awkward slip or fall can have serious consequences.

From various lookout points along this stretch of the route you will get your first real intimation of what all the Karakoram fuss is about. Lining the northern edge of the Baltoro and its tributaries are the legendary rock towers of Paiju Peak, Trango, Uli Biaho, Cathedral, Biale and the Lobsang Spire – vertical granite edifices soaring skywards from the broken serpent's back of the glacier to heights in excess of 6500m. **Urdokas** commands absolutely stunning views of all this and the way ahead from its elevated position above the glacier at 4200m. The sparse grass and colourful alpine flowers are the last hint of vegetation you will see until your return.

Urdokas to Concordia

Immediately before the trail out of Urdokas plunges down onto the glacier again, there's a small graveyard where your porters will probably pause and say some prayers. The graves are of porters who have perished here, and are a stark reminder that in bringing these folk up here, you have a duty to look after them. If your crew are not properly clothed, equipped and provisioned, it is ultimately your responsibility.

The view looking back along the Baltoro Glacier towards Concordia, from the route to Gasherbrum I Base Camp

Gasherbrum IV, 'the shining wall', glows at sunset

The surface of the glacier is very convoluted here, and still strewn with loose rocks, debris and gravel. Ahead, alluring strips of white ice finally appear from beneath the rubble with the prospect of easier going. Six hours or so from Urdokas brings you almost all the way across the glacier via a lunch-stop at Biange to the camp at **Goro** (4500m), and during this hike you will be treated to yet more jaw-dropping vistas. Gasherbrum IV (7929m) commands the skyline ahead and, from Biange especially, the formidable defences of Masherbrum (7821m) are revealed to the south. The final stretch to Concordia (4700m) is in fact slightly easier, but given fine weather you will have difficulty remembering the day's exertions, so awesome are the views.

It is about four hours' walk from Goro to Concordia, but most people have to stop every few yards to gawp and get their cameras out. The Mustagh Tower (7284m) appears briefly at the head of the Biange Glacier to the north just out of camp, but excitement really mounts as you approach **Concordia**. Superlatives are lost on vistas such as this. Finally K2 is revealed, so impressive that it almost defies you to look at it, let alone contemplate climbing it. But the whole place is sensational. Five glaciers come together at Concordia, ringed by what is undeniably as breathtaking a mountain vista as any on the planet. Broad Peak, Gasherbrum IV, Baltoro Kangri, Mitre Peak, Crystal Peak and Marble Peak all tower overhead, while lurking just out of view are the likes of Chogolisa and Gasherbrum I.

Beyond Concordia and return

Most commercial trek operators design their itineraries around a best-case scenario, assuming flights operate, you have good weather and a fit group. Few trips pass off with all these conditions being met, and are almost always subject to serious time pressures. Try to allow several nights at and above Concordia. A day's rest on arrival, for example, followed by an overnight excursion to K2 Base Camp and possibly another to Gasherbrum I Base Camp. These are big days out, but among mountains like these you'd expect nothing less. Fantastic days! You may then retrace your steps to **Askole** in six days – unless you've decided to make a crossing of the challenging Gondokoro La (5585m) and out south via the village of Hushe...

The green oasis of Askole marks the start of the Snow Lake trek ▶

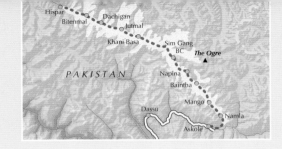

Trek 2

Snow Lake

by Steve Razzetti

At the heart of the Central Karakoram range in Pakistan, the 5151m Hispar Pass forms the vertex of the longest stretch of glacial ice outside the Polar regions. Like an enormous geographic fulcrum, this remote and difficult watershed gives rise to the mighty ice floes of the Biafo and Hispar glaciers, which drain east into Baltistan and west into Hunza respectively. Immediately below the pass to the east lies the vast white basin known as Lukpe Lawo or Snow Lake, and together these span a distance in excess of 130 kilometres.

Route summary

Location	Central Karakoram, Pakistan
Start	Askole, Baltistan
Finish	Hispar
Distance	about 140km
Duration	Minimum of 13 days' trekking; allow 16–20 days
Maximum altitude	Hispar Pass 5151m
Trek style	Camping
Restrictions	Open zone; no permits required
Grade	Expedition
Guidebooks	*Trekking in Pakistan* by Isobel Shaw (Odyssey, 1993); *Trekking in the Karakoram & Hindukush* by John Mock and Kimberley O'Neil (Lonely Planet, 2002)

Sunset anywhere in the Himalaya is one of nature's Oscar-winning performances, but watching it from the Hispar Pass you really are in the royal box. Exiting at stage west, the sun defiantly flings its last golden rays straight across the level snowfields of the pass and onto the lofty summits of the mountains beyond. Beneath you, invisible beyond a foreground of undulating snows, the awesome defile of the Hispar Valley is already fading into the obscurity of gathering dusk. One by one the shadows leap from their daytime lairs and invincibly stalk their way skywards up the slopes, eventually reclaiming even the highest peaks from the glorious dying light.

Turn to the east and your elongated shadow stretches far into the distance, finally disappearing where the slope eventually falls more steeply away. Even when viewed from such a seemingly boundless and level snowfield, the assembled peaks conspire to induce an attack of vertigo, such is the gravity-defying arrogance of their thrusting verticality. Inexorably the great ice-sea sinks back into the blue chill of night, the falling temperature once again congealing the slush into a pale sapphirine lustre and seizing in its icy grip the raging meltwater torrents that by day carve

bobsleigh runs across the surface. Above this frost-bound silence, the highest castellated towers defiantly fling back the sun's parting pinks before joining their lesser neighbours and succumbing to the inevitable night. The last to surrender is a peak of such stupendous and daunting proportions that the first man to set eyes on it was moved to give it a name that to this day strikes a note of awe in the hearts of mountaineers the world over. The date was 18 July 1892, the man was Martin Conway, and the name he gave the mountain was The Ogre.

Thirty years earlier, during his seminal expedition to the Karakoram in 1861, Henry Haversham Godwin-Austen succeeded in exploring much of this region. Most famously he discovered the Baltoro approaches to K2, but he also ascended many other glaciers, including the Kero Lungma. At the head of this, he reached the Nushik La, and from this col became the first Westerner to behold the Hispar Glacier. Martin Conway continued Godwin-Austen's work during his 1892 expedition, exploring both the Hispar and Biafo, and the upper Baltoro to Concordia and beyond.

Eric Shipton's two Karakoram expeditions of the 1930s finally filled in the blank on the Karakoram map – indeed the painstaking survey

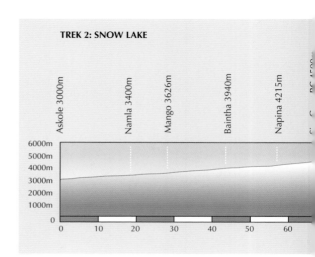

TREK 2: SNOW LAKE

En route to Dachigan. Conditions on the Hispar Glacier are always challenging

work they undertook produced a map of such accuracy that photocopies are still widely carried in the area today. Shipton and his famously phlegmatic companion Bill Tilman inspired generations of climbers with both their actual achievements and their philosophy of lightweight

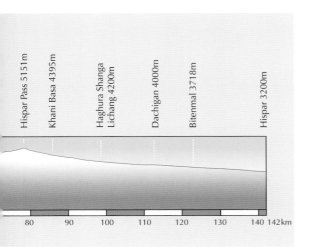

Hispar Pass 5151m
Khani Basa 4395m
Haghura Shanga Lichang 4200m
Dachigan 4000m
Bitenmal 3718m
Hispar 3200m

80   90   100   110   120   130   140 142km

mountaineering, of which legends have arisen. In his obituary of Shipton, Tilman wrote that 'I must content myself with this slight tribute to the most outstanding mountaineer-explorer of our time. Lord Montgomery's highest praise for a man was that "he would be happy to go into the jungle with him". Eric Shipton was undoubtedly such a man.'

My own Karakoram odyssey began unwittingly in a bookshop in Srinagar, Kashmir, in 1986 when I bought a first edition of Shipton's celebrated book about the Karakoram, *Blank on the Map*, for the princely sum of Rs50. Returning to my houseboat, I opened the dusty covers and started reading. Well after midnight I closed them again, having read the entire book. These words in particular still quicken my pulse at every reading: 'That evening for me was one of the greatest moments of the expedition. Warmed by the unaccustomed luxury of a blazing fire, its leaping flames fed with unstinted wood, I felt that after long days of toil and disappointment we had at last arrived. East and west of us stretched an unexplored section, eighty miles long, of the greatest

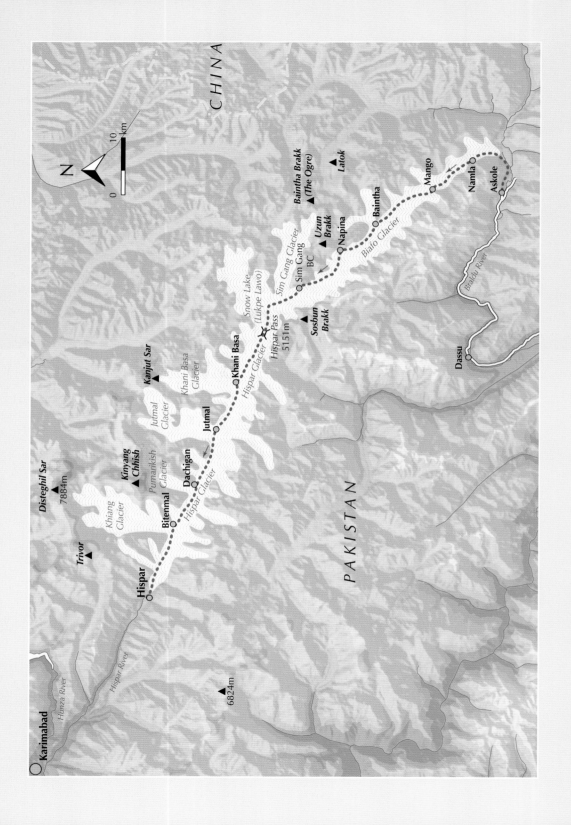

watershed in the world… To share all this, I had three companions as keen as myself, supported by seven of the most stout-hearted retainers in the world. We had food enough to keep us alive for three months in this place of my dreams, and the health and experience to meet the opportunity. I wanted nothing more.'

The following summer I crossed the Hispar Pass and explored the Sosbun Glacier with Stephen Venables, and in 1988 led the first-ever commercial trek over the Hispar. I have now been back there seven times. Eric Shipton was definitely onto something!

I mentioned the rigours of travelling through northern Pakistan to reach Skardu and Askole in Baltistan in Trek 1. This route demands the same level of preparedness, but it is even more committing and serious. On the Baltoro you are never far from an army base, and the number of trekkers and climbers travelling the route make communications and logistics relatively easy. On the Biafo–Hispar you are likely to be completely alone, demanding a higher level of self-reliance. You must be competent navigators and familiar with the techniques of glacier travel and rescue. Obviously, you should also be equipped for such contingencies. You must also have the experience to be able to make mountaineering decisions rationally.

My points about environmental considerations when travelling in the Karakoram, mentioned in Trek 1, need to be reiterated. Looking after yourself physically is crucial – these mountains are not kind to those who are cavalier about such things as protection from the sun, and dehydration. Martin Conway's description of the Indus Valley in 1892 could equally apply to any in the Karakoram, and should make the need for care in this regard obvious: 'I have never seen any valley that compared to it either in kind or dimensions. It was barren as an Arabian wadi; it was floored with the strewn ruins of countless floods, bleached and blasted by the suns of countless summers; it was walled along with rocky cliffs, a maze of precipices and gullies… The naked skeleton of the world stood forth, with every stratum displayed and every mark of the sculpturing chisel undisguised.'

Askole to Baintha

Do not be lulled into a false sense of security as you stroll along the first few easy miles of trail out of **Askole**. Gaggles of sun- and wind-blasted expedition porters trot by on their way back from Concordia and beyond, eager to reach the flesh-pots of Askole again. Returning mountaineers, lungs full of the rich lower-altitude oxygen supply, sprint past in their sponsors' colours, eyes hidden behind glacier glasses, ears full of the sounds of their iPods. One lonely and easily missed cairn marks the point just before the snout of the Biafo at which a barely discernible trail sneaks away up to the left (north) and over onto the glacier. Suddenly you are on your own in a sea of rubble.

Karakoram glaciers – especially ones the size of the Biafo and Hispar – are desolate, inhospitable

The fashion-conscious porter models his latest creation on the Biafo Glacier!

Above Baintha the dying light outlines a ragged silhouette of peaks

places in their lower reaches. Their flanks consist of terrifying yawning chasms of blackened, convoluted and rubble-strewn ice through which routes have to be chosen carefully. Mistakes can be extremely costly in terms of time and effort. Conditions underfoot are often treacherous. Loose rocks baking in the sun only just cover the fast-melting ice below and are ready to skate away the second your foot alights. Local hunters often mark their routes onto the ice with tiny cairns, but the constantly shifting and changing terrain means that these are frequently wrong or absent. It takes a practised eye to spot what is often just one stone placed atop another amid a sprawling confusion of boulders and rocks.

Fortunately, nature has conspired to create ablation zones beside these glaciers, and these provide camping sites of almost miraculous luxury amongst such geological carnage. The first three camps on

the ascent of the Biafo are at such places – namely at **Namla**, **Mango** and Baintha. After hours of exertion and intense concentration on the glacier you scramble up the almost vertical lateral moraine to be confronted by a tiny pocket of Eden. Green grass, alpine flowers, tamarisk scrub offering sparse shade, spring water, birds singing – and, of course, fabulous views! On the slopes far above you may spot ibex grazing, and at the muddy perimeter of shrinking spring meltwater pools you may see the footprints of a Himalayan brown bear. Unless you are incredibly fortunate you almost certainly will *not* spot the snow leopard peering out of her lair amongst the rocks above.

Baintha (3940m) lies on the northern side of the Biafo, just below its confluence with the Uzun Brakk Glacier, and is reached after a longer day's walk of maybe 10 hours. On the positive side this is the day when you reach the first of

Sim Gang Base Camp is the last stop before the Hispar Pass

those alluring strips of white ice that appear in the centre of the glacier and at last give some easier going. On the negative side you have to negotiate some truly horrible ground to get there. Baintha sports the last greenery you will see until you reach Jutmal on the Hispar, and it is sensible to spend at least two nights at this fabulous spot. Your porters will want to prepare bread for the days ahead, and you will need to acclimatise. You should also think about spending a further day here and make an ascent of the ridge that runs eastwards from the junction of the Uzun Brakk and Biafo glaciers. This is about a kilometre on from camp, and an altitude in excess of 5000m is easily attained, giving breathtaking panoramic views in every direction. South and east down the mighty ice highway of the Biafo, northwest towards the Hispar Pass, east to the Latok peaks and – most staggering of all – due north to the impregnable ramparts of Baintha Brakk: The Ogre. Pure Karakoram magic.

Baintha to Sim Gang Base Camp

In extremis I have covered this stretch of glacier in a single epic day, but it is far more sensible to take two. The going is good once you attain the centre of the glacier again, but if the weather is inclement you may encounter snow cover here and have to rope up. The crevasses start to get serious as you approach Sim Gang Base Camp, which is situated right on the eastern corner where the Biafo flows out of the Sim Gang/Snow Lake basin. If you are making this trek after mid-August, be prepared for absolutely enormous crevasses by the base camp. The Biafo at this point is 5 kilometres wide, 1000m deep and moves 100 metres annually. If you sleep on the ice here, you will wake up in the morning six inches closer to Askole and hear the incredible creaks, cracks and groans of the ice as it ploughs along.

The best place to camp overnight here is **Napina**. You may be tempted to stay out on the ice and save the considerable time and effort spent getting off the glacier at this point, but your porters and crew will thank you if you do. This is the only dry campsite this far up the valley and the location is beyond spectacular, being immediately below Lukpilla Brakk, the first of the famous Biafo Spires. Galen Rowell, Kim Schmitz and Ned Gillette stopped here on their seminal 1980 ski-traverse of the Karakoram, during which they travelled a staggering 285 miles from Khapalu and the Bilafond La, via the Siachen, Kondus, Godwin-Austen, Baltoro, Biafo and finally the Hispar glaciers. Unsupported, they were out for 43 days; it was a monumental achievement. Interestingly, Rowell thought the Biafo was the most impressive of all. He wrote in the *American Alpine Journal*: 'Here, lining the sides of the upper Biafo, was the greatest display of granite spires in the entire Karakoram, marching up the glacier like organ pipes in an ordered procession of design... The Bilafond and Saltoro valleys also had considerably more large granite faces than the fabled Baltoro, but for esthetics the Biafo won, hands down.' Rowell returned in 1984 and made the first ascent of Lukpilla Brakk.

Sunset lights the Ogre for trekkers camped on the Hispar Pass

Across the Hispar Pass

For suitably equipped and experienced parties, the possibilities for exploration above **Sim Gang Base Camp** are almost limitless. Immediately to the north lies **Snow Lake** – Lukpe Lawo – the vast névé basin described so extravagantly in 1892 by Conway: '...bounded to the north and east by white ridges, and to the south by a splendid row of needle peaks, the highest of which, the Ogre, had looked at us over the pass two days before. From the midst of the snowy lake rose a series of mountain islands white like the snow that bounded their bases, and there were endless bays and straits as of white water nestling amongst them. It was the vast plain that gave so extraordinary a character to the scene, and the contrast between this and the splintered needles that jutted their 10,000 feet of precipice into the air...'

Lukpe Lawo is only part of the story here, for immediately to the east lies another basin of similar magnitude: the Sim Gang. At the head of this enormous glacier the Sim La leads over to the Choktoi Glacier, the Skam La to the Nobande Sobande and the Lukpe La to the Braldu and Shimshal. Surely you are not going to come all this way to such a place and rush through it in a single day?

Having come up the Biafo, the Hispar Pass is the easiest of all the possible onward routes, but it is still a very major undertaking and must be treated with due respect. An early season crossing in the 1980s could reasonably be expected to be straightforward, with winter snow still covering the icefalls that protect either side of the pass. More recently – possibly due to climate change – these icefalls have become steeper and more challenging, the snow cover less complete. Stephen Venables and I only roped up here in 1987 because neither of us wanted to carry the rope on our backs, but today you will want to rope up all the way and take great care zigzagging your way through the crevasse systems.

Needless to say, an alpine start is required on the day you ascend to the pass. Picking your way out onto the ice by the light of your head torch, there is surely nowhere more dramatic to watch the sun rise. Turning west to cross the southern edge of Snow Lake, an apparition appears over your shoulder that will induce an adrenaline rush. Hidden since Baintha, The Ogre is suddenly with you again, its terrifyingly steep North Face rising straight above the Sim Gang. This is the mountain upon which, after completing the first ascent in 1977 with Chris Bonington, Doug Scott famously fell just below the summit, breaking both his legs. Years later, I showed him a picture I had taken of the North Face from Snow Lake, and his comment was succinct; 'F*** me – is that The Ogre?!' Twenty-four years passed and over 20 attempts failed before a second ascent was made in 2001 by Thomas Huber and his team.

If you are blessed with fine weather, a camp on the crest of the **Hispar Pass** is almost obligatory. Hopefully you will have arrived by midmorning and then have the luxury of lounging in the sun and feasting your eyes on the surrounding Karakoram giants and wondering how it is possible that such a vista remains relatively unknown. Perhaps it is better that way.

Down the Hispar

If you think that the mountain views you have been treated to thus far cannot possibly be bettered, think again. The Hispar is a much more difficult glacier to travel on lower down than the Biafo, for it receives no fewer than four major tributaries from the north, all of which bring down vast quantities of rubble and conspire to convolute its surface into a labyrinthine mass of icy mounds and valleys. The Khani Basa, Jutmal, Pumarikish and Khiang glaciers all descend from the watershed between the Hispar Valley and the Shimshal to the north. On this watershed lie a series of enormous mountains, many just short of 8000m. Kanjut Sar (7760m), Pumari Chhish (7491m), Kinyang Chhish (7852m) and Disteghil Sar (7884m) would all be world famous if they were anywhere else. Fortunately, the Hispar is

The Hispar Pass makes an unforgettable site for a camp

flanked on the north by some of the most beautiful ablation valleys I have come across, and there are some truly idyllic spots to camp.

Conversely, there are some very wide and difficult glaciers to cross, and vertical moraines that tower hundreds of feet above them to be negotiated. The initial descent from the pass follows the centre of the Hispar until it is chopped up by the intrusion of ice flowing from the **Khani Basa**, and most parties leave the glacier to the northern flank here and camp just before the actual confluence. Five days should see you to the road at Hispar village, but resist the urge to make a beeline for it. Savour the delights of camping at Haghura Shanga

Lichang and **Bitenmal**, and ascend the small peak above the latter for one last jaw-dropping view back up the valley to the Hispar Pass. Even from here, the tip of The Ogre is visible, peering ominously over the col. Soon enough you will be back amongst the trappings of civilisation, but be mindful of Kim Schmitz's reply to Galen Rowell after completing that epic ski-traverse. Rowell asked 'Isn't it wonderful to return to hot water and cold beer?' to which Schmitz replied 'The special things I miss are not what we are finding here, but what we've left behind in the dusty villages and campsites in the snow.'

Shortly before reaching Fairy Meadows, Nanga Parbat seems to fill the horizon ▶

Trek 3
Nanga Parbat
by Bart Jordans

Standing above the great bend of the Indus at a height of 8126m, Nanga Parbat is the world's ninth-highest summit and the most westerly bastion of the 2400-kilometre-long Himalayan chain. This tremendous mountain is a huge massif of rock and ice whose several sky-high peaks rise almost 7000m above the river. It has three major flanks: the North Face above the Rakhiot Glacier; the West-Northwest Face above the Diamir Glacier; and on the south side, the magnificent Rupal Face. Nanga Parbat is among the most difficult of the 8000m peaks, and its climbing history is both long and tragic. By contrast, the trekker has several short and easy routes that can be made to the various base camp areas, while a longer and more challenging trek makes a partial tour of the mountain. The easiest of these itineraries leads to the Fairy Meadows and the foot of the Rakhiot Face; another heads for the Diamir flank; while a third goes to the Rupal (or South) flank. The most difficult is the Mazeno Circuit.

Route summaries

Location	Punjab Himalaya, northern Pakistan
Start	Tato, Dimroi, Tarshing
Finish	Rakhiot Bridge, Dimroi, Tarshing, Fairy Meadows
Distance	**A** 30km **B** 40km **C** 45km **D** 85km
Duration	**A** Fairy Meadows and Rakhiot Base Camp 4–6 days **B** Diamir Face 4–5 days **C** Rupal Face 4–5 days **D** Mazeno Circuit 10–16 days (including rest days)
Maximum altitude	**A** 3967m **B** 4000m **C** 3650m **D** Mazeno Pass 5377m
Trek style	Camping
Restrictions	Currently none; but check when planning
Grade	Gentle/Moderate (except the Mazeno Circuit: Demanding)
Guidebook	*Trekking in Pakistan* by Isobel Shaw (Odyssey, 1993)

Sky and mountains are one in northern Pakistan, where the Himalaya, Karakoram and Hindu Kush challenge each horizon. Within a radius of 180 kilometres there are more than 100 summits above 7000m, many of them still unclimbed. Drained by the mighty Indus, which divides the Himalaya from the Karakoram, this is a harsh and unforgiving land, in which hardy mountain folk inhabit beautiful villages, their crops watered by complicated irrigation systems, their link with the rest of the country being along the famous (or infamous) Karakoram Highway.

Since 1989 I've had the privilege of spending seven summers guiding in these mountains, tasting the desolate wilderness of this magical area, sparsely occupied as it is by friendly, hard-working people. Accompanied by a group of porters, each and every visit has been a special experience. Pack

The tents of a trekking group are dwarfed by the massive Rupal Face (photo: Meikel Beek)

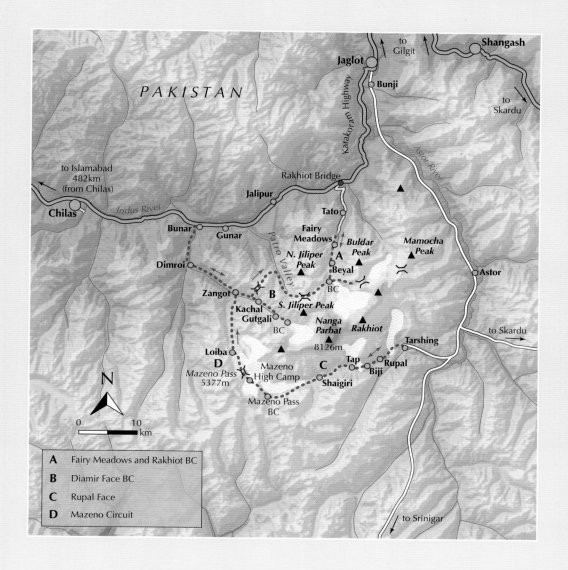

A	Fairy Meadows and Rakhiot BC
B	Diamir Face BC
C	Rupal Face
D	Mazeno Circuit

animals are rare, and the porters really earn their money by exchanging for a few weeks the hard life of the farmer for perhaps the even more demanding work of carrying loads on behalf of foreign expeditions and trekking parties. Being Muslims they daily chant or sing their prayers on trek, which at times can seem like living in a scene from an opera with an endless array of dramatic peaks as a backdrop. At the end of each journey as we clamber aboard jeeps to ferry us back to a world of hotels and hot showers, the porters have become our friends and the farewells are heartfelt.

In 1895 Mummery was lost, along with two Gurkha companions, when seeking a route on the Diamir Face

These men may be tough and resilient, but they're well looked after, for there are precise regulations for handing out food and clothing for use on trek, and all porters are protected by insurance. Their hardy nature was made clear on one occasion when we were camped on top of the windy and exposed Hispar Pass at 5151m (Trek 2). The porters were sleeping in either snow holes or in the mess tent, which was anchored to the snow and ice with climbing ropes and ice axes. During the night a storm blew the mess tent away. On hearing what was happening, I chased after it, eventually retrieved the tent and took it back to the porters, who were still fast asleep with snow falling on them.

Nanga Parbat

Northern Pakistan is unsurpassed as a mountain region, for this is the meeting point of three major ranges: the Himalaya, where Nanga Parbat reigns supreme; the Karakoram (with three 8000m peaks); and the Hindu Kush, whose highest summit is the 7706m Tirich Mir. As if this were not enough, the Pamir range also presses in from the north – so spare a moment to consider the immense powers of uplift that raised such a concentration of sharply pointed summits in an area of just 180 square kilometres. What a magical setting!

The name Nanga Parbat is a derivation of the Sanskrit, Nanga Parvata, which means 'The Naked Mountain', but it's also known as Diamir (King of the Mountains), or Dardi meaning 'The Dwelling Place of the Fairies'. First sketched and painted in 1856 by the German Adolf Schlagintweit, it was also described by Martin Conway in 1892 as 'a great white throne set in heaven'. But once it became a focus for mountaineers, Nanga earned the title of 'Killer Mountain' as a result of its many deadly avalanches. The well-known Victorian alpinist AF Mummery was lost during a reconnaissance of the Diamir Face in 1895, along with two of his Gurkha companions. By the time of its first ascent 58 years later, Nanga Parbat had claimed the lives of 28 other climbers and porters.

While British climbers concentrated their Himalayan efforts on trying to find a route to the summit of Mount Everest, German and Austrian mountaineers were mesmerised by Nanga Parbat, whose first ascent (via the Rakhiot Face) had to wait until 1953 – just five weeks after Everest had been climbed. The story of Hermann Buhl's heroic solo storming of the summit, followed by a lonely and shelterless bivouac at around 8000m, has passed into mountaineering folklore, as has the solo ascent of the mountain's Diamir Face by Reinhold Messner in 1978.

The approach

In the old days approach to the mountain was on foot from Srinagar, 125 kilometres to the south in Kashmir, taking up to two weeks, including two pass crossings, and there would be as many as 600 porters required to bring an expedition to its base. But today – weather permitting – a 60-minute flight from the capital Islamabad carries trekkers to the mountain town of Gilgit at 1500m, on the way passing very close to Nanga Parbat itself. It's an amazing flight during which you are transferred from the lowlands into the glistening kingdom of the world's highest peaks, while a slower and much more time-consuming approach by road follows the Indus River all the way from Islamabad.

Before going on trek spend some time in and around Gilgit, where you can visit the bazaar, watch a game of polo, and stock up with the delicious local apricots. Growing up to an altitude of

3000m there are many different species available in these northern areas, which, it is said, help local people stay young! Every bit of the apricot is used: as a fruit to eat, the shell for fuel, the nut for oil and the pulp as animal feed. Sometimes an alcoholic brew can also be found, but keep quiet about that!

The main trekking season extends from May until September; there are currently no restrictions and you can travel independently, or with a guided group. Since the local people are not always easy to deal with, taking a guide is strongly recommended; this can be organised either through an agent in Pakistan, or via one of several international trekking companies who will take care of the logistics.

Fairy Meadows and Rakhiot Base Camp trek

From Gilgit the hot, two-hour approach to the start of this trek is made by vehicle along the Karakoram Highway, which was opened in 1978 – an open jeep will reward with some cooling air in the stifling heat. As you travel southward note the intricately decorated trucks and buses passing by, for this is a busy road, a lifeline, not only for the northern regions, but also for carrying

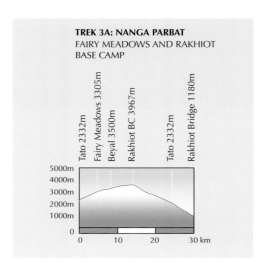

TREK 3A: NANGA PARBAT
FAIRY MEADOWS AND RAKHIOT
BASE CAMP

*High above Base Camp, the Diamir Face blushes
with the alpenglow*

trade between Pakistan and China. In the barren
wasteland of the Indus Valley, the highway suffers from dramatic landslides; sometimes trucks
run out of road and tumble down to the river

– but as you progress, so Nanga Parbat grows in
stature ahead.

At **Rakhiot Bridge** you transfer to local jeeps
that use a private dirt road leading to the village of
Tato (2332m) in a little under an hour. From there
it is only a short walk of two hours or so to **Fairy
Meadows** at 3305m, during which the landscape
undergoes a total change from hot, arid desert to

a dense forest and meadows full of edelweiss and wild roses, all at pleasant temperatures. It's almost like being in the Swiss Alps, with farmhouses and hay barns, and should you arrive without a tent, there's accommodation similar to that offered in a Nepalese teahouse, with showers and even a full meals service available. From here the view of the Rakhiot Face is 'overwhelming' – according to Karl Herrligkoffer in *Nanga Parbat: the Killer Mountain*.

The next village is **Beyal** at 3500m. This can be reached in one-and-a-half hours on an easy trail, and on arrival the same kind of facilities as at Fairy Meadows can be found. It then takes another four to five hours to reach the **base camp** area, set at the moraine end of a gigantic river of ice at

3967m, where a muted version of the groaning sounds of the glacier can be heard. While this may still be a place fit for human habitation, above the moraine the Rakhiot Face seems ready to collapse onto your camp. High up, hanging glaciers with delicately chiselled snow ridges, vertical snow ribs and ice runnels, produce a deadly bombardment of huge avalanches. At this camp there are memorials to a number of mountaineers killed by such avalanches, as well as one for the German climber Alfred Drexel, who died of pulmonary oedema on the mountain in 1937.

As well as the short trek to base camp, you could make side-trips to the summer alps at Susarboin (4200m), with grand views towards the massive North Face, or even more challenging, try climbing either the technical Southern Jiliper Peak (5206m) from Beyal, or Buldar Peak (5600m) to gain even better views towards Nanga Parbat.

After having spent several days exploring the area, should you wish to walk, rather than take the jeep back to the Rakhiot Bridge, follow the old route on the opposite side of the river at **Tato** to enjoy views towards the Rakaposhi and Haramosh ranges in the distance, with the Indus River swirling below.

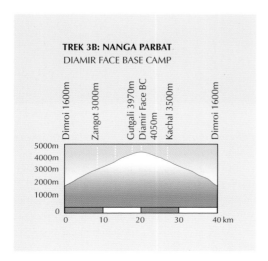

TREK 3B: NANGA PARBAT
DIAMIR FACE BASE CAMP

Trek to the Diamir Face

Some years ago I accompanied a BBC film team to the Diamir Face where Chris Bonington, Jim Curran, Sigi Hupfauer and Charles Houston were to make a documentary about Nanga Parbat. On our flight to Gilgit the overloaded Fokker Friendship struggled through a major monsoon storm that denied us the hoped-for close views of the mountain, but once our stranded luggage finally caught up with us a day later, we tackled the summer heat of the Karakoram Highway on open jeeps for two-and-a-half hours, heading beyond **Rakhiot Bridge** towards Chilas, the principal town in this part of the Indus Valley. Before reaching Chilas, however, an old jeep track led away to the south, climbing steeply into the **Bunar Valley**.

Near Bunar Bridge the village of **Dimroi** (or Diamorio) is worth exploring to see the basic conditions in which these mountain people live, but please be sensitive in your cultural interactions to avoid friction, and make sure you are appropriately dressed in this Muslim land. Depending on the condition of the jeep road, this is where the trek begins; if not, it will be somewhere along the way to Bunar village. For two days follow the Diamir River upvalley to the Diamir Face Base Camp, passing through the villages of **Zangot**, **Kachal** (3500m), and **Gutgali** (3970m); a route involving several exposed and questionable sections of trail. Gaining height the dry landscape changes into a more lush region where hard-working farmers till the soil. Two hours more and **Base Camp** is reached at 4050m, and the walk is finally rewarded with grand views of the Diamir Face, on which it is thought Mummery died in 1895.

Trek to the Rupal Face

From Gilgit drive by jeep to **Astor** (2345m) and onwards to **Tarshing** (2911m) in the Rupal Valley, which is dominated by Rakhiot Peak to the west. Here you either camp for the night, or use the simple Tarshing Guesthouse near the village. Spending an extra day here in order to acclimatise, you could make a side-trip of four hours in a northerly

Tarshing herders, and it has an amazing outlook onto Nanga Parbat's South Face and the Mazeno Peaks – a traverse of these to the summit of Nanga Parbat was one of the 'last great challenges' of Himalayan climbing until it was finally achieved in July 2012 by a British expedition. At least one day should be spent at Shaigiri, and since porters in Pakistan expect to receive some meat on trek, this is where a goat will be bought, followed by a feast and an inevitable evening of song. Join in and enjoy it. One possible use of a day here is the opportunity to explore the area towards Mazeno Pass Base Camp at 4200m, from where the Mazeno Circuit continues (see below). To return to the Tarshing roadhead from Shaigiri will take one day.

The Mazeno Circuit

This, the most rewarding of Nanga Parbat treks, could be started at one of several places along the Karakoram Highway, but it's often combined with one of the three treks described earlier. Including rest days you should count on 10–16 days of trekking. Although graded 'Demanding', the only

real difficulty will be found when crossing the Mazeno Pass, for on its northern side a steep and icy stretch of 200–300 metres requires the use of rope, ice axe and crampons. Despite this, the pass was crossed in the 19th century by men from Chilas without any technical climbing gear when they raided Tarshing, Rupal and other villages.

Here we will consider the Circuit as an extension of the trek to the Rupal Face, described immediately above.

Having arrived at **Shaigiri** (3750m), the trek continues to the **Mazeno Pass Base Camp** on a good, mainly flat trail parallel with the Rupal Glacier. Nanga Parbat views now disappear, and as the five- to six-hour climb to the next camp leads to 4750m it is important to be aware of the altitude gain and the need to be well acclimatised.

From **Mazeno High Camp** to the Mazeno Pass (Mazeno Gah) at 5377m is a fairly straightforward trek in a rugged landscape, with superb views to be won over the Loiba Glacier once the pass has been gained. This crossing is, of course, the crux of the route; difficulties include the advanced altitude, and a minor technical

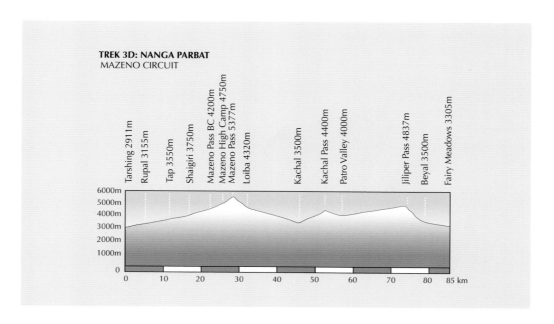

TREK 3D: NANGA PARBAT
MAZENO CIRCUIT

Descent from the Mazeno Pass takes you down to the Loiba Glacier (photo: Meikel Beek)

descent that not only involves the use of rope, ice axe and crampons, but assistance for porters and members of the trek crew when reaching the Loiba Glacier. After a night disturbed, no doubt, by sounds of glacial movement, the trek continues down to the meadows of **Loiba** and Eirel, both of which are used by herders.

There are two options to consider when deciding how and where to conclude this trek. The first and most direct leads steeply down to the hamlet of **Zangot** in order to reach the Karakoram Highway by way of **Dimroi** and **Bunar**, while a more challenging route goes via **Kachal** near the Diamir Face Base Camp, then over the Gotgali Pass (Kachal Pass) to the Patro Valley, and by way of the Jiliper Pass to eventually reach **Fairy Meadows** below the Rakhiot Face. Much will depend on the available time, energy and experience of your party, but with Nanga Parbat as a perpetual backdrop, each day will be truly unforgettable.

Dwarfed by the landscape, trekkers make their way to camp before tackling the Zalung Karpo La ▶

Trek 4
Zanskar Dream Trek
by Steve Berry

A bruise on the map that the eye cannot escape, the Greater Himalaya arcs from east to west before it collides at its western end with the Karakoram. Tucked away behind the Himalayan range, and before reaching the granitic vastness of the Karakoram, lies the former kingdom of Ladakh. This timeless, mystical land of levitating monks, hermit retreats and eyrie monasteries was the point of impact 40 million years ago between the tectonic plates of the sub-Indian continent and Eurasia. Little wonder then that it is characterised by grandiose gorges, alluvial fans, contorted strata and snow-capped peaks, with the Dream Trek passing through the most spectacular gorges on its way to the kingdom of Zanskar and beyond.

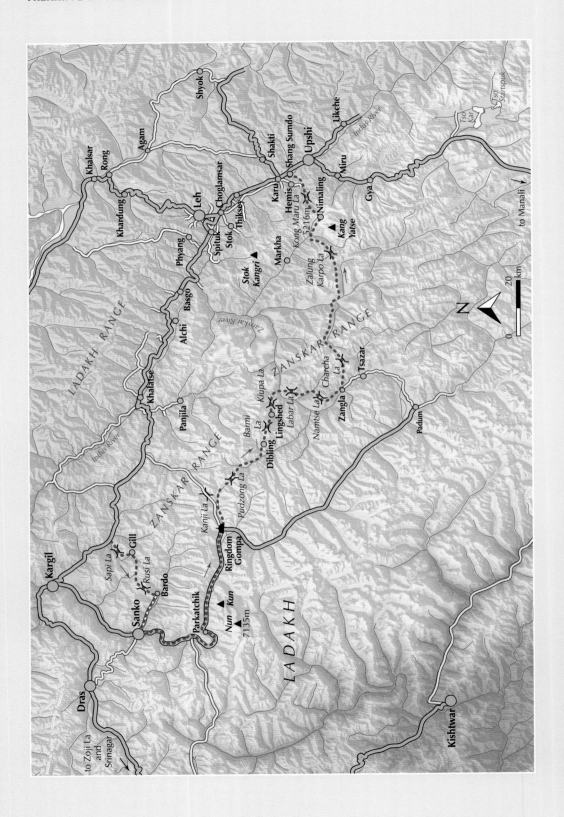

Route summary

Location	Ladakh, northwest India
Start	Gill
Finish	Shang Sumdo
Distance	275km as the crow flies
Duration	3½ weeks (20 days' trekking plus 2 rest days)
Maximum altitude	Kong Maru La 5216m
Trek style	Camping
Restrictions	None
Grade	Demanding
Guidebook	*Trekking in Ladakh* by Radek Kucharski (Cicerone, 2012) – includes small sections only

The tiny Tibetan Buddhist kingdom of Zanskar is roughly 190 kilometres long, and virtually closed off from the outside world by snow-bound passes for all but a few summer months. Its deep and spectacular valleys run roughly west to east in the centre of a veritable maze of mountains, which themselves lie south of the Indus Valley. In ancient times Zanskar paid annual tribute to the line of more powerful kings in Leh, the capital of Ladakh, whose Potala-like palace still stands serene above the bustling streets and narrow alleyways.

A violent incursion by a Kashmiri army led by General Zowara Singh in 1837 changed the balance of power in Ladakh. The king was shelled out of his palace, and Ladakh, a once proud and powerful nation, came under the yoke of the Maharaja of Kashmir. The British inherited 'Little Tibet' (as Ladakh is often called) during the Raj, and after Independence it became part of the Indian State of Jammu and Kashmir.

Ponies are sometimes used to ferry trekkers across the many rivers

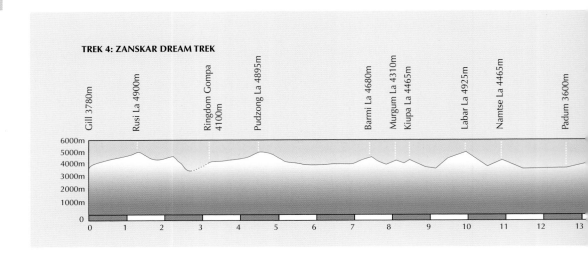

TREK 4: ZANSKAR DREAM TREK

The Ladakhi people have their roots in Tibet; they wear Tibetan-like clothes, their language is closely akin to Tibetan, and their sects of Buddhist religion are the same as those found in Tibet and Bhutan. Indeed, even after the Kashmiri invasion, Ladakh continued to pay annual tribute to the Dalai Lama in Lhasa. The kings of Ladakh and Zanskar are direct descendants of the early kings of Tibet, long before the line of reincarnate Dalai Lamas came into peaceful being.

After World War II my father, then a major in the British army, attempted to climb Nun (7135m), the highest mountain in Kashmir and Ladakh. He and his friends succeeded in climbing a subsidiary, White Needle Peak (6400m), but the big prize eluded them. In 1981 my brother Richard and I, with a group of our friends, finished the job off. The staggering views from the summit of Nun were of snow-capped peaks as far as the eye could see in every direction, and we gazed on whole swathes of mountainous country that I knew had as yet received virtually no European footsteps. Maps, further research, and many visits to various parts of Ladakh and Zanskar over the years left an imprint on my imagination, and I often have vivid dreams of wandering high forgotten trails in an age before technology began

to touch this ancient civilisation. Inevitably I was drawn to seek out the remotest paths in the hope of finding those places of my dreams. The Zanskar Dream Trek discovers those places.

Best tackled in September when the river levels are low, the trek falls naturally into three sections. The first is an acclimatisation stage of only three days from the Indus Valley towards Nun peak. Vehicles are needed at the end of this section to drive you past Nun and on to the Ringdom Gompa. At the end of my father's climb in 1946 the expedition had all but run out of food and Dad went off to hunt a bear they knew was in the area. Venturing far from base camp he came across Ringdom Gompa sitting on top of a hill in a wide valley, with a village nearby. The people had never seen a white man before and he was received by the Head Lama and given presents of a prayer wheel, a *mani* stone and a large crystal. To this day, this fantastic monastery is imbued with all the atmosphere of hundreds of years of prayer and continually burning butter lamps.

The second section is a trek from Ringdom to the kingdom of Zanskar, which takes nine days and crosses six passes. Halfway through it intersects with the better-known classic trail from Padum to Lamayuru, and you may well see other

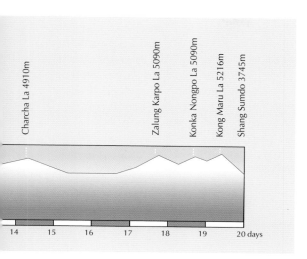

Charcha La 4910m

Zalung Karpo La 5090m

Konka Nongpo La 5090m

Kong Maru La 5216m

Shang Sumdo 3745m

14   15   16   17   18   19   20 days

Westerners at the village of Lingshed, but apart from that the adventures of this route will almost certainly be yours, and yours alone.

Having reached Zanskar you will deserve a rest, and from the village of Zangla you could take a jeep to visit the small township of Padum.

The third and final section of the trek now takes eight days, crosses another four major passes, and explores even more spectacular gorges on its way to the Indus Valley, east of Leh.

Leh to Ringdom Gompa

The flight from Delhi to Leh takes just over an hour and passes right over the top of the Greater Himalaya. It must be one of the most sensational daily scheduled flights anywhere in the world, and after your trek, on the return flight, you will be able to see from the air the scale of your achievement. In Leh you need time to acclimatise to the altitude, as the town sits north of the Indus River at a height of 3500m. Time spent here is not wasted, for it is a fascinating town. The Tibetan-like palace that dominates the scene has been sold by the royal family to the Archaeological Society of India, thankfully preventing its

In Ladakh private houses are often used by trekkers for homestays (photo: Kev Reynolds)

complete collapse. Take time to wander the bazaars, the Tibetan refugee market, and the main street where you will see Ladakhis wearing traditional stove-pipe hats and felt boots with turned-up toes, women selling vegetables from the pavement, and monks mixing with Kashmiri traders. Although Ladakh is primarily a Buddhist culture, Muslim influence has spread from Kashmir, and in the early morning be prepared to be woken by the plaintive cry of the *muezzin* calling the faithful to prayer. It's all a rapid culture shock after the frenetic hustle of Delhi.

From Leh it's a two-day drive to the roadhead near the village of Gill. It is possible to do this journey in a day, but you still need acclimatisation, and breaking the drive gives the opportunity of visiting a few of the most important temples in Ladakh. Alchi is a convenient stopover and a UNESCO World Heritage Site. The temples were built by the great Tibetan translator, Rinchen Zangpo (AD958–1055), and for a thousand years have escaped destruction by ravaging armies and the occasional Himalayan earthquake. Certainly you must visit the largest monastery in Ladakh, Lamayuru, which is a few minutes' walk from the road. Luckily when the Kashmiris invaded, the monks had prior warning and hid all the monastery's treasures in the surrounding mountains until the danger was past.

The audacity of the Indian army engineers who built the road astounds those travelling on it. High passes are crossed via countless looping hairpins through a barren moonscape country, punctuated by village oases. The main road eventually leads over the famous Zoji La and on down into the Vale of Kashmir, but before reaching the sordid town of Kargil you turn off south to cross the **Sapi La** (4350m). It is now only a short trundle to camp beyond **Gill** (3780m) next to the river. The Tibetan-looking villages nearby have small mosques, for indeed the people here are Muslim.

Two passes are crossed over the next three days – the **Rusi La** (4900m) and the 4380m Chardo La – providing excellent further acclimatisation. From the top of the Rusi La in clear weather you should obtain views of Nun. By now you are in wild country where the valleys are populated not by people but by marmots – try tempting them out of their burrows with a line of biscuits.

Descending from the Chardo La, the valley eventually leads to the roadhead village of **Bardo**. Having met your vehicles you then drive through impressive scenery to meet the much larger, prosperous Suru Valley, which, with its many orchards and larger settlements, leads

directly towards the sister peaks of Nun and Kun. Rounding a corner they stand framed in a picture-postcard setting at the head of the valley. Break the journey with an overnight at Namsuru, and next day drive past the snout of the Parktik Glacier. With vehicles straining at the altitude, you gain the high wide valley that is the transition to Buddhist Zanskar and the setting for the ancient monastery of **Ringdom Gompa**.

Ringdom Gompa to the kingdom of Zanskar

Now the real fun starts! Armed with the 'good luck' prayers from the lamas at Ringdom Gompa, you head into regions of box-canyons, gorges, snow bridges, high windswept passes and river crossings. The unknown beckons, and round each corner is the excitement of discovering fresh, awe-inspiring scenery.

A long, slow, snow plod eventually leads to the Pudzong La at 4895m

Dibling at harvest time, a secluded 14-house Shangri La (photo: Barbara Roberts)

From Ringdom the path leads east-northeast towards the Kanji La, but instead turn off right towards the Pudzong La. For the first hour or so follow the riverbed before contouring up the right-hand mountainside. A huge contorted cliff, hundreds of metres high, appears on the other side. Below the river emerges from a square-cut box-canyon made up of glacial deposits that, over countless millennia, have been eroded by the river. Eagles soar and marmots squeal at your approach. There is a small campsite almost opposite the turn-off for the Kanji La, but if time and energy allow, it would be better to continue another hour and a half to 'Hell Camp'. Quite why this place is so named I cannot say, but nearby there are magnificent views of Nun and Kun framed at the end of the valley. Camped at over 4300m, there is a long and inspiring day ahead to cross the Pudzong La.

From Hell Camp you turn up a stunningly beautiful valley with a snake-like stream coming down from a wall of snow-covered peaks at its end. It looks seriously difficult, but the pass is hidden from sight. Contour all morning before descending to the main riverbed, then follow this ever upwards, boulder-hopping from one side of the stream to the other until reaching the remains of winter snows forming bridges over the stream. Cross these and begin the agonisingly slow snow plod to the prayer-flagged **Pudzong La** (4895m). Shouts of '*Ki ki so so lha gyalo*' rend the air, praising victory to the gods; there are handshakes, backslapping and picture-taking, and the inner glow that comes from achieving a hard task. The views are superb, with snow-covered peaks in every direction.

Leaving the pass behind you still have 900m to descend to the valley. It will take roughly two hours to the next camp among an area of clumpy small trees and bushes. There is a small, solitary mud-brick house nearby that a yak herder uses in the summer – but watch out for his Tibetan-mastiff guard dogs.

The next morning stroll leisurely down this miniature Shangri-La valley, wading a small river before arriving at the 14-house village of **Dibling**, watched over by its small Yellow Hat (Gelug-pa) sect monastery. It's incredible to think that this solitary village is closed off from the outside world by high passes and deep gorges; it makes you wonder how the tiny population has attracted new blood to share in the hard life there.

Now follow the main river, which flows down for 30 kilometres to join with the Zanskar River to the east. Two hours from Dibling you arrive at the first river junction, or *sumdo*, where there is a delightful campsite.

Next day, after breakfast in the sunshine, you climb for 10 minutes to a col with prayer flags, before the path traverses down into a massive confined gorge. Vertical cliffs force major river crossings as the exposed path peters out. It is only possible to wade the river in September; at one point you have to wade some distance as the cliffs forbid a path on either side. The scenery is jaw-dropping – beetling cliffs with pigeons and choughs soaring the heights. Even eagles might come to see who these strangers are. You now criss-cross the river to Lingshed Sumdo (3745m) where a river and a path come down from the left. This is the route you now follow to a camp before the Barmi La. Stream hop and climb the ever-tightening side gorge, up and up, backwards and forwards, under gigantic cliffs to a traverse leading into a 'narrows'. The stony campsite lies just beyond, with impressive cliffs angling 45 degrees down to the stream edge.

The **Barmi La** (4680m) is some three hours of gradual ascent from camp, though the last 300 metres steepens and there are places where you would not want to slip from the narrow path. The pass itself is broad and the new views inspiring. The huge valley below contains **Lingshed** village

and *gompa*; it's a long and hot descent, but the views just go on improving.

Dropping past houses and fields you then climb up past the monastery to a camp near a small shop where, if you are lucky, they might sell bottles of beer. At the monastery each evening visitors are welcome to sit in on the daily *puja* ceremony. Enter the gompa through dark corridors and a kitchen straight out of Gormenghast, leading to a small meditation room where you can sit quietly, listening to the hypnotic chanting of prayers and being served yak butter tea and *tsampa*.

From Lingshed there are two passes to cross; first, the Murgum La (4310m), followed a few hours later by the **Kiupa La** (4465m). The latter follows a most improbable-looking route up a steep mountainside, and the path is pretty exposed in places. From the summit head straight down a shallow slope where rhubarb grows, until a sort of secret path funnels between two large rocky outcrops to emerge above the hamlet of Yulchung. Dwarfing everything is an amphitheatre of mountains containing slender spires of rock, and cliffs laced with quartz.

Three more sensational days lie between you and Zanskar. The first is probably the hardest physical day of the entire trek. Descend from Yulchung to cross the Zanskar River on an ancient cantilevered bridge, then climb over 1200m up the other side through the village of Nyerak to a camp before the **Labar La** (4925m).

The next day must rate as one of my best trekking days ever. Crossing the pass we saw definite bear tracks and plenty of evidence of ibex and blue sheep. The way heads down into the depths between imposing rocky mountains with gigantic contorted strata, past two unusual white cliffs where it looks as though the gods have literally torn the cliffs apart. Having passed through you find yourself in a sharp valley with a river running in its flat base. On either side eroded pinnacles have boulders perched improbably on their tops. Suddenly the cliffs squeeze together until the path is barely wide enough for a horse to pass through.

A series of tight canyons follows with hairy paths, gigantic slabs of rock coming straight out of the earth, and difficult man-made rock stairs where you may have to unload the horses. Finally leaving the gorges behind, only adrenaline will keep you going a long way down the valley to camp.

The last day into Zanskar is also fabulous trekking, over the **Namtse La** and down past impressive 300m-high vertical cliffs to emerge above the wide Zanskar Valley. It is then an hour's flat walking from Honia to camp on the river meadows before **Zangla** village.

Zanskar to Shang Sumdo

It seems sheer luxury to have a rest day, and it's well worth a jeep ride to visit Padum, the main township of Zanskar, where a relatively civilised lunch can be had at the Ibex Hotel in its pleasant green courtyard.

The final section of the Dream Trek can only be undertaken when the river levels are low, and it is rarely trekked. The gorges are arguably even more impressive, if that is possible, than those passed through previously. These eight days are through uninhabited country, over passes with powerful

names, such as the Zalung Karpo La (5090m), and some days there are up to 50 or 60 river crossings to be made. The scenery is so grand, so awe-inspiring, that in some sections you will want to stop every 50 paces just to take it all in.

The first challenge is the mighty **Charcha La** (4910m); from Zangla you enter the Zumlung Chu gorge where superlatives cannot do the scene justice. After an hour pass under a huge fin of rock on top of which is perched the remains of a very ancient fortress. Who built it and why? The gorge contains the bizarre and the unusual

The wide Zanskar Valley on the way to Zangla

– arching rock slabs, a painter's palate of coloured rock strata, small fish swimming in side pools – and after six hours the gorge spits you out at a river junction to camp and gird your loins for tomorrow. Start early in order to keep in the shade for as long as possible before huge scree slopes lead to an improbable-looking path that weaves its way through cliffs to the emotional summit.

Trekking below the spectacular coloured cliffs on the approach to Tilat Sumdo

The days via Chupchak, Tomto, Nyari Nyarsang and Rabrang become a blur of leviathan cliffs rising straight out of the earth in titanic twisted slabs, countless river crossings, and snow peaks peeking into your world of endless gorges. Question is, does one ever tire of cliffs that crick your neck? In 2009 we saw fresh snow leopard tracks, herds of blue sheep, holy caves, mountains of glacial conglomerate, and intricate ancient paths engineered from old tree trunks and stone.

Then there is the long exhausting climb to the **Zalung Karpo La** (5090m) from where, looking back, you can pick out with binoculars the peak of Nun. It will give you a sense of pride to know you have walked nearly all the way from there, while ahead the highest peak in the Zanskar range, Kang Yatse (6400m), can be identified by the striking steep snow ridge leading to the summit.

You still have to cross the **Konka Nongpo La** in order to reach the plains of Nimaling that lie on the other side of Kang Yatse, where yaks graze and the tented summer settlement may sell beer. One more day now to civilisation over the highest pass of them all, the **Kong Maru La** (5216m) before a knee-buckling descent to the roadhead at Shang Sumdo. Back in the real world, drive the short distance to Leh and a deserved celebration at completing what must surely be one of the finest adventure treks in the Himalaya.

With its tantalising location, Dibrugheta is as near to the Nanda Devi Sanctuary as you're currently allowed to go ▶

Trek 5
Nanda Devi Sanctuary

by Steve Berry

*T*he inner sanctuary of Nanda Devi was dreamt of, schemed over, and attempted by a gaggle of famous climbers over a 70-year period until Eric Shipton and Bill Tilman, the most important explorers of the Himalayan golden age, bravely forced a way up the Rishi Ganga gorge in 1934. Theirs is an incredible story, for not only did they succeed in entering the Sanctuary, but they spent literally months inside mapping, exploring, and climbing fine peaks. The ultimate prize, the first ascent of Nanda Devi herself, succumbed to Tilman two years later. Today permits are available to retrace their steps part way up the Rishi Ganga gorge – a fantastic outing in its own right.

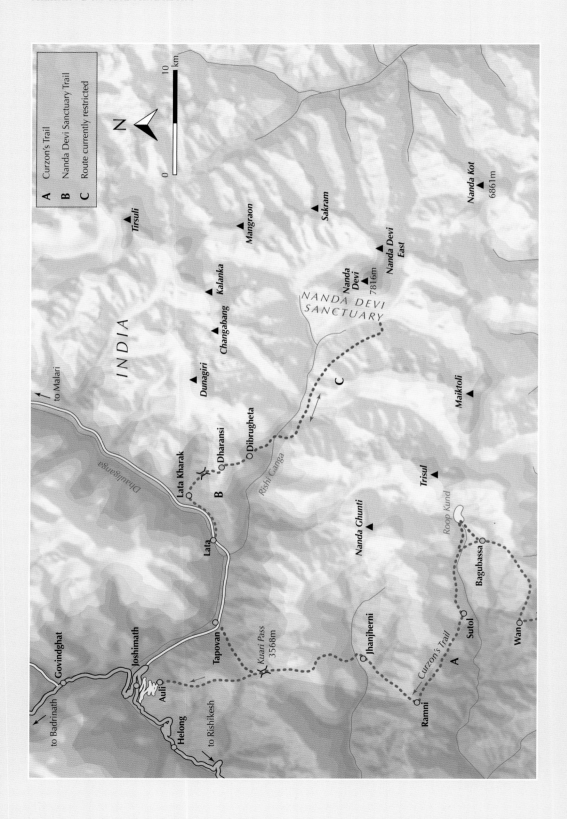

Route summary

Location	Garhwal, Indian Himalaya
Start	Curzon's Trail: Lohajung Nanda Devi Sanctuary: Joshimath
Finish	Joshimath
Distance	about 80km Curzon's Trail 48km Lata – Dibrugheta – Lata
Duration	Curzon's Trail including Roop Kund 11 days Sanctuary Trek, Dibrugheta return 7 days
Maximum altitude	Roop Kund variation 4724m Kuari Pass 3568m Nanda Devi Sanctuary Trek 4250m
Trek style	Camping
Restrictions	Special permits required
Grade	Expedition
Guidebook	*Nanda Devi* by Hugh Thomson (Weidenfeld & Nicolson)

At 7816m Nanda Devi is the highest peak wholly within India, and was once the highest of the British Empire. To Hindus, however, it is one of the main sources of the Ganges, India's holiest river, while Nanda Devi herself is believed to be a manifestation of Lord Shiva's wife Parvati. For explorers it was the holy grail of the Himalaya, for this monster peak sits within an almost impenetrable ring of mountains, at least 12 of whose summits exceed 6500m, including Changabang and Dunagiri to the north, and Trisul and Nanda Kot to the west and south. This concentration of peaks is connected by massive walls that dip no lower than 5200m and form an enormous amphitheatre enclosing some 650 square kilometres of land. The only place where this mountain stockade is broken is the Rishi Ganga gorge, which acts as a drain for the snowmelt from Nanda Devi and her sisters.

Little surprise, then, that finding a way into the Sanctuary became a *cause célèbre* and that many famous explorers tried their luck. GW Traill ascended the Pindari Glacier in 1830 and crossed a pass into the Milam Valley, but the first

real attempt to assay the Rishi Ganga gorge was by the redoubtable Himalayan explorer, WW Graham, in 1863. His party failed when the porters deserted, believing the route to be infested with devils. The next to try was Dr Tom Longstaff who took Swiss guides in 1905 and gained the Sanctuary rim, thus becoming the first man to look down into it. However his party found it impossible to descend into the Sanctuary itself and gave up. Returning in 1907 with a very strong team, he became the first person ever to climb a 7000m peak (Trisul), but failed to penetrate the Rishi Ganga gorge. Hugh Rutledge and Howard Somervell of Everest fame tried in 1926 and 1932, and they also failed. And so we come finally to Shipton and Tilman in 1934.

In the first of their great lightweight Himalayan expeditions, with a budget of £300 for five months, and accompanied by three tough Sherpas, they forced a way up the Rishi Ganga gorge and became the first human beings to set foot in the Sanctuary. There they found herds of mountain sheep completely unafraid of man's presence grazing pastures full of alpine flowers, while 3000m above them towered Nanda Devi herself. With more than a month's supply mainly of rice, flour, ghee and tea, they explored the Inner Sanctuary, and after the monsoon returned to complete their survey. Two years later Tilman was back as a member of a British/American expedition, when he and Noel Odell reached the summit – at that time the highest climbed by man.

The way in was open, and between 1934 and 1982 no fewer than 18 expeditions added their names to the history books. Some succeeded, some failed, and Nanda Devi claimed the lives of at least 11, among them Nanda Devi Unsoeld, who had been named after the mountain. One of the strangest of tales recalls that between 1965 and 1968 joint American/Indian army expeditions attempted to place a nuclear-powered tracking device on the summit to monitor Chinese missile tests in Sinkiang. However, the device was swept away in an avalanche at 6700m, never

From the town of Ranikhet, Nanda Devi and her great ring of peaks make an alluring sight

to be seen again. In 1978 revelations of the spy story appeared in the press, and members of an innocent British expedition were arrested at base camp on espionage charges.

This was the principle reason for the closure of the Inner Sanctuary in 1982 amid fears that India's holiest river could be polluted by this nuclear device. It wasn't the only pollution, however, for several expeditions accused each other of leaving piles of garbage in the Sanctuary. And as local shepherds were now taking flocks of sheep and goats there, this was also said to be doing irreparable ecological damage, while expedition porters were taking the opportunity to dig up rare medicinal roots and plants. There was an outcry, so the authorities decided to 'rest' the Sanctuary and allow it to recover.

Prior to 1982 the Indians themselves had been fielding many expeditions. Their first successful ascent of Nanda Devi in 1964 was led by Major Narinder Kumar, affectionately known to his friends as 'Bull'. Arguably the most accomplished Indian mountaineer of all time, Bull was deputy leader of his country's first successful ascent of Everest in 1965, and led the first Indian expedition to climb Kangchenjunga in 1977. Thanks to his immense influence, and his tireless pursuit of the elusive permits down the corridors of Indian bureaucracy, in the year 2000 I was afforded the rare privilege of entering Nanda Devi's Inner Sanctuary. By lucky coincidence, at a conference in Delhi I met George Band, who made the first ascent of Kangchenjunga and was a member of the 1953 Everest expedition, and he and his friend Ian McNaught-Davis, then president of the world's mountaineering body the UIAA, both accepted my invitation to join the party. Also by wonderful coincidence Bull's son Akshay is an old friend of mine, and he and his father both wanted to come, as did Eric Shipton's son John, who I had also known for many years. The idea was to carry out a survey and produce a report for the Indian Mountaineering Federation on the way forward for the Sanctuary; should it remain closed, or perhaps be opened in a controlled manner by the use of special permits?

Curzon's Trail to Joshimath

Although our group did not take this route in 2000, it would be the best approach, for it was the one Shipton and Tilman followed on their way to the Rishi Ganga's gorge. Known as Curzon's Trail, the famous Viceroy of India had the path improved sufficiently for him to make the journey; however, legend has it that he was prevented from crossing the Kuari Pass by a swarm of bees.

Beginning at **Lohajung**, there are several slight variations of this 11-day trek, one of which takes you to **Roop Kund**, where in 1942 a British forestry officer discovered a frozen lake located in a remote mountain valley at an altitude of almost 4800m. In and around it were the skeletons of between 500 and 600 people; carbon dating proves the bones date from AD850 but what the people were doing there, or how and why they died, remains unknown.

Curzon's Trail gives vital acclimatisation, an insight into the scale of Shipton and Tilman's efforts to reach Nanda Devi, as well as a real taste of the life of the village people, and an introduction to the mountains of Garhwal. It takes you over mountain passes, through dense forests where troupes of monkeys play and monal pheasants hide from hunters. It traverses

Teetering along a narrow cliff path, a trekker with a prized permit works his way into the Rishi Ganga's gorge

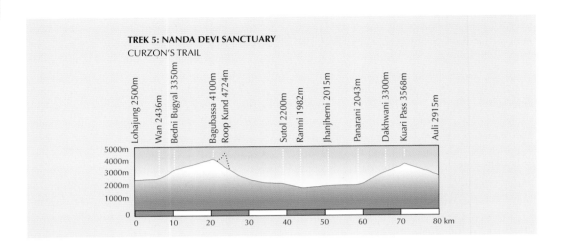

TREK 5: NANDA DEVI SANCTUARY
CURZON'S TRAIL

bugayals (meadows that serve as high-altitude summer grazing grounds), descends through gorges, and crosses suspension bridges over five major rivers: the Pindar, Kaliganga, Nandakini, Briehiganga and Dhauliganga. There are sections of untamed country where you need to be mindful of black bears, and you are not a million miles away from where Jim Corbett shot the

The scenic camp below the Kuari Pass (photo: John Earle)

legendary man-eating leopard at Rudrapryag – leopards still live in these hills.

Much of the trek though takes you through a dozen or so villages busy with farming folk whose rough houses are roofed with huge slabs of slate, and the older ones show intricately carved windows and door-frames. Old men sit on verandas smoking hookahs, women milk buffalo, and shy young girls, dressed in their traditional homespun woollen blankets, giggle as you pass by. Don't be phased as people gather round and stare as the circus comes to town; their cheerful grins and hospitality are utterly genuine.

In just over a week you climb the zigzag path to the 3568m **Kuari Pass**, said to be one of the finest vantage points in the Himalaya. On his way to climb Kamet with Eric Shipton in 1931, Frank Smythe described reaching the pass: 'We breasted the slope and halted, silent on the path. No words would express our delight. The Himalaya was arrayed before us in a stupendous arc.'

Among the mountains on show are Kamet (7756m), Nilkanth (7141m), Dunagiri (7067m) and Changabang (6864m), with Nanda Devi herself visible if you wander up the ridge for a while. Five hours of steep descent end at the roadhead and hot springs at **Tapovan**, from where a short drive leads to the pilgrimage town of **Joshimath** (1860m) for a well-deserved rest. Alternatively, many people now descend to Auli, from where a ski lift deposits the weary trekker in the valley below.

Joshimath to Dibrugheta

It's a 30-kilometre road journey to camp below the village of **Lata**. At the ancient temple, dedicated to the goddess Nanda Devi, we were greeted by drums and cymbals, and met an old man claiming to be 95 years old, who said he had been a porter with Shipton and Tilman. After cross-questioning we believed him; he was visibly touched to meet Eric's son, John, 66 years after the 1934 expedition.

In 2000 we had 15 Europeans, Colonel Bull Kumar and his son Akshay, 9 camp staff, 2 liaison

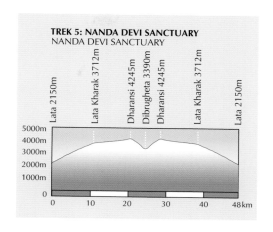

TREK 5: NANDA DEVI SANCTUARY
NANDA DEVI SANCTUARY

officers and a large, pre-booked team of porters. Of the 65 porters due to arrive, some turned up drunk and were dismissed, some had decided to go to a wedding, others could not be brought in from the harvest, and some gave up halfway on the first day. Even with the legendary colonel in our midst, the local workforce was a law unto itself, and none too reliable. However, those who did stick with us were truly among the bravest, hardest men I have ever met.

That first day is a killer! Before you looms a climb of 1562m to reach **Lata Kharak** at 3712m. However, taken slowly and given good weather, the day should pass pleasantly enough and the forest grants shade. Our porters drifted in some time after us; thankfully we'd managed to rent a few horses, which arrived long after dark. Some loads had been unceremoniously dumped halfway, but an acclimatisation and rest day enabled these to be recovered. A few more porters absconded.

On our rest day we went for a walk along the ridge leading to Lata Peak. With no path to follow, Shipton and Tilman climbed this from Lata village and returned the same day – a stupendous excursion that shows how fit they must have been. From the ridge there are fabulous views of Trisul, Devistan, Nanda Devi and many others.

From Lata Kharak we had intended going as far as Dharansi where we were told there was a

Extensive views make a diversion along the ridge to Lata Peak worthwhile

spring and a campsite. Shipton and Tilman had tried repeatedly to find a route there and eventually found a path along some cliff ledges. This is what Shipton had to say about these: 'We found a well-defined track running along the face of a steep precipice. The rocks still held a good deal of ice and snow, especially in the gullies, and much step cutting was required in order to get along the track. It was a remarkable place. The cliffs were exceedingly steep and dropped in an almost unbroken plunge for some 8000 feet, and yet there was this narrow ledge, along which it was possible for the shepherds to take their sheep in the summer time.'

This description induced some nervousness for the day ahead.

From camp it takes about three hours to reach a small 4260m pass, from where you gain a first view of the cliff path. The ledges traverse massive rock buttresses, the path is well worn and presents no difficulty, but the exposure is heart-stopping! You must concentrate on every footfall, and it is

best to look down only when stationary. Eventually the buttresses peter out and you enter a large bowl of dun-coloured grasses. This is **Dharansi**. When we reached it in 2000 the spring was almost dry. A small pass above the meadow looks straight up the Rishi Ganga gorge to Nanda Devi framed perfectly at the end, but cast your eyes down 760m and you can see the next meadow campsite of Dibrugheta (3390m) where we knew there would be water. It looked a long, steep way down into the fir and birch forest at the bottom, and the sting in the tail was a short rock wall to down-climb, which landed us on the banks of a stream followed by a short haul up to the meadow. Arriving at **Dibrugheta** – which Tilman described as 'a horizontal oasis in a vertical desert' – in the afternoon, it soon became obvious that many of our party would be overtaken by darkness. Some of the porters had an ingenious way of lighting the way; they pulled rolls of bark from birch trees and fashioned torches. The last to arrive at 10pm was

Dunagiri captures your attention on the trail to Dharansi

Bull who, having lost his toes to frostbite climbing Nilkanth many years ago, was slower downhill than most.

The headman of Lata turned up next day and showed us a bulging file of press cuttings and letters. He and his friends had been campaigning for years to open the Sanctuary as their village needed the valuable work of portering for expeditions and trekkers. They also wanted to be able to take their herds into the Sanctuary once more for grazing.

When we returned home and submitted our report, an unholy row broke out within Indian mountaineering circles. Some factions wanted what we recommended: a system of special permits and a cap on the number of annual visitors, with strict conditions regarding waste disposal and protection of the environment. Others, however, vehemently opposed any opening of the Sanctuary at all. Finally the IMF sent their own team to conduct a survey, but regrettably they

came under heavy criticism, and returned carrying animal skins, which showed that poaching was still a fact of life. The resulting compromise is where we are today; Dibrugheta is as far as you can go into the Sanctuary. It's a grand trek in its own right, and combined with Curzon's Trail is well worthwhile. Certainly if there is a change of policy and the Inner Sanctuary ever opens up again, the authorities would be forced to place and maintain safety ropes, build bridges and install a checkpost. Without safety measures the route beyond Dibrugheta is far too dangerous for regular trekking parties.

Dibrugheta to the Inner Sanctuary

Read Shipton and Tilman's superlative books and the classic understated narratives describe harum-scarum cliff paths, wading through torrents, and teetering along narrow ledges – you cannot help but get caught up in the excitement of real 'out-there' exploration. Take for instance Shipton's

The northern stem of Nanda Devi's Inner Sanctuary

description of just one of the difficult sections beyond Dibrugheta: 'Towards the end of the traverse, the links became very fragile. One spot in particular caused us such trouble that it produced a fairly forceful protest from Angtharkay, and caused Kusang to pause momentarily in his monotonous flow of song. But above and below us the cliffs were smooth and sheer, and the passage could not be avoided. This section came to be known as the "Mauvais Pas" and was certainly the most hair-raising bit of the traverse.'

Personally I found it all hair-raising! From Dibrugheta it was three days to reach the lip of the gorge and set foot in the actual Inner Sanctuary. All three days were high adventure, but the last day was the best, or the worst, depending which

way you look at it. I remember crawling on hands and knees under an overhang, pulling hand over hand up a knotted line that hung down a long steep gully, rock climbing round a rocky corner, then up and across very steep slabs, thankfully clipped into fixed line, joking with the porters, feeling the hot sun, hearing the thunder of the river far below. The wall of the gorge opposite

made me giddy just to look at it; such fantastic cliffs – no wonder Shipton and Tilman had pronounced that way impossible.

As the afternoon wore on, with two friends I watched as the best Indian guide, an old and wiry man, moved further and further ahead of us. We saw him climb a chimney, stand silhouetted for a minute then disappear. It looked as though that

If restrictions are lifted, the way into the Sanctuary will involve climbing this 'Stairway to Heaven'

might mark the end of the main difficulties, but when we exited the chimney half an hour later we were confronted by a wall of rock 300m high. My first emotion was to rebel against going up – it was too frightening, too difficult altogether, but on closer inspection we could see how it must be done. As we gazed awe-struck at the narrow terrace halfway up the cliff we involuntarily started singing bars from a Jimi Hendrix song: 'There's got to be some way out of here'. There was!

Firstly height had to be gained up a mountainside steep enough to necessitate pulling on clumps of grass to make progress. Then we edged across to the ledge itself, which was actually quite wide, and after 150 metres there was another rocky chimney. We found out later that the locals call this 'the Stairway to Heaven'. Even then our nerves had to be stretched a little further. Another steep slope and another chimney this time really did take us over the top of the final cliff and into the Inner Sanctuary of the Nanda Devi Basin.

There was Nanda Devi herself so close, so white, so gigantic. We were safe. The sense of relief was a great wave, the feeling that we could rest and savour a patch of earth that was reasonably level was the day's reward.

That evening the sun crashed slowly through the horizon, and we sat in the 'gods' applauding the last act as Nanda Devi blushed her subtle colours.

Mount Kailash rises abruptly from the Lha Chu Valley ▶

Trek 6

Mount Kailash Kora

by Siân Pritchard-Jones and Bob Gibbons

Hidden and isolated for centuries behind the almost impenetrable barrier of the Himalaya, there stands a mythical mountain close to the source of four major rivers: Indus, Sutlej, Karnali and Tsangpo-Brahmaputra. Revered by millions, the lonely peak of Mount Kailash rises from Tibet's barren plains as a great white dome of the gods. Capturing the trekker's imagination, and inspiring all who visit, Kailash stands majestic and alone. Yet across rolling hills not far away is another seductive gem waiting to be discovered – the lost Buddhist kingdom of Guge. Go soon if you can, for Kailash, Guge and Tibet itself are magical places where dreams and legends, folklore and mysterious mountains blend in a cocktail of adventure.

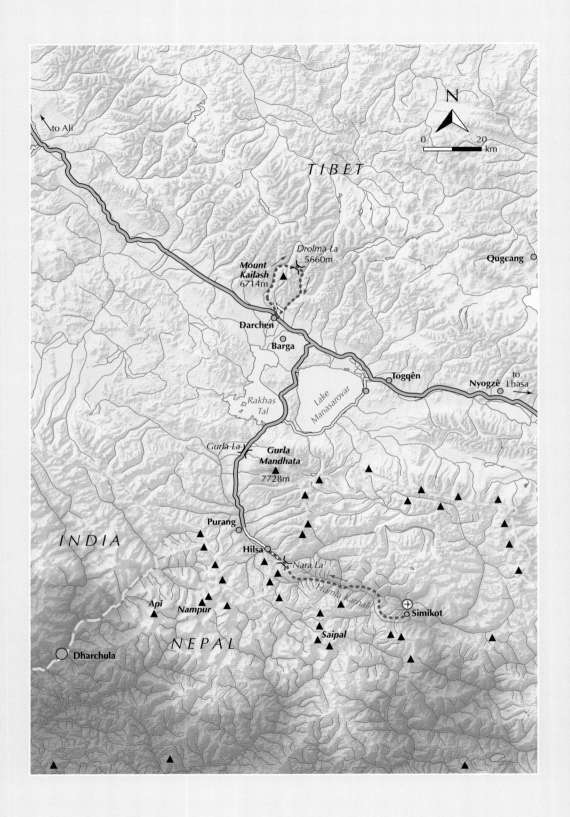

Route summary

Location	Southwest Tibet
Start/Finish	Darchen
Distance	55–60km
Duration	4 days
Maximum altitude	Drolma La 5660m
Trek style	Monastery guesthouses, lodges or camping
Restrictions	Permits required from the Chinese authorities
Grade	Demanding
Guidebook	*Mount Kailash: A Trekker's Guide* by Siân Pritchard-Jones and Bob Gibbons (Cicerone Press, 2006)

At 6714m Mount Kailash stands northwest of the borders of Nepal, India and Tibet, a pilgrimage site for some of the world's major religions for more than a thousand years. Sacred to Hindus for whom it is the home of Shiva, the god of destruction, Buddhists revere it as Kang Rinpoche (Precious Jewel of the Snows) – a vast *chorten*, a pyramid of nature that can cleanse the sins of a lifetime. For the Bon-po, the first religious people of Tibet, it is Yungdrung Gutse, or 'the nine-storied swastika mountain'. And for Jain pilgrims from India it is the sacred peak of Asthapada, where their first prophet gained enlightenment.

For many people Kailash is the spiritual centre of the universe. In the words of Lama Anagarika Govinda in *The Way of the White Clouds*: 'To see the greatness of a mountain one must keep one's distance; to understand its form, one must move around it.' It stands like a sentinel, a landmark of inspirational beauty, a place in which to seek spiritual peace. No one can venture below its mighty ramparts and remain unaffected. A circuit, or kora, of Mount Kailash will take one's breath away, for being located on the Tibetan plateau at over 4000m a trek around its mighty parapets is not an undertaking to be lightly entertained. It's impossible not

At Toling, west of Mount Kailash, the ancient kingdom of Guge stretches towards Kamet and the Nanda Devi range

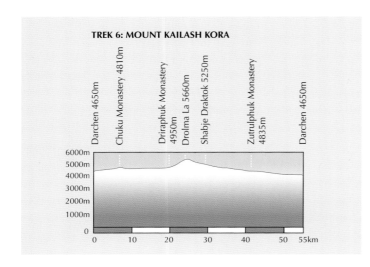

TREK 6: MOUNT KAILASH KORA

explore the weird chasms of the Khyunglung cliffs, where sacred Bon remnants remain. And after the privations of the trek, the hot springs at Tirthapuri offer a very special place for relaxation. South of Kailash, the mesmerising Lake Manasarovar is a place so holy it was born of the Hindu god of creation. Pilgrims may hike around the lake, but most visitors have higher aspirations; the shimmering turquoise waters are said to wipe clean the sins of a hundred lives.

to be in awe of its surreal canyons; to marvel at the striking, often contorted rock formations, and to fight for breath on reaching the highest point, the Drolma La – the pass of the goddess Tara.

But there are other sensational jewels hidden behind the endless ranges of the Indian Himal and the Trans-Himalaya. Where the headwaters of the sacred River Sutlej rise, there exists a vast maze of crazily eroded sandstone towers, troglodyte caves and fantastically contorted organ-pipe features. The ghostly ruins of the ancient kingdom of Guge are largely unknown. Exotic, intriguing, mysterious, it's a stupendous place; an odyssey into the unbelievable. The ethereal fortress ruins of its former capital, Tsaparang, house Tibet's greatest and most secret treasures: Buddhist monasteries, devotional art and exquisite, ancient paintings. Nearby, the monasteries of Toling were celebrated in the 11th century for their excellence as learning centres; from them the Indian master Atisha, and translator Rinchen Zangpo, led a Buddhist revival in western Tibet that would eventually spread across the vast Himalayan regions.

Western Tibet is entrancing, the true lost horizons of Shangri-La, where dreams and realities mix in an unfathomable blend of beauty and mystery. Those with sufficient time could

Remote, rugged, and invigoratingly wild, Tibet is barren and bitterly cold, but fantastic for all that. Even today, merely getting into the country and on to Kailash and Guge will never be easy. But that is half the challenge. The road to Kailash is studded with wonders; the stupendous scenery, the clear luminescent light, the crumbling history and vast rolling plains – this is a harsh land with quaint villages and large yak herds, set in a timeless landscape. Its curious yet friendly people, and its ancient religion, make it a very special place.

The approach from Nepal

Kailash hides its gifts well, whether you travel there by road from Kathmandu or hike into Tibet via Simikot in western Nepal. Commercial treks often use the **Simikot** airstrip as their means of approach, and work their way to the sacred mountain via the Upper Karnali's gorges. This is some of the wildest country in Nepal, where until recently remote villages had scarcely seen an outsider. Snow leopards and wolves, elusive bears, yaks and yetis are left to roam unhindered, while circling high above, vultures and lammergeiers watch and wait to feast on the fallen. The route passes through Tuling and follows the upper reaches of the Karnali to Kermi, Yangar and on

Gurla Mandhata and Lake Manasarovar dominate the plateau between Kailash and the Nepalese border

to Muchu. After Yari the trail crosses the 4620m **Nara La** to the frontier settlement of **Hilsa**. Then across the border in Tibet, a rough dirt road leads through Sher to **Purang** before climbing around the western flanks of Gurla Mandhata to **Lake Manasarovar** and Darchen.

For those travelling by road, Kathmandu is the most convenient place from which to begin the long drive to Kailash. The route takes three or four days and is full of interest as it crosses a series of high passes above 5000m, to reveal endlessly varied vistas of the northern flanks of the Himalaya. At the village of **Darchen** (4650m) you'll open a window to excitement, for the kora you are about to experience is an out-of-this-world trek of personal discovery in the enchanting landscapes that encircle holy Mount Kailash.

Darchen to Chuku Monastery

The Kailash kora trail begins appropriately enough at the chorten and mani wall at **Darchen**,

and soon after leaving there are the first prayer wheels, which you are strongly recommended to turn (clockwise) in order to send a prayer for a safe and rewarding trek. The trail climbs steadily but not steeply to the first auspicious site, a *chaktsel gang* (devotional spot), marked by stones – some covered with texts, cairns and prayer flags – while far to the south, the great mass of Gurla Mandhata and the Nepalese peaks of Api, Saipal and Nampur rise dramatically.

From here the kora trail turns north into the dark defile of the Lha Chu, meaning 'divine river', and the sacred summit of Mount Kailash can soon be seen peering above the forbidding canyon walls. A tall flagpole, festooned like a maypole with hundreds of prayer flags, dominates Tarboche. The flagpole is replaced each year on the full moon in May/June during the spring Saga Dawa festival, which celebrates the enlightenment of the Buddha.

The rugged grandeur of the canyon's west flank is simply stunning at dawn, its sheer walls shining with a luminescent pink light. On a raised plateau area nearby is the burial ground known as Drachom Ngagye Durtro; few trekkers will visit this sombre plinth, for this is the place of the dead, the haunt of the 84 Mahasiddhas – those mystic Tantric saints who have attained enlightenment. Revered lamas, sages and saints have passed into the next life from this burial ground, and the Bon magician Naro Bonchung used a cave nearby in which to meditate – a footprint of the Buddhist saint Milarepa is reputed to be above the cave opening. According to Tibetan mythology, it was here that Naro Bonchung and Milarepa first fought for control of Mount Kailash.

Close to Tarboche, the Chorten Kangyi is an archway that theoretically marks the beginning of the kora. The symbolic moon and sun on top of this chorten help to purify pilgrims against bad karma: the negative effects of one's personal actions. It is considered auspicious to proceed under this archway, or pass it on the left. The path then crosses a wide open area known as Sershung, or 'pot of gold', which is also linked to an ancient legend. The Lha Chu defile narrows, with the imposing ghost-like walls seeming to tower overhead, and excitement mounts in anticipation of the wonders to come.

At 4810m the Chuku Monastery clings perilously to the cliffs of the Nyenri mountain, and is considered to be the abode of the local Buddhist protector, Kangri Lhatsen. Belonging to the Kagyu-pa sect, the monastery was founded in the 13th century by a sage called Gotsangpo, who is credited with discovery of the kora route around Kailash. Care is needed here, for some of the rocks are unstable, and at this altitude one's concentration is apt to be below par.

Views from the monastery are amazing, with Kailash dwarfing the canyon. Across the valley there are considered to be 16 *arhats*, learned sages, revealed in the rocks of the cliff faces. Only well-informed pilgrims are likely to be able to see or appreciate these mythical figures, however, while it will be extremely hard to find the nearby Elephant Cave in which the Tantric master, Guru Rinpoche, meditated.

Chuku Monastery to Driraphuk Monastery

Continuing along the Lha Chu, an occasional gully or side ravine tempts with tantalising views of Kailash's sheer buttresses. Three peaks on the western side of the canyon represent the three Buddhist disciples of longevity: Drolma, a female deity; Tsepame, an aspect of Amitabha, the west-facing Buddha; and Namgyal-ma, a female deity representing victory. A few small streams cascade from these craggy summits, although they are often frozen into spectacular snakes of ice.

With the sun illuminating the valley, the next stretch to Damding Donkhang is a very pleasant and peaceful walk – unless there is a bitter wind blowing. A second prostration point, or chakt-sel gang, is located along the trail here. Hindus consider a squat, ghost-like outcrop on the right, known as the Guru Rinpoche Torma, to be a vision of Hanuman, their monkey god. Close to Damding Donkhang several nomad tents offer sustenance other than that of a spiritual kind to weary pilgrims and hungry trekkers. The West Face of Kailash towers improbably high above, its dark striated horizontal layers clearly displayed and a plume of spindrift constantly blowing from its icy summit.

The trail follows the main valley, swinging northeast to reveal a glimpse of the sacred mountain's North Face. Grassy banks are a delight along the river, which is braided here and there. The effects of the altitude begin to bite, and this stretch is surprisingly tough – until you look behind to be uplifted by the significant height gained so far. The degradations of once-mighty peaks can be observed in these crumbling hillsides. Only Kailash resists such decimation, remaining boldly sublime and little disturbed by the geological erosion of passing millennia. Then the peak is lost to view as the path climbs more steadily towards the monastery of Driraphuk.

A line of chortens directs the way to Driraphuk Monastery

Built around a small cave at 4950m, the monastery belongs to the Kagyu-pa order and its name means 'cave of the female yak horns'. Legends relate that the sage Gotsangpo was led to this shelter by a yak. Of course, this was no ordinary yak, but none other than a *dakini*, a protective flying female deity.

From the monastery the stunning North Face of Kailash is displayed like a gigantic ogre, guarded by craggy black sentinels. Rising around 2000m, the face is reminiscent of the north wall of the Eiger seen from Grindelwald, but unlike the Eiger's this North Face is not to be desecrated by the ungodly feet of man. If you are well acclimatised to the altitude, take a hike to the Kangyan Glacier at the foot of the great north wall.

Driraphuk to Shabje Draktok via the Drolma La

From Driraphuk the trail climbs steadily via Jarok Donkhang towards the pinnacle of the trek, the Drolma La. Be sure to avoid the alternative, higher pass of the Gangpo Sanglam La, for this is strictly for pilgrims who have completed 12 circuits of Kailash. In case you should entertain notions of taking it, remember that the spirit Khandroma guards the pass, and she might adopt a wrathful countenance if you invade her territory!

Along the way, the northeast wall of Kailash is a testimony to nature's grandeur. Passed en route at 5330m, the Shiva or Shiwal Tsal burial ground is an extraordinary place, resembling an untidy rubbish tip for worn-out clothes. To both Tibetan

Buddhists and Hindu pilgrims this is the place of death. Pilgrims may be seen cutting off strips of clothing, or depositing some of their hair; some even lie down, feigning death. Such symbolic acts are rituals that mark the death of the pilgrim's past life, as they await a rebirth free from their sins on the pass ahead.

Another significant place before the pass is the Bardo Trang, a large rock with a narrow hollow beneath it. This gap is a measure of a pilgrim's level of sin. Anyone who becomes stuck under this rock is deep in sin – could any foreign trekker pass beneath it? Various other sacred spots delay pilgrims, but trekkers will be enraptured by the last temptress, the Drolma La itself. On the last hard slog to the pass, a brief distraction is the forbidding peak of Sharma Ri, considered to be a vision of hell, and it casts an eerie, demon-filled shadow late in the day.

The final ascent is unrelentingly steep and energy-sapping, but it's a challenge to be faced with much anticipation. At over 5600m, an overdose of glucose tablets may be required. The altitude produces a strangely uplifting, yet lethargy-inducing trance, but wake up, or you might miss the Mila Shugri rock, carved with the Buddhist mantra: *Om Mani Padme Hum*. Innumerable prayer flags festoon the summit of the **Drolma La** (the 'hill of salvation'), and almost completely obscure the actual Drolma boulder.

The view is truly breathtaking. At 5660m we are on top of the world in a land of dreams (or nightmares), and the release of tension at having reached the pass is palpable. Pilgrims leave prayer flags at the pass; trekkers might wish to do the same, for everyone needs a little luck here as the descent can be icy and sometimes treacherous in deep snow. According to another legend, 21

Above Driraphuk, tantalising views are won of the elegant northeast wall of Mount Kailash

wolves once melted into a nearby rock, leading the sage of Kailash, Gotsangpo, to the correct pass and not to the Gangpo Sanglam, the pass of the evil dakini.

Descent is immediate and rocky underfoot, for this is a land of shattered, decaying cliffs and peaks. Below the pass lies the Gauri Kund – the pool of compassion – while ahead, views unfold like magic, revealing distant valley walls and the peaks above the eastern Lham Chu Valley. Nature's power is much in evidence; fractured crags guard an astonishing outcrop known as the evil Axe of Karma, but fortunately it is powerless under the spell of the goddess Drolma.

Nomadic families gather at the foot of Mount Kailash; their children are naturally inquisitive

The kora trail slips and slides down to the valley floor of the eastern canyon of Buddha Akshobhya, and the sight far below of the nomad encampment of Shabje Draktok, with the promise of hot butter tea, is enough to revive anyone's flagging spirits.

Shabje Draktok to Darchen

From Shabje Draktok the wide, gentle valley sweeps down below less severe peaks and ridges to provide a relaxing walk with some grassy spots and streams of clear water. A third chaktsel gang is located at the entrance to a side tributary. It is here that the often obscured eastern 'crystal face' of Mount Kailash deigns to show itself again. This eastern valley of the kora is known as the valley of Milarepa, the poet, ascetic and hermit. According to storytellers, another of his legendary fights with Naro Bonchung took place in the vicinity.

Below the confluence of the Lham Chu and Topchen Chu, and overshadowed by dark crags, is the miracle cave of Milarepa, the Zutrulphuk Monastery.

Legends recount that both Milarepa and Naro Bonchung sheltered in the cave before contesting the last battle for supremacy of Kailash. The duel concluded with Naro Bonchung falling from the summit of the sacred mountain, and as he fell his drum is said to have gouged out the step-like features on the South Face. To compensate for the loss of Kailash, the vanquished Bon deity was given a mountain near Lake Manasarovar on which to reside.

The path now heads down the Trangmar gorge, with its amazing mix of yellow, orange, green, red, purple and black features. A rocky knoll along the way makes one last attempt to drain the weary trekker or pilgrim, but beyond that a dream panorama opens to the south – the glittering morning splendour of Gurla Mandhata and the Nepal Himalaya. This sensational view is enough to make anyone drop to the ground in thanks, and indeed, a very short descent brings you to the final prostration point.

The final glorious amble passes some picturesque mani walls before arriving back in **Darchen**; and the fabulous Kailash Kora trek is completed. But remember, although your previous sins may have been forgiven, to be cleansed forever you must make 13 circuits of the mountain. So keep on trekking!

Trek 7

Inner Dolpo: Shey Gompa and the Crystal Mountain

by Stephen Goodwin

Dolpo, Shey Gompa, the Crystal Mountain: is the journey to these evocative places a trek, a quest, or perhaps a pilgrimage? Already, only months after returning from this remote western Nepal region, the memory of our three-week meander through deep river gorges and over wind-scoured 5000m ridges has assumed a dream quality. Did I really wake and part the tent flaps to see the Crystal Mountain, sacred to the Dolpo people probably long before Padma Sambhava brought Buddhism to these high borderlands of Tibet in the eighth century? Dolpo is a succession of revelations for inquiring trekkers, but its stony ways and cold passes test the muscles as well as expand the mind.

A short distance from Ringmo village, camp is set on an idyllic site overlooking Phoksundo Lake

Route summary

Location	Northwest Nepal
Start/Finish	Juphal (Dolpo airstrip)
Distance	about 220km
Duration	3 weeks (17 days' trekking plus 4 rest days)
Maximum altitude	Kang La c5300m
Trek style	Camping
Restrictions	Special permits required
Grade	Demanding
Note	Maps of Dolpo are poor, altitudes and place names inconsistent; altitudes quoted here should be regarded as approximate

Politically Dolpo has been a part of Nepal since the second half of the 18th century when the Shah kings from the tiny kingdom of Gorkha united the

country. But it does not look or feel like the Nepal of the Kathmandu Valley or even of the Everest region. Culturally and economically, until recent times its closest ties have been with Tibet. Indeed since the Chinese occupation of Tibet in the 1950s, Dolpo has been one of the last relatively undisturbed remnants of an authentic Tibetan culture, and also a redoubt of the little understood Bon religion, elements of which predate Buddhism.

This 'Tibetan' Dolpo is more precisely called Inner Dolpo, comprising four valleys close to the border – Panzang, Nam Khong, Tsharka and Tarap – and the Shey gompa area. Further south, from Phoksundo Lake to the Thuli Bheri River, is known as Lower Dolpo; greener hills cut by densely wooded valleys.

An Englishman, an American and a Frenchman put Dolpo on the map for Westerners. In 1956 David Snellgrove, a Tibetologist from the London School of Oriental and African Studies, laid the trail with his book *Himalayan Pilgrimage*, recounting a seven-month journey to the sacred places of the Tibetan regions of western Nepal. In his footsteps in 1973 came Peter Matthiessen, heading for Shey Gompa on a quest part spiritual and part naturalist's inquiry, described in *The Snow Leopard*; then in 1999 Eric Valli brought Dolpo to the screen with *Himalaya*, the first film in the language of the Dolpo-pa, a human drama set against the travails of a yak caravan over the snowy passes.

Literary and movie exposure, however, have hardly made Dolpo a busy tourist destination. During our 21-day trek in 2011 – I was leading a group for UK-based Mountain Kingdoms – we saw just four other small parties. There are good reasons for this exclusivity; only a limited number of visitors are allowed into Inner Dolpo each year and permits are expensive – US$70 per person per day at the time of writing. Anything less than a

Living in a land of harsh seclusion, the Dolpo-pa have a ready smile

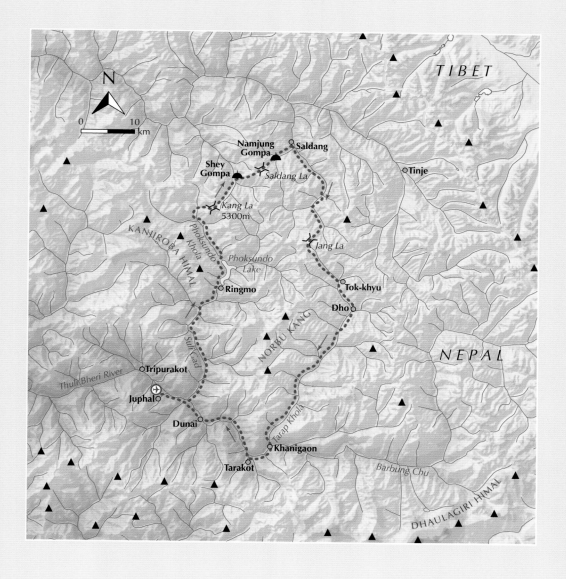

three-week visit would hardly do the area justice, and would certainly not enable you to reach the heartland valleys. And then there is the weather: while within Dolpo itself it is likely to be dry and bright during the ideal trekking season of mid-September through October, the tail end of the annual monsoon can cause problems getting into the airstrip at Juphal.

The logistics of travel to Dolpo bring home just how remote the area is. It's a land behind the clouds, ringed by mountains – including Dhaulagiri. The usual route from Kathmandu is

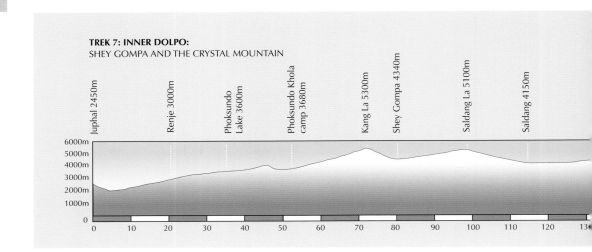

TREK 7: INNER DOLPO:
SHEY GOMPA AND THE CRYSTAL MOUNTAIN

a flight to Nepalganj by the Indian border in the Terai, followed by an early-morning hop over an outlying range to Juphal. It's one of Nepal's most exhilarating white-knuckle flights, the Twin Otter skimming through a 4000m col before dropping on to a sloping field. If cloud blankets the col or the airstrip there can be no flight; trekkers have been known to spend days either sweating in the heat of Nepalganj or playing cards at Juphal waiting for a clear window. The overland alternative, hiking up the valley of the Bheri, would take a week to 10 days.

But do not be deterred; in all my years of climbing and hiking in Nepal I have never enjoyed my days on the trail as much as in Dolpo. Peter Matthiessen drew me there, his descriptions of this 'hidden land' as luminous as the canopies of stars we witnessed spread above mountains on the Tibetan border. But it is the land itself, riven and bleak yet somehow serene, and the Dolpo-pa who exist in harmony with its seasons and their confusion of gods, that will draw me back.

Juphal to Phoksundo Lake
The unlovely settlement of **Juphal** sits at about 2450m on a hillside above the Thuli Bheri, one of the principal rivers of western Nepal; further upstream it is known as the Barbung Chu. With an assortment of traders, soldiers and policemen and women, Juphal has grown in an ad hoc way to serve the planes that land and take off at the top of its single winding street. It is here that trekkers meet the Sherpas, kitchen staff and porters who will comprise their caravan through this enchanting land. Since labour is scarce hereabouts, baggage is likely to be carried by mules.

With luck you'll be on the trail by midday, descending on narrow paths through terraces of millet and maize, looking north to the ramparts of Dolpo. Little is revealed, but that first winged silhouette high above the valley, a lammergeier in all probability, is a harbinger to quicken the senses.

Ten minutes below Juphal is the village of Dangi Bhara. One of the first things that Nepal regulars will notice is that prayer banners streaming from poles above the flat roofs are yellow and maroon rather than traditional Buddhist colours. This part of the valley is not a Buddhist area at all, and it will be two or three days before mani walls and other symbols of Buddhism and Bon become common. Hinduism has penetrated this area and appears strong in trading settlements like Dunai, but indigenous villagers cling to the older mountain gods; at village entrances and on some

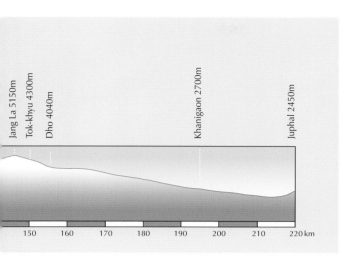

staged. The Bheri is followed for a couple of hours before crossing on a 99-metre-long suspension bridge, where the clear water of the **Suli Gad** flows into the glacial grey of the major river. The roar of the Suli Gad now accompanies the traveller all the way to Phoksundo; sometimes the trail is on rough causeways lapped by the river, sometimes on narrow balconies along gorge cliffs; and always 'undulating', as the itineraries so coyly put it.

In its lower reaches you push through dense clumps of marijuana and troupes of langur monkeys watch your passing; jungly trees and wild walnuts give way to pine and juniper, and each

dwellings crudely carved figures known as *dok-pa* ward off evil.

From Juphal to Phoksundo Lake takes three or four days, depending on how the camps are

At Juphal the crew gathers baggage and equipment into loads for the pack mules

High above the Suli Gad river a narrow trail supports trekkers on the way north to Phoksundo Lake and Inner Dolpo

night the Suli Gad lulls you to sleep and enters your dreams. Matthiessen wondered if 'anywhere on earth there is a river more beautiful than the upper Suli Gad in autumn'.

In the last hours of this stage the trail zigzags steeply up a hillside of juniper and thorns well above an energy-sapping 3000m. What breath you may have left is taken away by the sight of Nepal's highest waterfall, crashing 300m from the outflow of **Phoksundo Lake**, before the revelation of the turquoise lake itself.

Phoksundo Lake to Shey Gompa

Phoksundo Lake was created either by a landslide or an angry Bon demoness. Cool-headed Westerners would normally opt for the former, but so unearthly is the intense blue of the water and its setting between towering ochre cliffs – save for one corner where monastery buildings appear between the pines and prayer flags – that a supernatural origin seems entirely plausible. Some five kilometres long, it is said to be Nepal's deepest lake, reaching a depth of 650m. Curiously, it freezes from the centre outwards, though rarely over the entire surface, and is devoid of fish, possibly due to

mineralisation. Plenty to contemplate then as you gaze across the water from a campground superbly situated between the lake and **Ringmo**, a village of old stone houses, their flat roofs battlemented with winter supplies of wood and fodder.

What better place for a rest day to acclimatise? Time to do some laundry, then take the path to the Bon monastery, Tshowa Gompa. *Tshowa*, which means lake, is also the locals' name for Ringmo. Superficially there seems no big contrast between this Bon establishment and the more Buddhist gompas of Dolpo; the most visible difference being that ancient symbol of good fortune, the swastika. Buddhists use it in the Indian fashion with the right angles pointing clockwise; the Bon swastika points anticlockwise. Similarly while Buddhists pass chortens and other sacred places on the left, Bon adherents do the opposite.

Four monks were living at Tshowa Gompa in autumn 2011, though many more gather at festival times. It has an ancient undercroft where a fearsome collection of dance masks inhabit the darkness; if no *lama* is present, a caretaker is usually happy to show visitors round in exchange for a modest donation.

Back in the dazzling light, the eye is drawn to cliffs along the western shore and the balcony path you will tread next morning at the start of the three-day journey to Shey. This precipitous gangway features in the most dramatic moment of Eric Valli's *Himalaya*, one yak falling to its death as the Dolpo-pa, with their caravan of salt, risk the lakeside shortcut to beat approaching snow. The film shows parts of the trail poised hundreds of metres above the lake on saplings hammered into the cliff and covered in branches and stones. Does that sound scary? Well it's true, and the path is so narrow that our mules went along it unladen, all loads ferried by the sure-footed crew. Thankfully the gangway is in much better repair than in the movie version, or than it seems to have been when Matthiessen negotiated it on hands and knees at one point.

From the northern end of the lake, the way continues up the wooded valley of the **Phoksundo Khola**, glaciers peeling off the Kanjiroba massif soaring to the south, cliffs confining the view north. Two more camps follow, one in the river gorge, a second way above the treeline at about 4600m on the approach to the Kang La – a key passage of the trek. By now we are in a land of scant vegetation and it will become even more sparse on the steep shale headwall below the pass. Expect a hard frost at the high camp, and for a chill wind to be snapping at strings of prayer flags when you breast the **Kang La**.

At an estimated 5300m, the pass is the highest point on the trek. The view is humbling, range upon range of bare hills and mountains, a dusting of snow here and there, the valleys treeless and seemingly empty. But not quite: occasionally *bharal* or 'blue sheep' can be picked out on the hillside, while overhead lammergeiers, with their distinctive diamond-shaped tails, wheel in the thermals. Blue sheep are a type of wild goat and a favourite food of the snow leopard – the elusive grail of Dolpo.

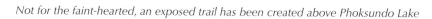

Not for the faint-hearted, an exposed trail has been created above Phoksundo Lake

From the Kang La, **Shey Gompa** is just a three-hour walk down the wild valley of the Hubaiung Khola. In the standard terracotta livery of sacred buildings, the monastery sits on a wide shelf, looking across the junction of three valleys towards the Crystal Mountain. Tents are pitched with a similar outlook a couple of hundred metres to one side. For Matthiessen devotees, as with Buddhist pilgrims, it is a singular moment.

Shey Gompa to Saldang

The monastery belongs to the Kagyu sect founded in the 11th century. As impressive as the building itself is the enormous area of mani stones to its western side, more a raised field than a wall; the inscriptions at its centre of unguessable antiquity and suggesting a time when spiritual life at Shey was more vital. It is likely that veneration of the Crystal Mountain predates Buddhism and may be earlier even than Bon; a circumambulation, or kora, of this pyramid of rock and snow is a meritorious act of pilgrimage, as it is of Mount Kailash (see Trek 6). The main festival at Shey is in late spring, not long after the valley is released from its winter isolation. During the trekking season the main activity is not at the monastery but down by the river junction where caravans of yaks encamp. For a day we shared the trail with scores of these magnificent black beasts, carrying timber from the south.

Less than a couple of hours' walk north of Shey on a winding path, Tsakang Gompa is one of the gems of Dolpo. Clinging to a cliffside above a wild gorge, this hermitage is a place of retreat for meditation, rather than a monastery. Matthiessen described it as 'plastered to the rock wall, like

Saldang Gompa is more than 500 years old

nests of swifts'. A tiny patch of potatoes sits on the lip above the abyss; beyond only snow-etched mountains can be seen.

From Shey a day and a half's walk, roughly northeast, leads to the village of Saldang in the valley of the Nam Khong. In between the **Saldang La** must be crossed at about 5100m. Hope for fine weather, then you can stand by its flag-bedecked cairn and gaze across a huge sweep of arid hills to the peaks of Tibet. If the wind is up, Saldang La is a very exposed spot indeed, but shelter for the night is only a couple of hours away, tucked in a gorge occupied by **Namjung Gompa** – a jumbly storehouse of dance masks and stacks of sacred texts – and the first terraces of barley and buckwheat since Ringmo.

Saldang to Tarap

Saldang is the most populous village in Inner Dolpo, but don't be misled. It's basically a scattering of crusted dwellings surrounded by small fields, with a school, a small clinic, and a gompa of the Nyingmapa sect dating back more than 500 years, including a large, walk-round prayer wheel. The settlement's fine location is best appreciated by walking up the ridge to the north. From here one looks over a ragged geometry of flat, rectangular roofs, terrace walls and *stupas* to where the silver band of the Nam Khong flows from the folds of dun mountains. This is our way southwards, over the Jang La to the Tarap Valley.

A trek starting late September will likely coincide with the harvest. It is the busiest time of year for villagers and the fields have the hyperactive look of a Breugel painting – men and women cutting barley and buckwheat with sickles, heaving it on their backs or on mules, thrashing the grain with short poles, children gleaning over the stubble, potatoes being buried in pits against the coming frost.

Soon the yaks will be brought down from higher pastures. Traditionally the herds would have overwintered on the Tibetan plateau, but 50 years of political upheaval in Tibet and Nepal have disrupted the old ways of Dolpo's farming-nomad-traders. The yaks of Nam Khong will probably spend the winter further south, in Lower Dolpo. Many of the villagers who in Snellgrove's day would have spent the frozen months holed up, telling stories, singing, drinking, spinning and tending to religion, will instead migrate to Kathmandu or go on pilgrimage to Buddhist sites in India.

The three-day walk to the Tarap Valley should be a joy. You're acclimatised, the weather should be set fair, villagers of Namdo and Sibu rise from their harvesting to wave and shout greetings, and on skylines you may see the silhouettes of blue sheep. After a high camp (c4800m), almost certainly in sub-zero temperatures, you gain the **Jang La** at approximately 5150m and take a deep intake of breath – part thin air and part exclamation of wonder. From a zone of rock, snow and frozen tarns the Tarap Valley plunges beneath broken cliffs, while hoist in the distance is the great white sail of Dhaulagiri.

Tarap to Juphal

Four hours' walk below the Jang La is the village of **Tok-khyu**, at about 4300m one of the highest permanent settlements on earth. It lies at a river junction in a landscape reminiscent of a Scottish strath, broad and open to an immense sky. In June these grassy slopes attract a Klondyke of fortune hunters, harvesting the *yartsa gumba*: a remarkable union of fungus and caterpillar, credited with powerful aphrodisiac properties. Prized in Chinese medicine, the dried and ground yartsa gumba can be sold for thousands of pounds per kilo.

At least one rest day should be spent in Tarap. A short walk from Tok-khyu, Crystal Mountain School, supported by French charities, is a good place to learn from the teachers about life in Dolpo and to be charmed by smiling pupils, keen to try their 'How are yous?' and have their photos taken. Barely two hours downstream is **Dho**, the main village of the valley. Above it is the imposing Ribo Bumpa Gompa of the Nyingmapa sect; the complex of ancient buildings includes

With the harvest gathered, Dolpo villagers thresh the barley with short poles

a small chapel in the form of a chorten enclosing a smaller chorten inside it, Russian-doll style. If time and energy allow, follow the prayer flags up the hill behind the gompa for a fine farewell panorama of Inner Dolpo.

In a side-valley a mile east of Dho is the Bon monastery of Sh'ip-chhok. When Snellgrove visited in 1956 he praised the recently painted murals depicting the Bon founder Shenrap and other deities. Sixty years later, by the light of a headtorch (an essential aid to gompa studies) we could make out the same images, finely executed, but fading.

Leaving Dho, there's a definite homeward feeling. But it is still four or five long days' walk to Juphal, and each has an entrancing character: repeatedly the trail descends to the edge of the Tarap Khola before climbing to traverse cliffs in hewn galleries; joining the valley of the Barbung Chu it undulates and winds through forest and fields of millet, maize and beans, skirts the old

hill fortress of **Tarakot** and follows the river to Dunai before finally retracing the climb up to the airstrip at **Juphal**. **Dunai**, on the south bank of the Barbung Chu, is the largest settlement in Dolpo district and the administrative headquarters, though by any traditional definition it does not lie within Dolpo at all.

The best place to camp here is in the garden of the Blue Sheep Inn – though blue sheep are by now but a memory. As to that other icon of Dolpo, the snow leopard, we saw its scat on the trail below the Jang La and heard that one had been prowling round the yaks one night during our stay at Shey. But, like Peter Matthiessen, we never actually saw one. Matthiessen drew a Buddhist lesson from his disappointment. Answering his own rhetorical question about the leopard, he wrote: 'Have you seen one? No! Isn't that wonderful?' The pilgrim had made peace with his own desire.

The Kanjiroba range is seen beyond the valley of the Maduwa Khola which leads to Phoksundo Lake ▶

Trek 8

Lower Dolpo: from Juphal to Jumla

by Kev Reynolds

olpo. The name resonates with the slap of a prayer flag, the snort of a yak, the echo of distance. Dolpo, a wild and mysterious land of seemingly barren, dun-coloured hills and the romance of high places. The highest inhabited land on earth, Dolpo is where the elusive snow leopard moves as soundless as a shadow, where small herds of bharal drift on forgotten hillsides. Remote and romantic, it has no major 8000m summit to entice with vertical adventures, but those who are drawn by its mystery are changed forever, for after a single visit this ancient back-of-beyond has a way of haunting one's dreams with a demand to return.

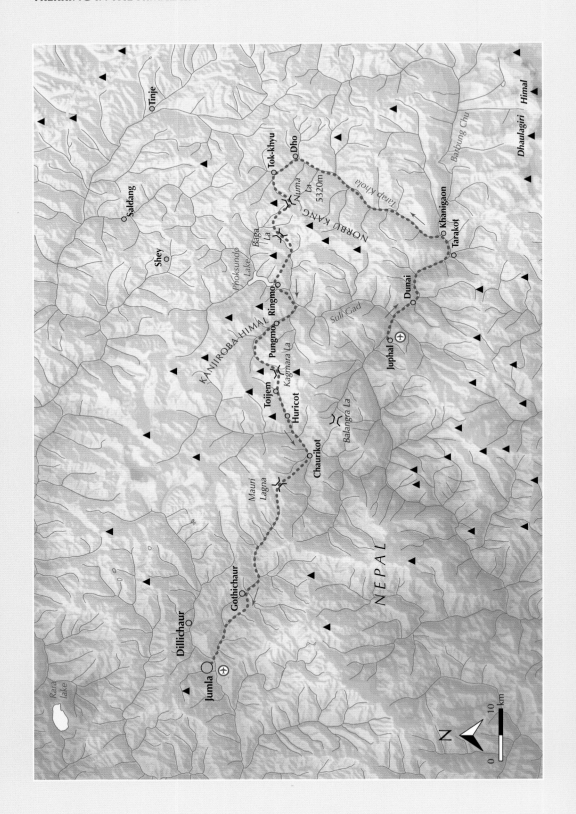

Route summary

Location	Northwest Nepal
Start	Juphal (Dolpo airstrip)
Finish	Jumla
Distance	about 190km
Duration	3 weeks (17 days' trekking plus 3 rest days)
Maximum altitude	Numa La c5320m
Trek style	Camping
Restrictions	None
Grade	Demanding
Guidebook	*Dolpo: A Trekker's Guide* by Kev Reynolds (Pilgrims Bookhouse, Kathmandu, 1997)

In 1989, more than 30 years after David Snellgrove travelled across Dolpo from monastery to monastery, recording with a scholar's eye for detail a landscape and culture that bore little relation to any other part of the country, the cautious Nepalese government finally allowed the first trekking party to make a journey through the hidden land. Dreams were born – dreams that now had a chance of becoming reality.

Study a map of the region. It may be inaccurate, peppered with inconsistencies and the cartographer's wild imaginings, but that is part of its charm and a spur to adventuring. The numerous *lekhs* and *dandas* drawn with tight brown lines; the arthritic *kholas* and rhythmic *las*; and the names of villages that hum like a mantra when spoken…all these summon a landscape to set the heart pumping with excitement. Trace journeys through that landscape over a series of high passes, and several possible tours leap from the sheet. But how much time do you have? How much money for permits? How much stamina can you muster?

These are pertinent questions, for this is an uncompromising land; it suffers no weakness, no lack of commitment from those who dare cross its borders. Should something go seriously wrong, there's no easy escape. But there's undoubted romance in the lure of wild places, and Dolpo is

certainly wild. Its very name may conjure dreams – but dreamers beware; reality can be harsh when storm clouds gather.

In his evocative chapter on Inner Dolpo (Trek 7), Stephen Goodwin describes a trek to Shey Gompa and the semi-mythical Crystal Mountain. That is a journey of raw beauty, trekking north and northeast of Phoksundo Lake in a restricted area for which premium rates are paid for a permit. However, the trek described here remains just outside the unmarked boundaries of that restricted area, and makes a demanding journey over several lofty passes heading roughly east to west, visiting a few remote villages but passing through uninhabited valleys too.

It begins where the trek to Shey Gompa begins, on the sloping meadow/airstrip of Juphal, but instead of heading north to Phoksundo, it first works a way southeast along the valley of the Thuli Bheri in search of another breach in the great Himalayan wall that will grant access to the hidden land, where every day is a gift to be treasured.

Juphal to Dho

A sense of relief on landing at **Juphal** can be seen on every face. That relief is three-fold: that you've landed safely after dodging the clouds and mountains that form Dolpo's outer rim; that you've escaped the oppressive heat of Nepalganj in the Terai; and best of all, the relief and joyous realisation that at last the trek can begin.

For the first couple of hours the trail is the same as that which leads to Phoksundo Lake and Shey Gompa, but when that classic route crosses the Thuli Bheri in order to strike up the narrows of the Suli Gad, we remain on the west bank of the main river and soon enter the district headquarters of **Dunai**. It may have taken less than half a day to get here, but this will be far enough; there will be plenty of tougher days ahead.

Out of Dunai another two days are spent in the Thuli Bheri's valley, a lovely deep trench with something of interest all the way. The upper

A makeshift footbridge in the Tarap gorge

sources of the river drain the northern side of the massive Dhaulagiri Himal whose 7000 and 8000m summits scratch the heavens to create a rain barrier, but for the brief time we follow it, mountains of 'only' 4000 and 5000m act as its flanking walls. Their summits are mostly unseen; though steep and forbidding they're just hills, but now and again the valley gives a kink and loftier snow-dusted peaks tease far ahead. Then they're gone again, leaving their icy breath to chill the river and the air around it.

Passing below **Tarakot** a morning's hike leads to **Khanigaon**, standing at the confluence of a river that flows from Tarap in the north, whose gorge holds the key that allows access to the hidden

land. A cypress grove makes a fine campsite, with a tantalising view along the **Tarap Khola** – a surprisingly small stream for one that comes so far – with its fringe of birch trees lending it an almost European character. When Snellgrove was here, he was enchanted by the numerous mani-carved rocks, and sensed that he was about to enter what he called 'some hidden and idyllic valley…where men and animals live in peace and harmony'.

It takes three days to trek through the Tarap gorge to enter Dolpo proper, and in that time you pass from about 2500m to somewhere in the region of 4000m, trading walnut, birch and cypress trees for a seemingly arid land. The trail is good in places, demanding in others. Never is it dull. In the early stages the gorge is almost park-like, with cropped meadows and waterfalls spraying over sheer cliffs, but then the way climbs abruptly, here on a stone stairway, there along an exposed ledge made of flat slabs laid on tree trunks fitted to the rock face. The gorge walls are sometimes no more than 50 paces apart and sunlight rarely penetrates. But elsewhere the constrictions are less severe, and tiny islands stand midstream. Often cliffs overhang the trail, and a whole series of bridges carry the route from one side of the river to the other. There are small meadows on which to camp, some used as yak pastures, or grazed by goats with strangely twisted horns, but on the third day after leaving Khanigaon you reach the head of the gorge, pass between its rocky portals and gain a first exciting view into the Tarap Valley, broad, flat-bottomed and flanked by big rolling mountains, and with a long line of mani walls leading to the village of Dho.

Dho is other-worldly. It has no apparent connection with the world left behind at your airport of departure (seemingly a lifetime ago), nor of Kathmandu or Nepalganj. Nor even of Dunai, Tarakot or Khanigaon. Dho belongs to Tibet – if it belongs anywhere beyond its home valley. Its sturdy stone-walled houses are flat-topped and covered with straw from the latest harvest; from each roof a prayer flag catches every breath that moves. Longhaired yak snort and snuffle in the dusty fields, and women whose faces have been scoured and scorched by the high-altitude wind and sun beat recently scythed barley with bamboo flails. And keeping a fatherly eye on both the village and its occupants, an ancient gompa stands on a shelf on the eastern hillside; a fabulous lookout over the whole valley.

Dho to Phoksundo Lake
Stretching northwest of Dho the Tarap Valley is a wide glacial trough. Perhaps it once contained a lake, for it's surprisingly fertile for such a lofty region, and after the harvest has been taken the outline of its numerous fields are easy to detect. A tall, elaborately decorated *kani*, or entrance chorten, marks the boundary of Dho village, and as you pass through it the mountains that fold away towards Tibet appear squat and shapeless, despite altitudes of almost 6000m. Though wearing neither glacier nor permanent snowfield they have an undeniable allure, for they suggest nothing less than the great unknown, beyond which must surely lie a forbidden kingdom.

The trail becomes a wide track rising gently, making its way to handsome **Tok-khyu**, beyond which the valley forks. The more northerly branch leads to Saldang by way of the Jang La (Jyanta

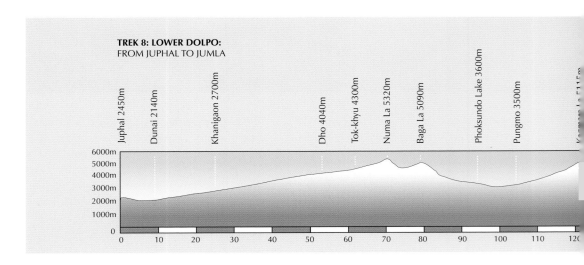

TREK 8: LOWER DOLPO:
FROM JUPHAL TO JUMLA

La); that is the route by which the Shey Gompa/ Crystal Mountain trek came to the Tarap Valley. The other option, which strikes northwest, is where our traverse of Lower Dolpo now breaks

Tok-khyu near the head of the Tarap Valley

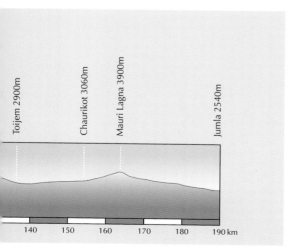

away, for it leads to the Numa La and Baga La; two linked passes whose crossing is the unquestionable highlight of our journey, in more ways than one. Although traders regularly cross with their yak trains, under fresh snow the route could be difficult to find without a guide who knows the way.

It takes two strenuous days to cross these passes, and it's essential to be well acclimatised and have settled weather by the time you set out, for both cols are well over 5000m, and the intermediate camp is not low enough to offer safe recuperation should any of the party suffer from altitude sickness.

From a camp between Tok-khyu and the Numa La an early start is needed, for it will be a long, tough day to cross the pass and descend to the valley of the Poyun Chu below the Baga

La. At first a reasonably clear trail climbs a bare mountainside over numerous spurs and folds, but as height is gained you come onto slopes that are black with shale and grit, then snow. About 900m above last night's camp, and four hours or so after setting out, the **Numa La** (c5320m) is a windswept saddle festooned with prayer flags, and with a memorable panoramic view. The great white block of Dhaulagiri dominates all to the south; to the north Dolpo rolls its mysterious hills into the wastelands of Tibet, while the Kanjiroba massif looms to the northwest – and it is this that will reappear again and again in the next few days.

Descent on the western side leads to a tight 'V' cleft between steep rock walls, then stumbles upon the headwaters of the Chhadha Chu that eventually empties into the Phoksundo Lake. In its upper reaches the stream (for that is all it is) courses its way through gorges of russet-coloured rock. Then the trail crosses to the left bank and makes a traverse while the stream cuts deeply below, giving the impression that you're gaining more height than you are in reality. In places the way is a little exposed before you turn into the valley of the Poyun Chu, which opens to scant meadowland backed by ice-crested mountains.

Next morning, after boulder-hopping over a stream near the head of the valley, a clear yak trail is followed on the steady ascent of a nose of hillside, then curving round a hollow the **Baga La** is seen some way ahead – a long saddle indicated by prayer flags and a pile of stones at about 5090m. (All altitude measurements in Dolpo are approximate, for it seems no two authorities agree – one gives the Baga La as 5090m, another 5190m, yet another quotes 5169m – but there's just one certainty: you'll be breathless on arrival.) As with the Numa La, a vast panorama is revealed; the Kanjiroba mountains rise among a sea of peaks,

The Baga La, at about 5090m, marked by a cairn and weather-bleached prayer flags

Pungmo, a village of thick stone-walled houses on the way to the Kagmara La

while near at hand a rim of ragged summits captures the imagination.

The way now descends to the southwest into the head of the idyllic valley of the Maduwa Khola, almost alpine in its comparatively lush vegetation after the arid high valleys you've come from. There are clumps of juniper and dwarf cypress, and lower down, stands of pine, for you're losing a lot of altitude here and the air is thick with new scents. And instead of the bald rolling mountains of Tarap, here the valley is flanked by soaring rock slabs with cascades pouring from them. The trail eases across meadows pitted with marmot burrows, and gaps in the left-hand wall expose snowpeaks full of promise. A camp here allows an exquisite morning's walk to the southern shore of **Phoksundo Lake**, with the village of **Ringmo** close by, and an old Bon monastery nestling just above the east bank.

Phoksundo Lake to Jumla

The Shey Gompa trek tackles the abrupt cliffs lining the western side of the beautiful turquoise lake, but to follow that exposed trail requires a special permit. Our route turns away from both lake and village and heads downvalley through poor meadows and between scrub and low-growing trees, then unexpectedly climbs to a high point where you look back to Phoksundo and down onto a huge waterfall pouring from the lake, its thunder drifting in the breeze. The trail resumes its downward trend, passing through Palam and Sumduwa before turning northwest into the valley of the Pungmo Khola.

In its lower reaches this is a narrow wedge of a valley whose flanking walls only ease back as you approach **Pungmo** village. Entered through a decorated kani and alongside several chortens and a small orchard, Pungmo is an attractive settlement, some of whose houses are three storeys high. Half an hour later you reach Doju, a haphazard collection of houses surrounded by fields. Above it the trail rises among trees and shrubs to gain a snatched view through a rocky cleft to Kanjirowa, a 6612m peak variously known as Kenchen Ruwa, Kanjirolba or Kanjelaruwa. To the northwest, but unseen from here, stands the higher Kanjiroba Himal with its several lofty summits and glaciers.

Two camps are now needed before tackling the next high pass; some way above Doju there's an idyllic meadow at about 3700m; another will be found 10 minutes beyond that, after which there's nothing for several hours.

The valley arcs west and southwest, the river's name now changing from Yulung (or Julung) Khola to the Kagmara Khola, as the trail makes a long steady climb through a gorge-like narrowing.

A porter labours up a slope into a hanging valley below the Kagmara La

Looking back Kanjirowa and its neighbouring snowpeaks make an impressive sight, while ahead the valley divides, with another fine snowpeak standing above the right branch. Our route follows the main (left) stem, emerging from the gorge to a high moorland. Ahead the valley is blocked

by a rim of glaciers and snow-covered mountains of the Kagmara Himal, the highest of which is a little under 6000m. Camp is made in the undulating meadowland near the head of the valley, at an altitude of around 4300m, leaving a climb of 800m or so for the next morning.

Meaning 'crow killer', the **Kagmara La** remains unseen until shortly before you reach it. At 5115m it's a wide open, wind-scuffed saddle, gained about two hours after leaving camp, and as you should be fit and fully acclimatised by now, you may be tempted to climb the ridge to the north for another 200m to gain a tremendous panoramic view that includes both Dhaulagiri and Annapurna in the southeast, as well as all the highest summits of Dolpo, and countless minor ones too.

Descent from the Kagmara La is steep at first, and after a slight easing it then resumes over endless moraine spills (punishing for the knees) before gaining the head of the Garpung Khola's valley. A rough stony trail now carries the way down to spectacular views of icebound peaks, then over a bluff starred with edelweiss in late October. A good, fairly level campsite can be found close to the river at about 4000m.

The Garpung Khola is followed downstream for a full day, steeply in places, with side streams to cross and a gorge-like section to negotiate, the valley becoming more colourful as height is lost. Berberis, cotoneaster and swathes of marijuana spread over the hillsides, while alpine asters colour open patches of meadowland.

About three hours after leaving camp you come to **Toijem**, which has an army post at a confluence of valleys. Below this you cross the Jagdula Khola, then resume high above the right bank of the Garpung Khola. Before long the trail leaves the Shey Phoksundo National Park through which you've been travelling since crossing the Numa La, then continues its switchback course to **Huricot**, a collection of sombre flat-roofed houses, an important gompa and several small mills, set in a sheltered basin at the junction of two valleys.

Passing above the gompa the trek slants along the hillside above the river, and beyond a flag-bedecked bridge leading to Kaigaon, continues through terraced fields before entering the untidy Chhetri village of Majgaon, whose square is protected by a carved wooden dok-pa effigy. One-and-a-half hours later you come to an open grassy saddle at 3135m to catch a first view of Chaurikot ahead. Pause here for a moment to look back, for an outlier of the Kagmara massif signals far off, while the Balangra La, across which lies a route to Juphal and Dunai, is evident to the southeast.

Chaurikot enjoys a charming outlook, but it's reached too soon to make a suitable overnight camp. However, between the village and the Mauri Lagna – the final crossing of the trek – an open slope of grassland between two dense belts of forest, makes a reasonable campground, leaving a walk of just two hours to gain the pass next day.

The **Mauri Lagna** (Mauria Bhanjyang) is a grass-covered saddle of about 3900m, whose name means 'honey pass'. It makes a fine outlook, with the snowy block of Saipal floating above lesser ranges a long way ahead, while much closer to the northeast a shapely duo of snow mountains rise above the brown hills of the Jagdula Lekh. A great bank of rhododendrons spreads across the slope below the pass, and through this you enter a forest of birch, pine and oak, then follow the boisterous Chotra Khola downstream to Chotra, beyond which there are several tempting sites for an overnight camp.

This leaves just one final day's trek through charming country to Mani Sangu, Kuri Santha and the meadows of **Gothichaur**. The valley is broad and gentle. Low terraces fold down to the river; there are no more challenges, and in the autumn children run bare-footed across the stubble fields to greet you. The small settlements you pass through suggest a life of comparative ease; the wild remoteness of Dho and the Tarap Valley belongs to another world, and as you enter **Jumla** the door to the hidden land of Dolpo closes behind you.

In cold but clear conditions, a trekking party arrives at French Pass (photo: Steve Razzetti) ▶

Trek 9
Dhaulagiri Circuit
by Bart Jordans

*E*very year tens of thousands of trekkers gaze in breathless wonder from the vantage point of Poon Hill above Ghorepani as Dhaulagiri emerges from night to receive the blessings of sunrise. It's one of the iconic visions of trekkers' Nepal, an essential part of the Annapurna experience. Yet Dhaulagiri is unconnected to the Annapurna range for it lies west of the Kali Gandaki, while Annapurna, its neighbour, dominates the east bank. Annapurna is a magnet that attracts vast numbers of trekkers. Dhaulagiri stands aloof, defiant, challenging. For a trekker to accept that challenge and tackle the classic circuit around it, the serious nature of the mountain's hinterland needs to be fully appreciated. It is essential to understand that the route encounters sections of difficult, remote and sometimes dangerous terrain where bad weather or poor visibility could have serious consequences for those unprepared. Yes, the Dhaulagiri Circuit is one of the most demanding, yet at the same time one of the most satisfying, treks in Nepal, and it should never be underrated.

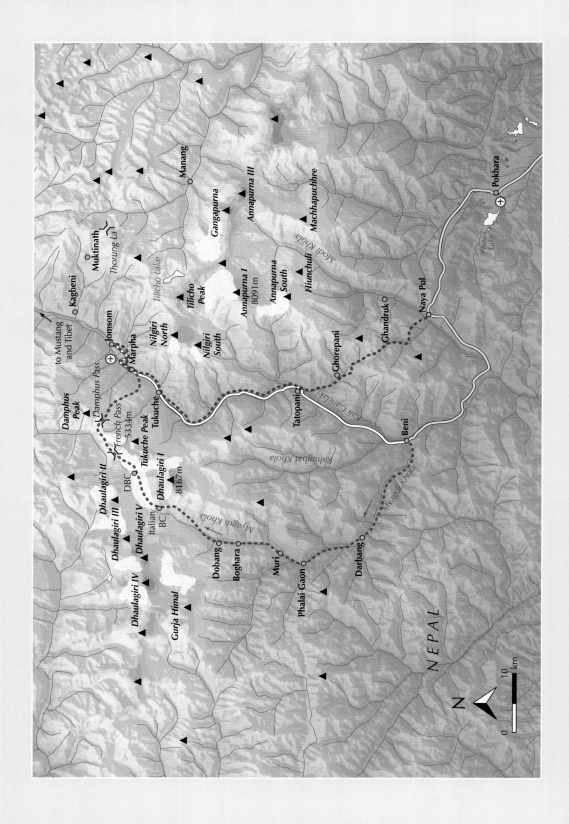

Pokhara

Phewa Lake

Manang

Gangapurna

Annapurna III

Machhapuchhre

Muktinath

Thorung La

Annapurna I
8091m

Annapurna South

Hiunchuli

Kagbeni

Tilicho Lake

Tilicho Peak

Modi Khola

Kali Gandaki

Chandruk

Naya Pul

Jomsom

to Mustang and Tibet

Marpha

Nilgiri North

Nilgiri South

Ghorepani

Damphus Peak

Damphus Pass

French Pass
5334m

Tukuche Peak

Tukuche

Tatopani

Beni

Dhaulagiri II

Tukuche I

DBC

Dhaulagiri I
8167m

Kahubhat Khola

Dhaulagiri III

Dhaulagiri V

Italian BC

Myagdi Khola

Myagdi Khola

Dhaulagiri IV

Dobang

Boghara

Muri

Phalai Gaon

Darbang

Gurja Himal

N E P A L

N

0   10   km

Route summary

Location	Central Nepal
Start	Beni
Finish	Jomsom or Pokhara
Distance	about 95km
Duration	2–3 weeks
Maximum altitude	French Pass 5334m
Trek style	Camping
Restrictions	ACAP permit required
Grade	Demanding
Guidebook	*Trekking and Climbing in Nepal* by Steve Razzetti (New Holland, 2000)

In Sanskrit Dhavala Giri means the White Mountain, and with its great snowfields, glaciers and formidable icefalls, it is an apt name for the seventh highest of the world's mountains. At 8167m it is easily recognised from Poon Hill by its symmetrical pyramid shape yet, rising to the south of the main Himalayan axis, Dhaulagiri is not a solitary peak but part of a large and complex massif with five ridges and no fewer than five other summits more than 7000m high ranging west of the main summit. There's also a neighbouring group of outlying peaks with its own appeal forming a massive 6000m wall that effectively shields the hidden land of Dolpo.

Although it had been surveyed as long ago as 1810, Dhaulagiri was not seen at close quarters by any Westerner until 1949 when Dr Arnold Heim, a Swiss geologist, made an aerial reconnaissance from an altitude of 4500m. The following year Frenchman Maurice Herzog arrived in Tukuche in the Kali Gandaki's valley with an expedition whose aim was to make the first ascent of either Dhaulagiri or Annapurna. Dhaulagiri was the first choice, and with little to guide them but imperfect Survey of India maps, several groups were sent out in search of a possible route to the summit. It was time-consuming and often frustrating work, but having crossed the 5250m Damphus Pass, and reached the 5334m col now known as French Pass on the far side of Hidden Valley, the highly experienced guide Lionel Terray saw the monstrous icefall on its North Face and considered the mountain to be 'absolutely unclimbable'. The decision was then made to abandon any assault on Dhaulagiri and to concentrate on Annapurna instead. That attempt succeeded, of course, and Annapurna became the first 8000er to be won – 'for the

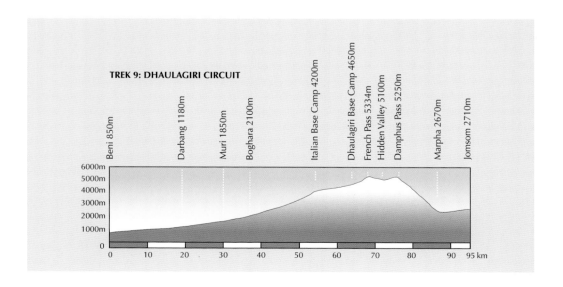

TREK 9: DHAULAGIRI CIRCUIT

Beni 850m — Darbang 1180m — Muri 1850m — Boghara 2100m — Italian Base Camp 4200m — Dhaulagiri Base Camp 4650m — French Pass 5334m — Hidden Valley 5100m — Damphus Pass 5250m — Marpha 2670m — Jomsom 2710m

honour of France' – but at great physical cost to the summiteers, it must be said. As for Dhaulagiri, in the decade following the French reconnaissance no fewer than six expeditions tackled the mountain without success. Then in 1960 a Swiss team (the third from that country), whose members included the 28-year-old Austrian Kurt Diemberger, managed to force a route to the summit by way of the Northeast Ridge, by which no fewer than eight climbers in two groups reached the top. Apart from this success, the expedition was noteworthy for its use of a single-engine Pilatus Porter aircraft to ferry both men and equipment to the Northeast Col at 5877m. Named *Yeti*, the aircraft crashed near the Damphus Pass eight days before the summit was reached. Remnants of the plane are still scattered on the mountain.

Fifty years on, the trekkers' circuit of Dhaulagiri has a real expeditionary flavour to it. There may be no major summits to aim for, but the valleys surrounding the massif have a remoteness unknown on the more celebrated circuit of neighbouring Annapurna, and there are two passes in excess of 5000m to cross. The route begins low down where for several days it keeps company with the Myagdi Khola, at first among terraced fields and thatched villages, later through dense jungle to reach the narrow Chhonbarden gorge and Dhaulagiri Base Camp, a wild and windy site on a glacier north of the main peak. But the crux of the route comes after leaving base camp, and this involves the linking of French Pass, Hidden Valley and Damphus Pass, which can be difficult and even dangerous to navigate in poor visibility. Several Nepalis have lost their lives there when the weather changed; on such occasions experience counts for much, and it's imperative to keep a close eye on each member of the party. Beyond Damphus Pass a long and steep descent to Marpha (between Tukuche and Jomsom) exchanges an arctic environment for the relatively balmy climate of the Kali Gandaki's valley, contrasting a sense of raw isolation for the conviviality of trekkers' lodges, apple pie and locally brewed brandy.

Observing village life in the trek's early stages, enjoying remote days with close views of Dhaulagiri's North Face, and the vision of the Annapurna massif in the distance from the Damphus Pass, make this a truly unforgettable trek.

My first experience of the circuit was in 1986 when I tackled it with a friend – just the two of us – which is something I wouldn't recommend to anyone. We suffered food poisoning, our stoves failed to work, we managed to get lost in a snowstorm in Hidden Valley and were 'rescued' by some expedition Sherpas coming down from the Damphus Pass. But of course it was a brilliant trip – as such epics often are in retrospect! Brilliant, but not one to emulate.

Beni to Muri

'Silvered by eternal snows, Dhaulagiri's crown shimmers beyond a heat-brewed haze.' Such was the vision described by one of the first Westerners to study the mountain; a vision to make any ambitious trekker reach for their boots…

This classic route makes a clockwise circuit of the mountain, starting in the lower reaches of the Kali Gandaki at the large bazaar village of **Beni** at a steamy altitude of just 850m. Nowadays accessible by bus from Pokhara, the village stands at the confluence of the Myagdi Khola and Kali Gandaki rivers; the first of which drains glaciers on the northern side of Dhaulagiri, the second rising in Tibet and flowing between Dhaulagiri and Annapurna before escaping the mountains at Pokhara.

Before setting out from Beni it is important to make sure your porters are well equipped for the high passes where warm clothing, good footwear and sunglasses are all essential items. If this is a tough route for fit and well-equipped trekkers, it's no easier for laden porters – those Himalayan juggernauts without whose support most Western groups would not get far. Look to their welfare as you would your own and treat them as friends instead of servants.

The trek has a very gentle start, which provides a good opportunity to acclimatise, and I

Small tent, huge peak – Dhaulagiri sweeps above base camp into the Himalayan blue

The long approach through the Myagdi Khola's valley is rewarded by the sight of the Dhaulagiri massif apparently blocking the way ahead

consider these first few days as a form of meditation when it's possible simply to concentrate on walking and enjoying the scenery, the life of the villages you pass through, and the abundant nature all around. A narrow dirt road continues beyond Beni to Darbang, thus saving time but also missing out on some rewarding opportunities for walking off the effects of long-distance travel amid the lush green beauty of the lowlands. One of the first campsites is near the hot springs of Tatopani, just one of many such springs in the Himalaya that have been visited for centuries by local people with medical problems like back pain or rheumatism; if you have the time, dip in and enjoy a bath!

For the next couple of days you pass through several villages and wander beside terraced fields with plenty of farming activity in the pre- and post-monsoon seasons, while ahead you may gain the occasional glimpse of the mighty Dhaulagiri and perhaps be a little daunted by the prospect of the increasingly remote areas that lie ahead.

The valley is wide in these early stages, and you slowly gain height while exploring prosperous settlements such as Babichor and **Darbang**, whose houses have been described as being strongly built of red and white clay bricks. Then come Phedi and **Phalai Gaon**, the latter nearly 1000m higher than Beni, and located where the valley forks. The inhabitants of these villages are mostly Gurung and Chettri, whose hard-working farmers grow rice, wheat and bananas. Historically this was a recruitment area for Gurkha soldiers, while a number of locals have migrated farther afield in search of more lucrative work – to the Middle East especially. Crossing the Dhara Khola the trail continues up the Myagdi Khola's valley and, weather permitting, when cresting a ridge near **Muri** (1850m) on day four you should be able to see Gurja Himal and Dhaulagiri I towering either side of the valley to the north.

Muri to Italian Base Camp

Muri is a large Magar settlement of traditional two-storey farmhouses, and by the time you arrive there you should be well into your stride in readiness for some tough days ahead. Longer and more committing stages now follow. There are fewer villages, and the trail becomes more demanding with several steep and sometimes exposed ascents and descents – look out for bees' nests attached to soaring cliffs. **Boghara** is the last big village at 2100m; it was once reached by a scary trail, but this has recently been improved. The valley is steeper and more rugged now, allowing less room for cultivation, and two hours beyond Boghara you arrive at the most remote village of the trek; a tiny settlement known as Jyardan. After leaving these last few houses it becomes an exciting prospect to walk for several days in uninhabited country between some of the loftiest of all mountains.

The trail becomes more challenging, the jungle denser and more forbidding – which is one of the reasons why porters and not pack animals are used on this route. The report presented by one early expedition to Dhaulagiri gives an idea of the problems to be faced here: '…the jungle was so thick that the expedition found great difficulty in making any movement at all. A way through had literally to be carved out with the help of bush knives and *kukris*, until at last the party arrived at the last birches of Tsaurabon at 3800m.' From here a damp trail through moss-laden woods brings you to Salaghari (3110m) where the jungle gives way to coniferous forest with tall bamboo and rhododendrons, a rewarding stretch that leads to the **Italian Base Camp** (4200m) on a tiny meadow among glacial moraines below the West Face of Dhaulagiri I. (Different maps fail to agree on the precise location of Italian Base Camp; a confusion that is part of the

A snow-covered moraine is crossed on the way to Italian Base Camp

appeal of such a route.) With even more committing days ahead, if the weather is set fair this is as good a place as any to take a couple of rest days, and to aid acclimatisation.

Italian Base Camp to Dhaulagiri Base Camp

On leaving IBC, the altitude will make the going slower, but when the going is slow, the rewards are immediate. You now descend steeply to the snout of a glacier and follow upstream through a narrow brooding gorge; note the layers in the limestone cliffs. Travelling on moraine and glacier for the next couple of days can be tricky. Clouds often drift up through the valley around noon when visibility can be greatly reduced. Make sure you stay together and keep an eye on your laden porters and the occasional cairns that guide the way.

Emerging from the gorge you come to the snout of the Chhonbardan Glacier where evidence of the power it has exerted by cutting its way between Dhaulagiri I to the east and Dhaulagiri

II, III and IV to the west, is to be seen in the rock faces on either side. The glacier is covered with rock debris chiselled from the cliffs and brought down by avalanches.

Suddenly one of the highlights of the trek is reached: the lonely yet magical site of the **Dhaulagiri Base Camp** at about 4650m below the mountain's enormous North Face, replete with the Chhonbardan Glacier's spectacular icefall. All around you other peaks in excess of 7000m reach to the sky; French Pass is to the northeast. This is the high Himalaya in all its savage beauty, and if you are familiar with the Eiger in Switzerland you will recognise the similarity with the lower section of Dhaulagiri's North Face and understand why it has sometimes been called 'the Little Eiger'. Expect a cold night with sounds from the glacier, from the wind hammering the upper slopes, and from avalanches released from the mountains. Some trekking groups choose to have another rest day here in order to acclimatise for the next stage.

Hidden Valley, a high plateau stretching between French Pass and the Damphus Pass (photo: Steve Razzetti)

Dhaulagiri Base Camp to Marpha

If it were possible, you should walk backwards here, for the route to French Pass and on to Dhampus Pass via Hidden Valley is one of the most beautiful sections in the Himalaya. The early morning view of Dhaulagiri's North Face improves with every hour as you climb towards French Pass. It is a long and steep ascent, at first on the Chhonbardan Glacier, then by way of a spur enticing you up towards the snowy saddle, but the surroundings are so breathtaking that you might have double trouble breathing – as if the advanced altitude were not bad enough!

When Buddhists cross a pass they will present something like a flower, a stone, or a prayer flag as an offering of thanks to the mountain gods. Bring your own prayer flags from Kathmandu, and on reaching **French Pass** at 5334m follow their lead and add them to those already flying on the pass, but before continuing into Hidden Valley, enjoy the view back the way you've come. In May 1950 Lionel Terray and Jacques Oudot were the first to set eyes on this scene when searching for a way onto Dhaulagiri. Oudot described the view: 'In front of us was Dhaulagiri...and straight down below us was a huge glacier, heavily crevassed... flowing down a canyon with walls thousands of feet high.' Terray added: 'It's all on such a terrific scale, it's a world in itself.' As indeed it is.

Northeast of the col Hidden Valley provides a panoramic view towards Tibet, and most parties choose to camp somewhere in the middle of this high plateau, which is poised between the lower valley and the broad slopes of Tukuche Peak. At around 5100m this is the highest camp of the trek, and you may depend on having a cold night here. Aptly named by Marcel Ichac during the French reconnaissance more than 60 years ago, Hidden Valley is used as a yak pasture in the summer months, but it's not unusual to find it covered with snow, which can make trekking across it both time-consuming and exhausting work. One route that descends from here leads to Mustang, but given sufficient time, energy and decent acclimatisation, the ascent of the non-technical Damphus Peak (also known as Thapa Peak: 6012m) is worth considering for the extent of its summit views that include Mustang, Dhaulagiri I and II, the Nilgiri peaks on the far side of the Kali Gandaki Valley, plus Annapurna and even Manaslu. Once again if visibility is limited or clouds are spilling into the plateau, keep alert for cairns, porters and the other members of your party. This is no place in which to get lost.

On leaving Hidden Valley, an easy walk up to **Damphus Pass** at 5250m will reward with yet more spectacular views into the Kali Gandaki's valley over 2600m below, while on the other side of the valley it will be the Nilgiris and the Annapurna massif that holds your attention.

Once across the pass there is still a long, four-hour section to traverse at high altitude with stunning views all the way, before cairns direct you onto the steep descent to the pastures of Yak Kharka, where a last high camp is usually made at about 3800m. Beware of exposed sections, which can be especially tricky with snow around.

The descent is not yet over at Yak Kharka, although your days of solitude are. Once you reach the Annapurna Circuit trail at **Marpha** (2670m) you can relax and celebrate with a beer or two in one of the many Tibetan-style teahouses. Or perhaps you will be tempted by the local apple brandy, but be warned – it's stronger than you think! But after those long days around Dhaulagiri you will have earned it.

The easy way out of the mountains now is to hike the short distance upvalley to **Jomsom** from whose airstrip daily flights take off for Pokhara, or if you're still in trekking mode you could head downstream and follow the popular Annapurna Circuit trail (Trek 10), which will take you below the mountain that has dominated your steps during the past two weeks or so, and on to Pokhara by the old traditional route. But whichever way you choose to depart, it will be a long time before you get Dhaulagiri out of your system.

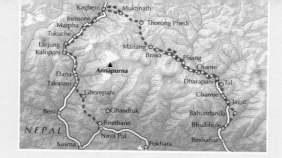

Trek 10

Annapurna Circuit

by Siân Pritchard-Jones and Bob Gibbons

Long before the former Himalayan kingdom of Nepal opened to outsiders, few could name many of the peaks apart from Everest. Today one other Nepalese mountain has become synonymous with high adventure – Annapurna. Superlatives are insufficient to do justice to its seductive trails, sublime scenery and the fascinating culture of this magical massif. It's no wonder that avid trekkers and mountaineers are drawn, as if hypnotised, by these mesmerising peaks. In his 1947 anthology The Mountain Top *Frank Smythe summed up the appeal of trekking when he wrote: 'Escape from the shell of your small affairs and tread for a while those mysterious paths of the spirit that lead nowhere and everywhere. Then you will know beauty.' Such is the essence of the Annapurna Circuit.*

solitary monk lives in a cave high above Manang, with an outlook that includes peaks of the Annapurna range across the valley

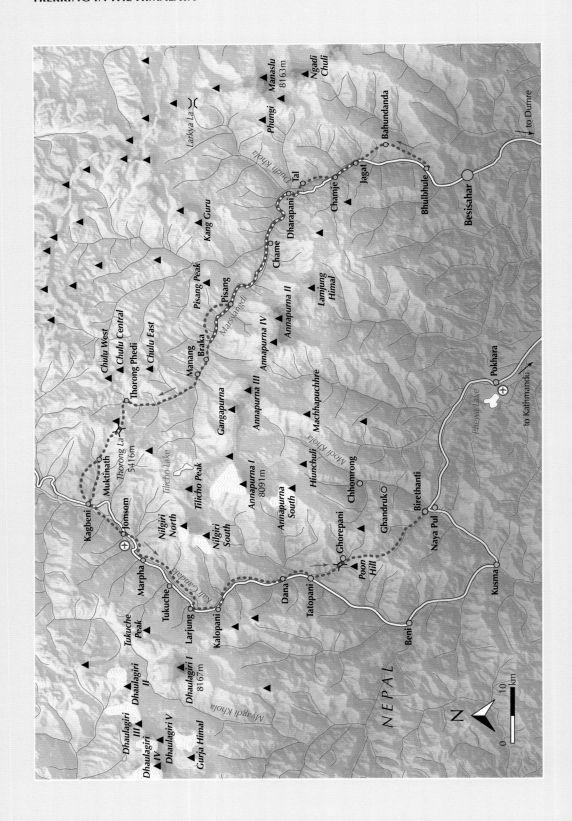

Route summary

Location	Central Nepal
Start	Besisahar
Finish	Naya Pul
Distance	200km
Duration	3 weeks (alternative finish in Jomsom: 2 weeks)
Maximum altitude	Thorong La 5416m
Trek style	Lodges or camping
Restrictions	ACAP permits required
Grade	Demanding
Guidebook	*Annapurna: A Trekker's Guide* by Siân Pritchard-Jones and Bob Gibbons (Cicerone Press, 2012)

What the early explorers found in Nepal was almost paradise on earth, a lush and plentiful land where the rhythms of life unfolded in daily rituals, strong religious beliefs and a tempo alien to those from more developed societies. Annapurna is an ancient Sanskrit name for the goddess of plenty, and indeed everything is found here in abundance – only such a divinity of the heavens could have sculptured such grandeur. The giants of the Annapurnas are engaging in all their moods; at dawn they are bathed in a soft, hazy light, but soon clouds drift in, leaving the jagged spires floating like benign ghosts. Throughout sunset they are cloaked by fiery demons, at night they shimmer in the moonlight. Sometimes tempestuous storms engulf the ramparts, while at other times they're reflected as a vision of earthly serenity in the cool blue waters of a lake.

Annapurna I, the highest peak of the massif, climbed in 1950 by Maurice Herzog and Louis Lachenal, remains one of the most enigmatic and inaccessible of mountains. Yet Annapurna is not just one peak. Four summits numbered in order of height, plus Annapurna South, bear that name, while the sacred Machhapuchhre, or Fishtail, lies within that refuge of the gods, the Annapurna Sanctuary.

Lying in the rain-shadow of the mountains, the country below Muktinath is reminiscent of a high-altitude desert

The range of sights across the region is astonishing: terraced hillsides, dense jungle, humid
bamboo clumps, canopies of cloud forest, dank
eerie woodlands and silent alpine glades. Quaint
farmhouses dot the landscape among buffaloes,
goats and chickens, while excited children scurry
across the fields to greet visitors. Women in
brightly coloured saris wash clothes by the river;
their menfolk sit and ponder the country's future.
Elsewhere a Hindu god may catch your gaze with
a smile of encouragement.

Higher up, the land is barren. Weirdly eroded
turrets support fairytale citadels, casting shadows over mediaeval villages and hermit caves.
Monasteries adorned with colourful prayer flags
cling to sheer cliffs where Buddhist monks chant
evocative mantras, half hypnotised by the aromatic incense of juniper. And all the while, impos-
sibly high bastions of ice and snow peer down.

Religion plays a vital role in the day-to-day
life of these hillfolk. The Hindu middle hills are
inhabited by Brahmins, Magars, Chhetris and
Gurungs. Thakalis, Manangis and others related
to Tibetan ethnic groups eke out a living in the
high country, sustained in their daily tasks by the
spinning of prayer wheels. An astonishing array of
vegetation hides numerous birds and elusive animals: Himalayan thar and snow leopard guard the

higher ramparts, where even the yeti keeps itself
well hidden.

Despite rumours of its demise through the construction of new dirt roads, the Annapurna Circuit
remains one of the truly great walks of the world.
After all, mountain roads criss-cross the Alps, yet
no one would deny that the trekking there is also
superb. Making a counter-clockwise tour, the
Circuit begins by trekking north through the valley
of the Marsyangdi Khola. Above Manang it crosses
the Thorong La at a lofty 5416m, then descends to
the stony bed of the Kali Gandaki, a river born
in Tibet. Where it passes between Dhaulagiri and
Annapurna, this is the deepest valley on earth: a
valley whose scale is almost impossible to define.

Besisahar to Manang

Reached by tarmac road from Dumre on the main
Kathmandu to Pokhara highway, **Besisahar** has
long been the start of this classic trek. From there
a rickety bus now rattles along the dirt road to
Bhulbhule, while jeeps ferry trekkers sometimes
as far as Chame, from where you'll have to start
walking. The road is expected to reach Manang
soon, but construction of new trails to attract
trekkers has already begun.

Many trekkers take the old trail from Bhulbhule
on the east bank of the river to the hilltop Brahmin

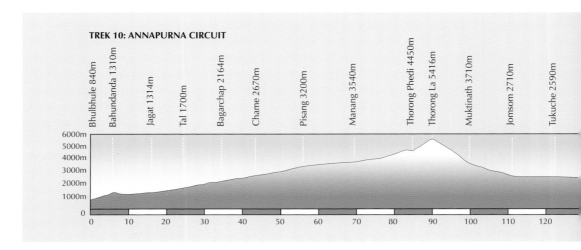

village of **Bahundanda**, and then among terraces of rice, mustard and millet to Syange on
the west bank. **Jagat** is a former trading customs
post, a quaint cluster of houses from where the
route leads to **Chamje.** Now the full drama of
the Marsyangdi's gorge opens its show as the
mighty Himalaya are pierced by the awe-inspiring

*A steeply winding trail climbs the true left bank
of the Marsyangdi Valley before reaching Tal*

geological forces of nature. The path to Tal climbs
in earnest beside the raging cascades and torrents
of the river, the canyon hemmed in by forbidding
cliffs draped with slender waterfalls. **Tal** has the
first of many colourful monasteries, and families
of Tibetan exiles run some of the lodges.

Traversing several attractive settlements, the way
continues along the steep-sided chasm to Karte.
Here you'll find the quirky Dorchester Lodge, but
don't expect a bellboy wearing white gloves, just
a typically warm Nepali welcome. Just across the
river is **Dharapani** and the once-forbidden village
of Tonje – it's worth a detour to see its tiny monastery adorned with ancient paintings and statues.
From here a quiet, alternative forest trail on the
river's north bank heads to Bagarchap by way of
an incongruously high suspension bridge. Sadly,
part of Bagarchap village was destroyed by a massive mudslide in 1995, and many of its inhabitants

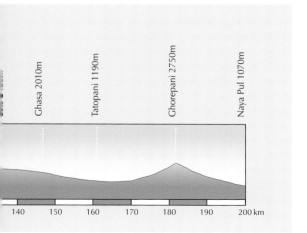

Chame enjoys a grandstand view of Manaslu at sunset

moved to the new village of Danakyu further up the valley.

A steep new trail climbs relentlessly to Timang, from where the panoramic view of Manaslu and Himalchuli is unforgettable. For a while the path is almost level, so take the opportunity to relax, turn round and enjoy the stupendous sight behind you.

Thanchok is a traditional settlement unaffected by passing trekkers, and soon a mysterious valley, guarded by a narrow defile, appears at Koto. Adventurous visitors, with a pre-obtained permit and local guide, can explore the recently opened last frontier of the Annapurnas – the region of Nar-Phu, which lies to the north. Typical of much of the Trans-Himalayan regions and nestling against the remote Tibetan border, the high-altitude valleys of Nar and Phu are predominantly arid and sparsely populated. Cut off from the outside world, the valleys have been gazed on by only a few favoured anthropologists like David Snellgrove, who described the region in *Himalayan Pilgrimage*. A monolithic outcrop guards the entrance to Phu where, it is said, spirits are trapped behind its fearful countenance. The villages have flat-roofed stone houses built in a style similar to those in Manang, with log-cut ladders giving access. Tibetan Buddhism is followed here, but some still adhere to the ancient Bon faith; a few dramatically located ruined *dzongs*, or forts, recall the region's tempestuous past.

Back on the main trail **Chame** (2670m) is the next village, with soothing hot springs, hot showers, flush toilets and fancy menus. Here trekkers can gaze at the sunset on Manaslu before tucking into *dal bhat*, the traditional rice and dal dish of Nepal. There follows a delightful stage of blue pines and woodland glades filled with birdsong and sweet aromas, and ascending from Bhratang beside the dramatic sweep of the glacier-etched rock face of the Paungda Danda, the altitude begins to bite. It's breathtaking as the path climbs relentlessly to Dhukuri Pokhari for a rejuvenating tea stop. Leaving the pines, the trail emerges into the desert-like landscape of the Manang district where the next settlement, Lower Pisang, has a long mani wall. But if you have sufficient energy, climb to the upper village and immerse yourself in its mediaeval ambience.

Decisions, decisions – there are two routes that link **Pisang** (3200m) and Mungji, and both are equally rewarding. The lower trail passes strangely fluted, troglodyte turrets and cliffs watched over by Pisang Peak and Annapurna III. The upper route is tough and enthralling as it climbs to the old flat-roofed Tibetan-style villages of Ghyaru and Ngawal. From this airy belvedere Annapurnas II, III and IV, and Gangapurna are the star turns across the valley, while far below lies Hongde airport, served by only two flights per week – weather permitting.

The two trails converge before the intriguing old village of **Braka** (Braga), whose picturesque,

The old village of Braka is dwarfed by the landscape; Tilicho Peak is in the background

Jhong, a mediaeval village below Muktinath. The pyramid-shaped peak in the background is Dhaulagiri

400-year-old monastery is set into the craggy hill-side, dramatically poised above the village. Do persist in trying to find the man or woman with the key, if you can. Aromatic bakeries, along with comfortable rooms and hot showers, are an irresistible temptation to stop for the night in one of the lodges, swapping stories with other trekkers in the cosy dining rooms.

High above Braka is the Ice Lake, with sensational views en route of Tilicho Peak and the 'Grand Barrier' of the Annapurnas. It's a rugged and dehydrating excursion, where the goats are failing in their duty to maintain the trails!

It's absolutely essential to spend a night or two in either Braka or Manang to acclimatise to the altitude. At 3540m historic **Manang** is a thriving settlement with plenty to do, see and buy. The Manangi people are famous traders, who in the past had a special dispensation to import goods duty-free; they were often encountered on flights into Nepal wearing several pairs of jeans and jackets, one on top of the other. ACAP (Annapurna Conservation Area Project) has an office here, while at the medical clinic a daily lecture on altitude sickness is given during the trekking season. If you're contemplating a ride to the top of the Thorong La, sure-footed Manangi ponies negotiate the precarious slopes on the trail ahead with consummate ease.

To aid acclimatisation, head up to the Buddhist cave retreat of Praken. A longer side-trip leads to the timeless village of Khangsar, while a thrilling but much more challenging three-to-four-day hike aims for the deep blue waters of Tilicho Lake, whose calm ambience is disturbed only by the thunder of ice blocks crashing from the glacier above. It's a tough climb from Tilicho Base Camp up through the wind-eroded outcrops that float in the soup of unstable sands blocking the eastern end of the lake.

Manang to Jomsom

With the 'lazy' days of Manang behind, attention focuses on the crowning pass ahead. It's high and wild country up here; herders eke out a meagre living, while modern lodge owners do rather better – and some pony men do even better still. The trail climbs steeply up to Gunsang, a great place to spend a night. Then views of Tilicho, Gangapurna and Annapurna III compensate for the effort required as the trail passes through Yak Kharka and Churi Lattar to the infamous **Thorong Phedi** where, at 4450m, a sleepless night inevitably awaits.

Next morning you feel as though you're in another world, with anticipation and adrenalin-bulging expectations about to be fulfilled. In the first flush of dawn, most trekkers will be climbing up the trail, its steepness masked by the darkness. After a while the rhythm of the climb sets in, as a great amphitheatre of peaks show off their finest – the captivating cirque of Putrun Himal and Chulu, with tumbling glaciers in abundance.

Unless you've experienced high altitude before, nothing can prepare you for the effects encountered on the 5416m **Thorong La**. The final stage is a bit of a killer, with endless false summits and pony men hovering like vultures, waiting to scavenge on falling and failing trekkers. You wonder why anyone wants to climb a Himalayan mountain. You gasp for breath and feel high as a kite, nose droplets freeze – and after all that you probably can't wait to do it all over again. Reaching the summit of the pass, festooned as it is with brightly coloured prayer flags, is mind-blowing in all senses; sometimes an icy blast threatens to tear the hair from your scalp as you're buffeted by ferocious winds.

The Thorong La marks an amazing landscape change as the trail drops into the Mustang district. From the pass a steep, seemingly endless and knee-jerking descent begins, wending its way

down to the holy shrine of **Muktinath** and the unholy, but most welcome, collection of restaurants and lodges, with hot showers, rock music and food enough to delight any palate.

A new trail from Muktinath to Kagbeni passes through three delightfully evocative, untouched villages, like the picturesque Jhong. The awe-inspiring scenery along the way includes a salt lake, mysterious rock caves dug into fluted sandstone, and a fabulous view back to the Thorong La. It's a magical day.

Kagbeni has retained its ancient flavour, with a mud citadel, a historic monastery, atmospheric alleys, tumbledown houses and low tunnels. It's a rare gem of a village (even if it does offer Italian coffee houses and YakDonalds). Another fantasy location is the remote settlement of Lubra, hidden high on the hillside where weird crags give sanctuary to a Bon community close to a stupendous outcrop. A diversion to visit Lubra is recommended on the hike from Kagbeni to **Jomsom**.

Jomsom to Pokhara

Jomsom attracts, not for its remoteness, but for its good food, shopping, electricity, TV and modern conveniences. Many trekkers nowadays think this is the end of the Circuit, but nothing could be further from the truth. Forget the dirt road and airport that whisk many trekkers away too soon. Don't succumb to temptation, but carry on down the Kali Gandaki's valley on foot and you'll be rewarded with the most extraordinary sights, both cultural and geographical. It's still a great experience and definitely not to be missed.

Treats in store include the paved streets and old white houses of **Marpha**; on the other side of the river, the priceless ancient monastery of Chhairo – enough to capture any culture vulture's imagination. The beautiful old Thakali settlement of **Tukuche** is famous for its quaint stone houses, old wooden windows, paved streets and apple pies. Japanese explorer Ekai Kawaguchi stayed here and his house is now the distillery for their most famous product, apple brandy. Another hidden treasure on the left bank, after a beautiful forest walk, is the clifftop village of Chimang, reached by intrepid visitors via a precarious log ladder. Above Larjung is the rarely seen Bon monastery of Naurikot, well worth a visit for its strange and colourful imagery.

For a short while the trail follows the riverbed, crossing the raging waters on a couple of rather dodgy log bridges. Be sure to spend the night in **Kalopani**, where the sunset view of the elusive Annapurna I is staggering – it's the only place on the entire Circuit where the mountain's extraordinary beauty is displayed. Except for a small section of road near Ghasa, an alternative trail now leads all the way to Tatopani, climbing up and down through the forest on steep staircases on the east bank of the river, while the dirt road stays on the opposite bank. There's hardly another soul to be seen on this peaceful trail, and the sight of the waterfall of Rupse Chhara from high above is stunning. A visit to the village of **Dana**, with its old carved window frames and classic houses, is definitely worthwhile. But be sure to cross the river back to the trail to **Tatopani**, which leads through little-visited settlements below the Miristi Khola.

Tatopani's famous hot springs will soothe any aching muscles, while superb enchiladas or apple pies energise and stimulate the taste buds. You might be running out of steam here until, that is, you see the bus to Beni, which makes the 1600m climb to Ghorepani a more attractive proposition. There's nothing for it, then, but to make the ascent through rhododendron forest to **Ghorepani** (2750m), above which the daily ritual of witnessing sunrise from Poon Hill should not be missed. This feast for the eyes includes Dhaulagiri, the Annapurnas, the Kali Gandaki Valley and endless misty blue ridges fading into the distance as far as the Indian border.

The options from Ghorepani are varied. For drama head north to the majestic Kopra Danda ridge; however, you'll need a guide for this section, as the trail is not so frequented, but teahouses and community lodges have been built. The Kopra Danda is higher than Poon Hill and the view of Dhaulagiri that much more exciting. The viewpoint often gets a dousing of snow, adding to the spectacle. Higher still is the holy lake of Khairetal, from where the blue-tinged Nilgiri peaks dominate the view north. But it is the sheer drop into the mist-filled morning haze of the Kali Gandaki that truly exhilarates trekkers.

West of Ghorepani is a new homestay-based trekking route through Nangi, where those keen to interact with traditional rural Nepalese culture may immerse themselves in the offbeat countryside. Alternatively, head for the Annapurna Sanctuary along a forested ridge and down past dramatic tumbling waterfalls by way of Tadapani and Chhomrong. If there is one place in the Annapurna region that truly illustrates the immensity of the Himalaya, it is surely the Sanctuary (Trek 11). Otherwise, simply descend from Ghorepani via the endless staircase of stone steps to Ulleri, and head for the warmer climes of **Birethanti** and transport to Pokhara.

Pokhara offers a well-earned rest beside the shimmering waters of Phewa Lake, a place for contemplative silence or a thirst-quenching beer in one of the many lakeside gardens. Apart from pizzas, pies or even paragliding, Pokhara rewards with some of the best panoramas of the whole trek.

Some hardy souls will always be drawn to climb the most formidable of Himalayan peaks, but for most ordinary mortals, the mere sight of such majesty is enough. To trek in the shadow of the mighty Annapurna range is to feel closer to the heavens, and to be at one with nature. The goddess of abundance gives plenty.

Machhapuchhre, the 'fishtail' peak, towers over the Modi Khola's gorge ▶

Trek 11

Annapurna Sanctuary

by Kev Reynolds

Imagine an almost complete ring of high peaks, six of which top 7000m and one – the enigmatic Annapurna – gracing 8000m. Picture this immense amphitheatre hung about with glaciers, plastered with snowfields, buttressed by massive walls of rock that erupt from a basin of old moraines and raunchy streams. Dream, if you will, of a silver moon lighting the scene; of sunrise staining summits, of mist thickening to cloud that slowly fills the basin. And the last summit to be swamped by it all is one of the most charismatic of mountains: Machhapuchhre, the unmistakable 'fishtail' peak, guardian of the Annapurna Sanctuary and seducer supreme, set in a landscape of imagination. But in this sanctuary, this abode of the gods, imagination is surplus to requirements, for reality exceeds even the wildest of dreams.

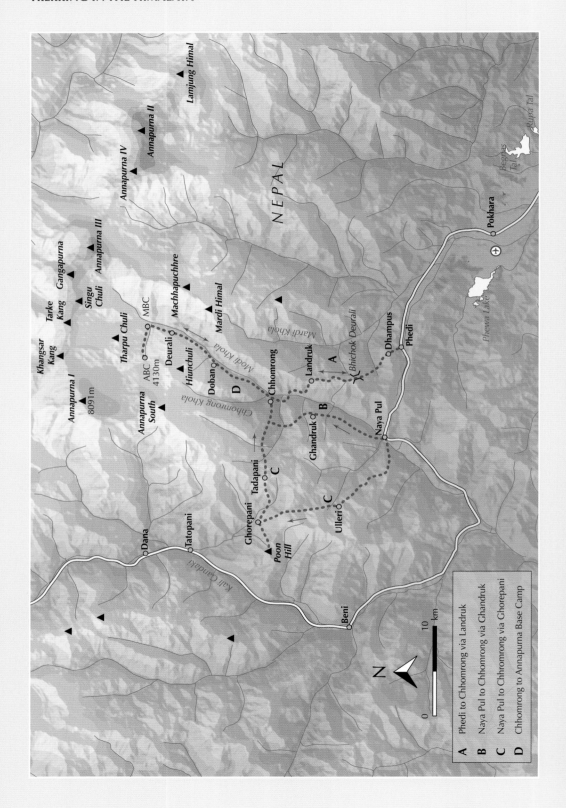

A   Phedi to Chhomrong via Landruk

B   Naya Pul to Chhomrong via Ghandruk

C   Naya Pul to Chhromrong via Ghorepani

D   Chhomrong to Annapurna Base Camp

Route summary

Location	Central Nepal
Start/Finish	Phedi or Naya Pul
Distance	84–100km
Duration	10–12 days (but allow at least 2 weeks)
Maximum altitude	Annapurna Base Camp 4130m
Trek style	Lodges or camping
Restrictions	ACAP permits required
Grade	Moderate/Demanding
Guidebook	*Annapurna: A Trekker's Guide* by Siân Pritchard-Jones and Bob Gibbons (Cicerone Press, 2012)

When Maurice Herzog wrote about the brief period he and Louis Lachenal spent on the summit of Annapurna on 3 June 1950, he made no mention of the great bowl of the Sanctuary on the southeast side of the mountain, only that the summit itself was a crest of ice from which precipices fell vertically away; they were terrifying, he said, 'unfathomable'. In his euphoria on having gained that elusive high point – the first of the Himalayan 8000m giants to be won – no mention was made of neighbouring peaks such as Annapurna South or Hiunchuli, nor of Glacier Dome, Singu Chuli, Gangapurna or Annapurna III. Neither did he mention Machhapuchhre, which rose directly opposite his hard-won summit on the far side of that tremendous glacial basin. But the specially drawn map that accompanied his book of the expedition contains a note that would have stirred the blood of any mountain adventurer of the time. It read: 'As the south side of the Annapurna massif has not been explored, it has not been possible to give the detailed relief of this portion.' Of such words ambitions are born.

Six years later Jimmy Roberts, a Gurkha officer and avid mountain explorer who became the 'father' of trekking in Nepal, was the first Westerner to penetrate the gorge of the Modi Khola, which

By mid-morning clouds often drift up from the gorge to fill the Sanctuary

opens into the Annapurna Sanctuary. His reason for being there was to study Machhapuchhre from close quarters, in advance of an attempt the following year (1957) to climb the fishtail peak by a British expedition of which he was to be leader. It was Roberts who gave the Sanctuary its name, for he learned from the village elders of Chhomrong that a powerful goddess lived at the top of the gorge, and she would have to be propitiated at a shrine near the Hinko cave.

Over the next few years a handful of mountaineering expeditions followed Roberts' lead by forging a way through the Modi Khola's gorge and entering the Annapurna Sanctuary in order to tackle a number of its peaks: a group of Japanese on Glacier Dome in 1964, Germans on Gangapurna in 1965, and an attempt on Annapurna I via Glacier Dome in 1969. But although local shepherds had long grazed their flocks in the upper basin, and a few hardy trekkers made their way there after the attempt on Machhapuchhre, it was not until the South Face of Annapurna – one of the most formidable of Himalayan walls – was climbed by a team led by Chris Bonington in the spring of 1970, that a proper awareness of the Sanctuary began to filter into the minds of ambitious trekkers. Before long Bonington's Annapurna Base Camp became one of the ultimate goals on the tick-list of 'must-visit' sites in Nepal.

The Sanctuary itself is a tremendously exciting and rewarding goal for all who love the drama of high mountain scenery. Its gateposts – Hiunchuli and Machhapuchhre – form a division between bamboo thicket and mountain fortress, rainforest and glacier. Fortunately the route through the gorge, which is the key to getting there, is neither as difficult nor dangerous as that of the Rishi Ganga leading to the Nanda Devi Sanctuary (Trek 4), and with plenty of simple lodges strung along the way the two or three days it takes to trek from Chhomrong to Annapurna Base Camp make the route highly attractive to independent trekkers. But as the standard approach is so short, it's important to acclimatise well before going up to

the base camp at 4130m; this is more than 2000m higher than the gorge entrance. Happily there are plenty of excuses to spend several days trekking in the foothills first, getting fit and coming to terms with Nepal's verticalities before being drawn into this abode of the gods.

Pokhara to Chhomrong via Landruk

With its attractive lake, boating opportunities and blatant tourist appeal, **Pokhara** is the nearest any Nepalese town can claim to being a resort. Easily reached from Kathmandu by either a half-hour flight or a full day's bus ride, the town sprawls below the Annapurnas at an altitude of just 820m. When he retired from the army, Jimmy Roberts set up home there, claiming that 'there is no other mountain view in the world to equal Machhapuchhare [sic] and Annapurna hanging in the sky above the green Pokhara plain'. It also happens to be the perfect place from which to set out on a trek into the Annapurna Sanctuary.

Although there's only one route into the Sanctuary through the Modi Khola's gorge, several options exist for trekking through the foothills on the way to it. All these converge on the village of Chhomrong at the gorge entrance, most of

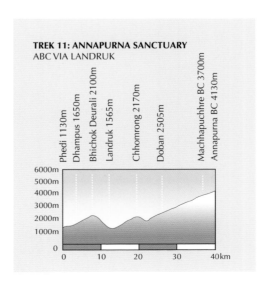

which take a basic two or three days, but could easily be extended by trekkers with plenty of time and a desire to see as much of this foothill country as possible. It's all spectacularly beautiful and as rewarding in its own way as the high mountains, which for many are the major lure.

The most direct approach begins at **Phedi**, a half-hour's taxi ride from Pokhara, where a trail climbs steeply through forest and alongside terraced rice fields to **Dhampus** (1650m), a village popular with tourists who come to spend a night there in order to capture sunrise over the mountains.

Above Dhampus a partly paved trail heads through rhododendron forest and on to Pothana, where Machhapuchhre makes its presence felt in a powerful way, while a clearing in the wooded ridge above the village extends the view to include Dhaulagiri and Annapurna South. The ridge is crossed at **Bhichok Deurali**, a pass of 2100m where there are two lodges, followed by descent into a broad hillside scalloped with terraced fields dotted with neat farmhouses and villages. The

At 7210m, Annapurna South – seen here at dawn above Chhomrong – is one of the many impressive peaks that rim the Sanctuary

largest of these is **Landruk** (Landrung), an attractive Gurung settlement perched on a steep slope at 1565m, with a number of circular thatched houses, good lodges and a narrow paved street from which Annapurna South and its neighbour Hiunchuli dominate the scene. To the west across the deep cut of the Modi Khola, Ghandruk is enticing. This, the main village south of the Annapurna Sanctuary, is visited by one of the alternative approach routes beginning at Naya Pul.

Two hundred metres below Landruk the Modi Khola is crossed by way of a large suspension bridge at a group of lodges prosaically known as New Bridge. At 1340m this can seem depressingly low, especially if you've taken aboard the fact that Chhomrong's altitude is 2170m and the sun is blazing. The uphill trail is remorseless, and the 800m of ascent can seem at least twice that long.

To those not yet mountain fit, Chhomrong remains an elusive dream until the very last minute.

Naya Pul to Chhomrong via Ghandruk

A second short approach to Chhomrong begins at **Naya Pul**, a scruffy collection of buildings beside the Pokhara to Beni road west of Phedi, served by public bus that takes about two hours for the 42-kilometre journey; a taxi will take about half that time, but cost considerably more. If this is your first Himalayan trek, the shanty will make you wonder what you've come all this way for, but within a few minutes you'll have crossed your first suspension bridge and entered the bazaar village of Birethanti, where things start to look up.

Birethanti marks the confluence of the Modi Khola and Bhurungdi Khola, and at 1025m is on a major trekking crossroads. One trail heads northwest to Ghorepani and Poon Hill (described below), while the Chhomrong route via Ghandruk

Several lodges in Ghandruk are run by ex-Gurkha soldiers

initially follows the Modi Khola northeastwards. Like a towering signpost Machhapuchhre beckons from afar, leading you out of town and along the river valley past a string of teahouses interspersed with fields of rice and millet. An hour from Birethanti lies Syauli Bazaar and another junction

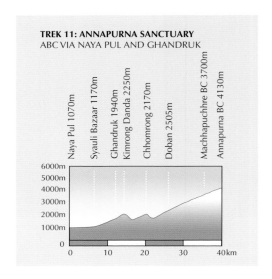

TREK 11: ANNAPURNA SANCTUARY
ABC VIA NAYA PUL AND GHANDRUK

of trails. One leads to New Bridge and Chhomrong, the other climbs to Ghandruk with 770m of ascent between immaculately terraced fields.

This is an artistic landscape, a land of vibrant colours. In springtime buffalo drag ploughs through the fields, while men and women stand calf-deep in muddy water planting the rice. In the autumn these same hillfolk are busy with the harvest, when fields are transformed as brightly clad villagers lay the yellowing rice low with short-handled sickles spreading fan-like swathes among the stubble. On threshing floors grain is tossed from large circular trays, the chaff floating away in clouds of dust; conical haystacks speckle the hillside and buffalo tramp an endless circuit as part of the winnowing process. Elsewhere women stand waist-deep in fields of millet, plucking the brown seed and tossing it over their shoulders into a waiting *doko*, while soaring above everything Annapurna South, Hiunchuli and Machhapuchhre hover among the clouds.

Ghandruk (1940m) is a large village of slate-roofed houses set upon an open terraced site with uninterrupted views of big mountains. Paved alleys twist through the village, with sufficient side-trails to cause temporary disorientation. There's a gompa, a Gurung museum, an Annapurna Conservation Area Project (ACAP) Visitor Centre, plus several shops, a post office, campgrounds and plenty of well-run lodges. Some of the best are managed by retired Gurkha soldiers and their families, and a night in one will be a night well spent, especially if you rise at dawn to watch as the new day drains its magic from the slopes of Machhapuchhre into the harvest fields below.

The trek from Ghandruk to Chhomrong crosses the Kimrong Danda, zigzags 500m down to the Kimrong Khola where there's a log bridge, then winds up a wooded slope to a crossing path near a teahouse. Forty minutes later you arrive at the first buildings of **Chhomrong**.

Naya Pul to Chhomrong via Ghorepani and Poon Hill

The previous two approach routes are more direct than this one, but the spectacle of sunrise from Poon Hill above Ghorepani is part of the Annapurna experience and deserves to be included in any trek to the Sanctuary. Allow yourself four days to reach Chhomrong via Ghorepani, and begin as described in the previous section with a taxi or bus ride from Pokhara to **Naya Pul** and a short trek from there to Birethanti. Now instead of answering the lure of Machhapuchhre, take the trail on the north bank of the Bhurungdi Khola, which leads through bamboo forest, passes several lodges and teahouses and arrives at Hille about two hours from Birethanti. Ten minutes later you go through Tirkhedunga (1540m), and soon after begin the long, steep ascent of more than 3500 well-made stone steps leading to the Magar village of **Ulleri** at 1960m. With its several tempting lodges and views of Annapurna South and Hiunchuli, this is as good a place as any to spend the night before continuing the climb to Ghorepani next day.

At 2750m, and crammed within a heavily used pass on a spur projecting southwest from

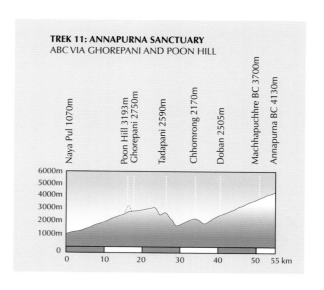

TREK 11: ANNAPURNA SANCTUARY
ABC VIA GHOREPANI AND POON HILL

Annapurna South, **Ghorepani** consists of a cluster of tin-roofed trekkers' lodges and shops, and a view north to Dhaulagiri. But some of the best views are to be had from the high point of **Poon Hill**, less than an hour's walk up the ridge to the southwest at 3193m. Go there for sunrise and you'll not be alone, for every fine morning during the trekking seasons hundreds of bleary-eyed trekkers gather there to capture daybreak over the Himalaya: Dhaulagiri to the north, Annapurna I, Annapurna South, Hiunchuli, Machhapuchhre, all bear witness to the new day; an experience not to be missed.

Sunrise over, descend back to Ghorepani and have a filling breakfast, then take off along the eastern side of the pass en route to Tadapani and Chhomrong; a two-day trek, the first section being through forest lavish with rhododendrons, Spanish moss, giant ferns and tree orchids. Occasional views are gained between the trees of Dhaulagiri, and later, Machhapuchhre and Annapurna South. Several of the **Tadapani** lodges enjoy spectacular views, but it can be a dank and chilly place when afternoon mists settle over the ridge on which it sits. But as you draw nearer to **Chhomrong** on the second day out from Ghorepani, so the countryside opens to a productive landscape of terraced hills stretching as far as the eye can see. Walking alone here one day I came to a fork in the trail and was unable to decide which was the correct branch to take. Both trails were of bone-hard earth with no bootprints to give a clue. I scanned the hillsides and saw no one. Then a cry could be heard far off. It sounded like 'upside...upside!' Again I scanned the hillside, and at last spied a figure almost completely buried in a field of rice; he was pointing to the upper trail, guessing that I was bound for Chhomrong. 'Upside,' he called again. 'Upside!'

Chhomrong to Annapurna Base Camp

Chhomrong is a prosperous Gurung village of two parts linked by a long stairway of more than 2000 paved steps. In the upper village there's an ACAP checkpost and a number of fine lodges, many of which have flower-bordered sun terraces, panoramic dining rooms and solar-heated showers. The lower village houses a kerosene depot (no cooking on wood fires allowed beyond this point), a dispensary, several shops and more lodges. Make the most of the comparative luxury of the lodges in this village, for accommodation within both the gorge and the Sanctuary tends to be rather more basic. In any case, Chhomrong has such a pleasing location, with magical views and good facilities, that it's tempting to spend at least two nights there before moving on.

Away from the lower village a suspension bridge takes the trail across the thunderous waters of the Chhomrong Khola, at the head of which stands Annapurna South. The way now makes a long twisting ascent of a spur falling from Hiunchuli, effectively dividing the valleys of the Chhomrong and Modi Kholas, then continues a little further to Sinuwa (2340m), a group of lodges with a stunning view of Machhapuchhre, Annapurna III and Gangapurna at the far end of the Modi Khola's gorge.

The trail through the gorge is something of a switchback, zigzagging among rhododendrons and dense bamboo thickets with plenty of steep uphills and descents where concentration is required, for in places the trail is rough underfoot and a fall could have serious consequences. Waterfalls spray down the mighty cliffs while mist often hangs for days at a time; even the air seems damp. Sections of trail are greasy with mud and for long sections views are virtually non-existent as the towering walls on either side crowd out any features of interest. But when views do appear, it's the graceful fishtail peak that holds your attention.

Lodges are grouped together in specially designated places, their siting controlled by ACAP, who also limit the number of rooms allowed to ensure no single building becomes too big. The location of these lodges is critical, for the threat of avalanche from the slopes of Hiunchuli is very real, particularly in the early spring or after a heavy fall

Above Ghorepani, Poon Hill is the ever-popular vantage point from which to study Dhaulagiri

of snow; the area between the Hinko cave and Machhapuchhre Base Camp being especially vulnerable. The so-called cave is not a true cave at all, but a huge overhanging boulder formerly used as a bivouac shelter by the shepherds and hunters who pioneered this route. For some years a simple lodge stood beneath it, until the ACAP authorities forced its closure.

The next section is often littered with avalanche debris. Approaching Annapurna in the spring of 1970, Chris Bonington found the gorge here almost entirely filled with debris, describing the mass of avalanched snow as being like a miniature glacier. When the danger area has been passed, you'll find another huddled group of lodges at **Deurali**, beyond which the valley broadens with Gangapurna ahead framed by massive

rock walls. An hour later, and after crossing more avalanche chutes, you emerge from the constrictions of the gorge to the lodges of **Machhapuchhre Base Camp** at 3700m.

In many ways this is an unsatisfactory site, for although you've at last gained access to the Sanctuary, views remain severely limited. The great shaft of rock, snow and ice of Machhapuchhre towers intimidatingly overhead but is so close, so foreshortened, as to lose any true sense of identity. And only the northeast aspect of Annapurna South gives any impression of the grand scene waiting to be absorbed 400m higher and another

Machhapuchhre guards the way out of the Sanctuary

two weary hours' walk away. If you're feeling the altitude, spend a night here at MBC before going any higher.

The hike up to Annapurna Base Camp (ABC), although not particularly steep, can seem a relentless toil. The trail wends its way through a grassy ablation valley below old moraines. Streams rush down from melting snows, and as you gain height, so one summit after another rises ahead as though on a pedestal.

Rimmed by glacial moraines at 4130m **Annapurna Base Camp** is a cold, often windy site occupied by a group of lodges. But given the legendary clarity of Himalayan views, it is a truly breathtaking location. The great wall of Annapurna's South Face soaring beyond the moraine rim naturally holds your attention, and to the non-climber (and to the majority of 'ordinary' mountaineers too) the prospect of forcing a route up it seems like a suicidal mission. But arguably more beautiful than this is the graceful shape of Annapurna South, a 'mere' 7210m outlier rising directly above the lodges.

Yet everywhere you turn a bounty of visual elegance is laid out for inspection. Go onto the crest of the moraine wall just beyond the lodges, and you'll gaze on soaring buttresses of rock and ice, hanging glaciers, snowfields, shapely peaks and ridges etched with cornices against the Himalayan blue. And maybe you will echo the words of Wilfrid Noyce, the poet-mountaineer who concluded his book about the attempt on Machhapuchhre, with the cry: 'If there be a Paradise on earth, it is now, it is now, it is now!'

The graceful, twin-peaked Manaslu is seen at its best from Syala (photo: Linda Reynolds) ▶

Trek 12

Manaslu Circuit

by Kev Reynolds

Flanked by the Annapurnas to the west and Ganesh Himal to the east, Manaslu is one of the most graceful of 8000m giants, while the circular tour around it counts among the truly great treks of the Himalaya. Physically demanding, culturally enriching and scenically uplifting, it takes you from the steamy lowlands – with their terraces of rice and millet – through the mighty gorges of the Buri Gandaki, to the snow-bound Larkya La close to the Tibetan border, then down the well-known Marsyangdi Valley to the verdant foothill country once more. It's a visual feast from start to finish – but you'll need to be fit.

Route summary

Location	Central Nepal
Start/Finish	Gorkha
Distance	about 200km
Duration	3 weeks (19 days' trekking plus 2 rest days)
Maximum altitude	Larkya La 5135m
Trek style	Camping or simple lodges
Restrictions	Special permits required
Grade	Demanding
Guidebook	*Manaslu: A Trekker's Guide* by Kev Reynolds (Cicerone Press, 2000)

Viewed from a ridge above Gorkha, the distant wall of the Himalaya rises above a foreground of terraced fields; a jagged wall of ice and snow often detached from its foundations by skeins of mist or a layer of cloud. Towards evening it turns pink, then purple, but holds onto its colours long after shadows have swamped the lowlands. Manaslu itself cannot be seen from here, for it is blocked by Ngadi Chuli. But Himalchuli and Baudha suggest a hidden wonderland 'lost behind the ranges', while the Annapurnas stretch the panorama leftwards, and the Ganesh peaks spread the great white wall to the right.

If that view fails to get your heart beating faster, you'd better head for home.

My first encounter with the Manaslu Circuit took place in 1992, just after it had been opened to a maximum of 400 trekkers per year. In those days a liaison officer had to accompany the group, and as we saw no other Westerners our journey

Larkya Peak and, far right, the saddle of the Larkya La which forms the crux of the route

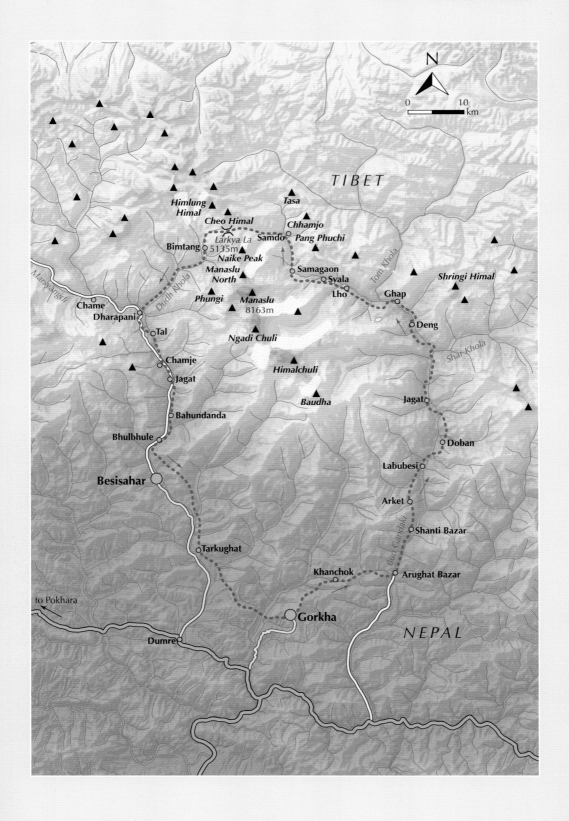

N

0   10
km

TIBET

Tasa

Himlung
Himal

Cheo Himal

Chhamjo

Larkya La   Samdo   Pang Phuchi

Bimtang   5135m

Naike Peak

Manaslu   Samagaon

North   Syala

Lho   Ghap

Shringi Himal

Phungi   Manaslu

8163m

Chame

Dharapani

Dudh Khola

Ngadi Chuli

Deng

Tal

Shar Khola

Chamje

Jagat

Himalchuli

Jagat

Marsyangdi

Baudha

Doban

Bahundanda

Labubesi

Bhulbhule

Arket

Besisahar

Shanti Bazar

Buri Gandaki

Tarkughat

Khanchok   Arughat Bazar

to Pokhara

Gorkha

NEPAL

Dumre

took on the nature of a pioneering expedition. The massive gorges through which the Buri Gandaki thundered both enticed and challenged; villagers stared as we wandered through their remote settlements; mani walls and prayer flags blessed and protected us; and the mountains shone a benediction. It was the most magical of journeys, and every subsequent trek there has further strengthened my love of the area.

Of course, we were not the first to penetrate this magical land. Members of Bill Tilman's small expedition had seen something of it in 1950; soon after, Japanese mountaineers launched a series of attempts to climb Manaslu, and in 1956 David Snellgrove, the scholar of Tibetan Buddhism, crossed the Larkya La and descended through the Buri Gandaki (effectively reversing a large portion of the trek described here), to find a trail resembling narrow cat-walks where small tree trunks were pegged against the rocks. He wrote of single-pole bridges across which shepherds carried their sheep one by one, and reported having to wade waist-deep through raging tributaries where a slip would result in almost certain death.

Since those early days the route has been treated to major improvements, but in common with just about every Himalayan region,

the annual monsoon rains and effects of climate change have a habit of reshaping the landscape, so it would be possible to trek the Manaslu Circuit every year and each time discover different trails, bridges and even views. But there is one consistency: a truly memorable experience is guaranteed for all who achieve it.

Beginning and ending in Gorkha, the route described here is based on the original circuit, which gives perhaps the greatest variety and most satisfaction. But there are those who prefer to start in Arughat Bazar, the important township in the Buri Gandaki's lower valley, which can now be reached by road, and if the trek concludes at Besisahar in the Marsyangdi's valley, its overall length can be shortened by about five days. However, this means sacrificing glorious views and a magnificent trek through lush farming country that makes such a contrast to the stark but sterile beauty of the higher stages.

A second alternative begins at Gorkha, heads north through farmland with Baudha directly ahead, and after five or six days of fairly tough trekking joins the main circuit at Khorlabesi. This too, is a magnificent route, but we'll concentrate on the main circuit here, the start of which can be reached by a long morning's drive from Kathmandu.

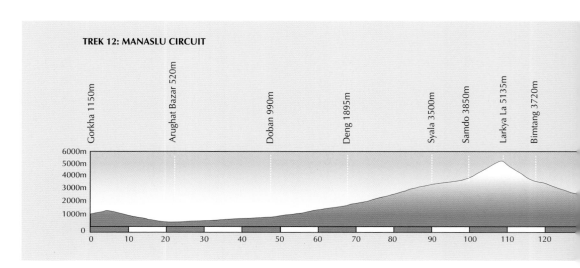

TREK 12: MANASLU CIRCUIT

From the ridge above Gorkha the Manaslu range is seen as an arctic wall beyond the foothills

Gorkha to Arughat Bazar

Standing at the end of a 17-kilometre spur off the Kathmandu to Pokhara road, **Gorkha** is the small but historic town from which Prithvi Narayan Shah began his 27-year campaign that led to the unification of Nepal in 1769, and his palace, or *durbar*, is perched on the wooded ridge-crest immediately above the town. Less than an hour after setting out, you come onto that crest to catch sight of the mountains around which you'll be trekking for the next three weeks. It's a tantalising view and one that holds your attention as you descend on the far side to a terraced site with a farmhouse nearby, and monkeys playing in the trees behind the tents.

Two easy days of trekking lead to Arughat Bazar, and as you descend from around 1300 to just over 500m it doesn't matter whether you're there in the spring or the autumn: they're likely to be hot and sticky. That being said, they're also full of colour and interest, with small groups of houses dotted among the terraced fields, with canna lilies and bananas in their gardens, and bougainvillea and lantern-like hibiscus hanging over the trail. Butterflies dance in the bright sunlight, spiders weave their nets in shrub and tree alike, and the sound of cicadas can be almost deafening. In the autumn huge meaty grapefruit are offered for sale by brightly clad villagers, while orange groves

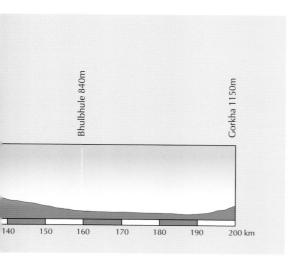

The trail through the Buri Gandaki's valley is often washed away by side-streams, leaving trekkers to use semi-submerged rocks

flank the approach to one or two villages. Goats and buffalo graze this verdant land; hens and their chicks dart to and fro across village streets as the life of lowland Nepal fills your senses to overflowing.

Although a dirt road has been ploughed across these foothills, this can be avoided for much of the way, and 'rush hour' is a once-a-day truck passing through.

On the second day out of Gorkha you cross the Maudi Khola – a major tributary of the **Buri Gandaki** – pass beneath a magnificent banyan tree shading a *chautaara*, and enter the little township of **Arughat Bazar**. Its buildings are cluttered with goods for sale and the streets busy not only with locals but also with villagers from outlying settlements. There's a police checkpost where permits must be shown, a bank with a shotgun-toting guard, and shops selling batteries, clothing, plastic footwear, Cadburys chocolate and Coca Cola.

If you've left something behind in Kathmandu, there's a chance you might find a replacement here, for this is by far the largest township en route until you're back in Gorkha. From here on you'll need to be self-sufficient.

Arughat to Syala

Allow sufficient time to take advantage of Arughat's facilities before moving on for another couple of hours to camp on a grassy bench above the river at **Shanti Bazar**. Early one morning hunched and hooded figures could be seen apparently floating through the mist that lay draped across the valley; they were local porters dressed in the brown cloak-like garment called a *bokkhu*, which doubles as a blanket and is also worn for protection by honey gatherers at work on the steep cliffs.

In these lower reaches the valley is broad and open, with flat, low-lying fields and groups of thatched houses. A few tributaries have to be crossed; some on suspension bridges, others on shaky temporary structures, or by simply wading through a ford. It's mostly gentle walking and you begin to question claims that this is one of Nepal's toughest treks. Until, that is, you enter the constrictions of the Buri Gandaki's gorge and the trail begins its switchback course, rising and falling with unsettling frequency. One moment you're down at river level, the next you're struggling up a steeply angled trail rising against a rock wall, bamboo growing at impossible angles, waterfalls cascading from notches cut in the sky.

The gorge twists this way and that, so you move from shade to sunlight and back again. Flights of stone steps lead to villages built on precarious ledges among a few meagre terraces. **Labubesi** is one, and when camped there recently a constant bombardment of rocks could be heard crashing down the east flank of the valley some way upstream. Villagers said this had been going on for three months, and next day we saw it for ourselves; a great dust cloud hung over the river where the opposite mountain was disintegrating before our eyes.

Summits are rarely seen on this stretch, for the soaring valley walls deny distant views for hours at a time. But on the way to Khorlabesi the snow-peaks of Shringi Himal make themselves known before you drop once more into the bed of the gorge to discover the hot springs and teahouses of Tatopani. When David Snellgrove passed through in 1956 he saw 'a little stream of hot water which ran from under the rocks'. Now this hot water has been diverted through three spouts set above a paved area, and it's not unusual to find members of your crew lathering up beneath them.

Shortly after leaving Tatopani a suspension bridge takes the trek across the river to the east bank for the first time, then climbs to a camp in **Doban** (990m). Another suspension bridge leads out of the village next day. This one spans a tributary, not the main river, which is crossed shortly before entering one of the neatest settlements in the Buri Gandaki. **Jagat** has a tidy paved street and a trim campsite

edged with flowers. The chorten standing at the far end of the street is one of the first visible signs of the Buddhist faith, but as the journey progresses, so these will become more numerous – not only chortens, but mani walls, water-driven prayer wheels, prayer flags and a few gompas.

A day and a half after leaving Jagat, you pass through a kani marking the entrance to **Ghap**. The walls and ceiling of this elaborate archway are decorated with Buddhist motifs, and as you emerge from it the trail runs alongside a prayer wall whose stones have been etched with illustrations of the Buddhist saint Milarepa. Unique to the valley, carvings like these have been painstakingly created by artisans from Bih, a village that stands high above the trail on the way to Lho.

Lho, or Lhogaon to give its proper name, is a full day's walk from Ghap, and set at around 3100m is nearly 1000m higher, so it's hard going for the porters. Reached through fields of barley, Lho is a large village whose houses are interspersed with more mani walls and chortens; there's a large kani and an impressive gompa; long strings of prayer flags catch every breeze, and the looming presence of Manaslu signals the fact that you've now emerged from the Buri Gandaki's gorge and, nine days out of Gorkha, have arrived at last among the mighty Himalaya. Your heart will leap, your smile grow wider.

Shortly after departing Lho the trail forks. One branch is the direct route to Samagaon (Sama), while the recommended alternative climbs through a wooded ravine to reach the expanding village of **Syala**, which gives another heart-in-mouth view of Manaslu ahead. Twenty years ago Syala consisted of a couple of stone-and-log huts in a small forest clearing. Most of that forest has since been cut down, and numerous houses have taken the place of once magnificent trees. But what a site!

A terraced campground makes a two-night stay here an option worth considering, as the altitude is around 3500m and it's time to think about acclimatisation. From the top of a huge moraine

wall above the campground, there's a stunning view not only of Manaslu but of Ngadi Chuli too (also known as Peak 29).

Syala to Bimtang

Samagaon (Sama) lies only an hour's walk away, at much the same altitude as Syala and reached through a broad, open yak pasture. Icy streams cut through it, and a line of white chortens march towards the village, while Manaslu spreads its glaciers and sun-dazzling snowfields in a pristine wall as if to block further progress.

The village lies in a sheltered scoop, its numerous low stone houses standing behind walled courtyards where snotty-nosed children call a greeting. A huge mani wall leads the way, but the building that gives it character stands on a rise just beyond. Sama Gompa enjoys a privileged view, its pagoda-styled roof rising above whitewashed walls, the group of tiny houses in which the monks reside spread out behind.

Beyond the gompa there's a yak pasture edged with berberis; above it an old moraine shelters an ice-bound lake at the foot of the Manaslu Glacier, but continuing upvalley the trail passes one of the longest mani walls on the circuit. Later, the Buri Gandaki is crossed on a wooden bridge; then comes a short pull up a slope to a large kani, through which you enter **Samdo**, a village of Tibetan refugees and the highest on the circuit at 3850m.

This is another good place in which to spend at least two nights to aid acclimatisation. The village is interesting, views spectacular, and there are some worthwhile objectives that would fill a 'rest day'

In contrast to the high country, the last few days of the trek pass through a series of low-lying rice fields

with useful activity. The first of these is the ascent of the steep hill that rises immediately behind Samdo. Its crown is at about 4600m, but almost anywhere between village and summit would be worth aiming for; one of the rewards being a clear view of the Larkya La to be gained along the way.

Another hike worth taking continues beyond Samdo on an old traders' route heading north towards the Tibetan border; yet another heads east towards the base of Pang Phuchi. And everywhere the landscape challenges the thesaurus for superlatives.

Out of Samdo the trek crosses the Buri Gandaki for the last time. Now little more than a modest

stream, it only takes two or three strides to cross the bridge before the trail rises in short bursts heading west above the ruins of Larkya Bazaar, one-time trading centre where salt, wool and butter from Tibet would be exchanged for rice and other grain from lowland Nepal.

It takes less than three hours to reach the solitary stone shelter of Duwang at 4450m where camp is made before crossing the Larkya La. From the meadow a fine outlook shows Pang Phuchi to the east, and southward to a cluster of peaks and mountain walls that shield Manaslu from view. It's a beautiful but frosty site. You'll need to make an early start next day, so be prepared to rise long before dawn with the aim of reaching the Larkya La before the wind picks up, as it often does at these altitudes around mid-morning. It will be a long and tough day, but one to enjoy to the full.

As day breaks the mountains appear to burn with a golden glow and, no longer being focused into the beam of a headtorch, it is then you will notice the long trough of moraine through which you've been picking a way from Duwang. A few small lakes lie below the trail; often these are covered with ice and snow, but on a recent crossing one revealed blue-green water littered with ice floes.

Marked by cairns and wind-thrashed prayer flags, and hemmed in by Manaslu outliers to the south and border peaks to the north, the 5135m **Larkya La** gives its clearest views to the east, back the way you've come. But by far the most spectacular view will only be won after you've left the actual pass and worked along a fairly level corridor to the west. Suddenly a great glacial cirque bursts into view. A stupendous wall created by Cheo Himal, Himlung Himal, Nemjung, Gyaji Kang and Kang Guru, casts down a stream of glaciers, while Annapurna II rises above the blocking ridge ahead. That view alone would make the trek worthwhile.

The way descends steeply, and if caked in snow or ice it may be necessary to cut steps and safeguard porters with ropes. But once the gradient eases you strike along the lateral moraine of the first of three glaciers, before descending into the vast **Bimtang** meadow, with yet more glorious views to soak in as you slake your thirst with several mugs of tea.

Bimtang to Gorkha

From Bimtang to Dharapani on the banks of the Marsyangdi takes one-and-a-half days of trekking along the valley of the **Dudh Khola**. There are tributaries to cross, an enchanting mixed forest to wander through, a few small meadows, fields of buckwheat and barley outlined by drystone walls, and the Gurung village of Tilje in which to spend the night. But once you reach **Dharapani**, it's like stepping into another world, with shops, lodges and teahouses, and numerous trekkers working their way anticlockwise along the Annapurna Circuit en route to Manang and the Thorong La. Given sufficient time and energy, it might be tempting to join them. But that is to desert the Manaslu trek, so the recommendation is to turn left and reverse the Annapurna trail, heading down the Marsyangdi's valley for two days or so, before trading this busy route at **Bhulbhule** for a cross-country trek to Gorkha.

There's a world of difference between the glaciers and soaring peaks that surround Bimtang, and the low-lying foothills through which you trek for the next three days. Bimtang is nearly 3000m higher than the fan of rice terraces, broken by houses of ochre and thatch that are so distinctive of these closing stages. In the high country vegetation was limited to juniper and berberis, but now orange trees and bananas grow among tiny settlements, cactus hedges line the trail, and lizards slither across sun-warmed rocks.

In places there is no clearly defined trail, so locals direct you along bare earth walls that line irrigation ditches. Camps are set in schoolyards, or on river banks, and it's warm enough at night to use your sleeping bag as a mattress.

A morning's walk short of **Gorkha**, the last night is spent beside the wide Darondi Khola, from which you have a clear view of the Manaslu Himal stained blood red as the sun goes down, while the river funnels cool air from distant summit snows to mingle memories with dreams.

The Langtang Valley opens out at Kyangjin Gompa, its walling mountains now higher, more dramatic and enticing ▶

Trek 13
Langtang and Helambu

by Kev Reynolds

From a logistical standpoint, this trek, which takes place among mountains that form a backdrop to Kathmandu, is one of the easiest of all Himalayan treks to organise. Although largely unknown to all but the most ardent of mountain buffs, the ice-hung peaks of the Langtang Himal are seductive in their beauty; the valley they overlook is an enchanting place flowing from east to west parallel with the Tibetan border, and conveniently reached by a day's drive from the city. There are no internal flights dependent on cloud-free skies to worry about, passes are not high by Himalayan standards, and the district is well served with lodges. And when linked with the Sherpa-inhabited hill country of Helambu, it's possible to walk right down to the Kathmandu Valley just an hour's bus ride from the capital. With its daily mix of challenges and rewards, the route through Langtang and Helambu makes a near-perfect introduction to the Himalayan trekking experience.

Route summary

Location	North of Kathmandu, Nepal
Start	Dhunche or Syabrubensi
Finish	Sundarijal
Distance	about 160km
Duration	2½–3 weeks (14 days' trekking plus rest days/exploration)
Maximum altitude	Laurebina La 4610m
Trek style	Lodges and/or camping
Restrictions	Langtang National Park permits required
Grade	Moderate
Guidebook	*Langtang with Gosainkund and Helambu: A Trekker's Guide* by Kev Reynolds (Cicerone Press, 1996)

On the proverbial clear day a ragged line of ice-bound summits forms a mesmerising wall to the north of Kathmandu. Seen from the tarmac of the city's airport white peaks and ridges tease and tantalise through a fug of pollution, and when viewed from a hotel rooftop those same mountains challenge distant clouds. This, surely, is what you came to Nepal to see!

But there are no Annapurnas or Everests here, no famous names in this choppy sea of 6000 and 7000m peaks, for this is the Langtang Himal, flanked on the west by the Ganesh, and to the east by the Jugal and Rolwaling Himals, while filling the spaces between the mountains and Kathmandu's valley lies Helambu, a district of fertile, intricately terraced hills scattered with farms and tiny villages – the quintessential Himalayan foothills with a charm all their own.

Legendary mountaineer Bill Tilman was among the first Westerners to visit Langtang when he arrived with a small expedition in 1949, and his book *Nepal Himalaya* richly describes his travels

The pilgrim site of Gosainkund lies a little below the Laurebina La, the link between Langtang and Helambu

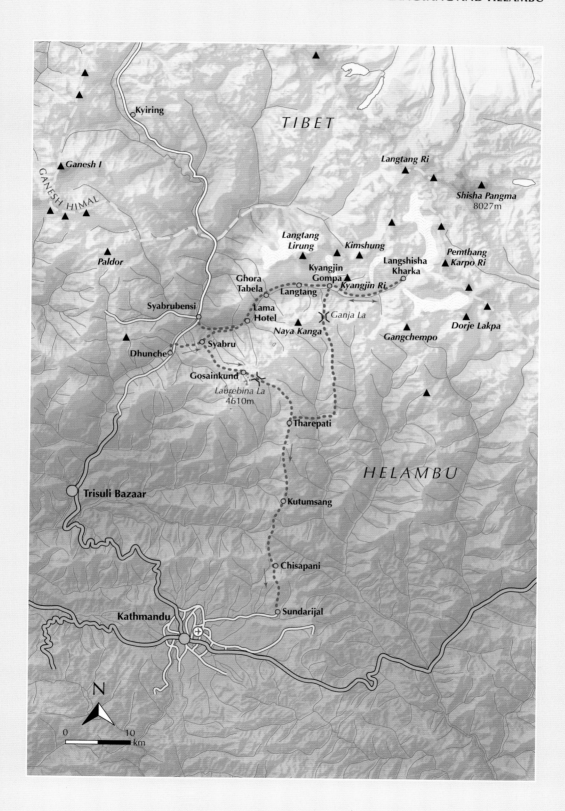

there. Although the expedition took place partly during the summer monsoon period, Tilman and Peter Lloyd climbed Paldor (now a classified 'trekking peak') in the neighbouring Ganesh range, and crossed a couple of difficult passes in upper Langtang. His observations are delivered with the inimitable brand of ironic humour for which he is noted, but he was clearly taken with Langtang, which he described as 'a fine, open valley, rich in flowers and grass, and flanked by great mountains'. Those mountains include broad-topped Kimshung, the mighty Langtang Lirung, Dorje Lakpa, Pemthang Karpo Ri and, best of all, the spectacularly graceful Gangchempo (6387m), which Tilman called Fluted Peak, its face 'of glistening purity framed between clean-cut snow ridges of slender symmetry'.

Long before Tilman's visit the valley was known to Buddhists across the border in Tibet as a *beyul*, a hidden, secret valley, to which those in the know could escape in times of trouble in order to keep their faith alive until it was safe to return to their homeland with the original teachings intact. Populated mostly by Tamangs who have retained their Tibetan heritage, the valley displays numerous signs of the Buddhist faith, including some of the longest mani walls in the country, which, together with chortens, prayer

flags and water-driven prayer wheels, add a spiritual dimension to the landscape.

Throughout the valley houses are built of timber and stone and often roofed with shingles weighed down with flat stone slabs, and a number of these have been adapted for use as simple trekkers' lodges. Though seldom as 'grand' as some of the so-called luxury lodges now springing up in the Everest and Annapurna regions, they offer basic overnight lodging and meals, and provide for those who use them a glimpse into the daily lives of the Tamang hillfolk. A network of these lodges reaches as far as Kyangjin Gompa in the Langtang Valley, while many more can be found throughout Helambu and the route that links the two districts via the holy alpine lakes of Gosainkund and the pass of the Laurebina La. Independent trekkers are well catered for here.

In 1971 the region was designated Nepal's first Himalayan national park, although it was not officially established until 1976. Today the Langtang National Park office is located close to the township of Dhunche in the Trisuli Valley, which also houses the administrative headquarters of the region, and serves as one of two starting points for treks into Langtang – the other trailhead being Syabrubensi, situated a few kilometres closer to the Tibetan border.

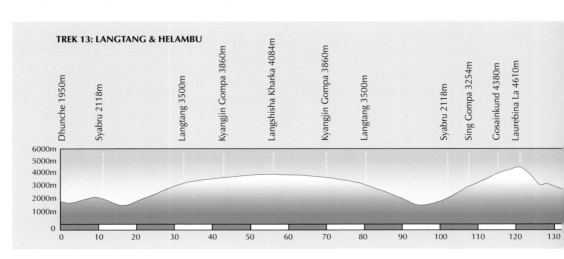

TREK 13: LANGTANG & HELAMBU

Dhunche (or Syabrubensi) to Kyangjin Gompa

Straddling a ridge spur in the foothills, Syabru acts as a gateway to the Langtang Valley

Public buses can take nine hours or more to make the scenic journey of a little under 120 kilometres from Kathmandu to Dhunche via Trisuli Bazaar, so many independent trekkers prefer to share a private vehicle that will take less time and provide more comfort. But however you make the journey, the road is rough, potholed and sometimes cut by landslides, and you'll surely be ready to get some exercise once you arrive at your chosen trailhead.

Allow four days to reach Kyangjin Gompa, whether you start in Dhunche or Syabrubensi. Of the two the one-time trading post of **Syabrubensi** offers a gentle

and more direct start by following the Langtang Khola all the way, while a trek beginning at **Dhunche** crosses a spur on which the interesting village of Syabru is perched. The two routes join near Dhomen (Doman) beside the Langtang Khola northeast of Syabru.

The Dhunche option does not begin in Dhunche itself, but in Thulo Bharkhu, the next village along the road towards Syabrubensi. The trail then climbs above the road on a flight of stone steps, continues through forest and emerges to a vista of snowpeaks ahead, and a bird's-eye view onto the houses of Mungra set among steeply terraced fields below.

Syabru (also known as Thulo Syabru) consists of a line of buildings strung along a narrow ridge above a cascade of terraced fields in which the main crops are wheat, maize and millet; when

the harvest has been taken the sound of thresh-ing with bamboo flails is the village soundtrack: 'thrap, thrap, thrap' resounding across the hills. Many houses have elaborately carved window frames, with panels beneath decorated with Buddhist designs. There's a gompa at the upper end of the village, where most of the lodges are clustered, and views to the west show peaks of the Ganesh Himal across the Trisuli Khola, while Tibetan mountains can be seen to the north. It's a charming place, which will also be visited on the way out of Langtang by trekkers heading for Gosainkund and Helambu.

When the Dhunche and Syabrubensi trails come together down by the Langtang Khola you wend your way towards the narrow, gorge-like western end of the Langtang Valley through luxu-riant mixed forest in which birds attempt to make themselves heard above the thundering river. Langur monkeys clamber among the trees, and it is said that both red panda and wild boar inhabit this part of the valley.

Between **Lama Hotel** (Changtang) and Ghora Tabela patches of holly oak are interspersed with rhododendrons, the latter becoming more numer-ous as you press on, and in the late pre-monsoon season blooms the size of car headlamps form banks of colour beside the trail. In other places tatters of Spanish moss hang from the trees, and huge ferns and delicate orchids all add to the magic.

At **Ghora Tabela** the valley begins to open out, and its origins are betrayed by the distinctive U-shape of glacial action. Meaning 'horse stable' Ghora Tabela was once a Tibetan settlement, but today it is noted more for the fact that it's home to an army and National Park checkpost where trekkers must show their permits.

Beyond the checkpost the trail climbs among more rhododendron and berberis to gain a higher level of valley with a few small lodges at Thangsep (Thangshyap). The way continues to rise above fields of buckwheat, barley and potato, with large stretches of open yak pasture now dotted with

temporary shelters known as *goths*, and about four-and-a-half hours from Lama Hotel you come to **Langtang**, the largest of the valley settlements at 3500m.

The upper village is a close gathering of houses with small walled courtyards that contain livestock. More than half a century after his visit, Tilman's description holds true today, for he found 'a settlement of some thirty families rich in cows, yaks and sheep'. Elsewhere the village now boasts a dozen or more lodges, a bakery and the head-quarters building of the Langtang National Park authority.

Half a day's trek is all that's needed to reach **Kyangjin Gompa** from here, during which the landscape is steadily revealed in all its wild, untamed beauty. Let Tilman's words sum it up: 'The Langtang has not only the austere beauty of ice mountains accentuated by the friendly smile of flowery meadows alive with cattle – but it has the charm of reticence and the witchery of the unexpected.' There are yak pastures sliced by meandering streams, an old moraine topped by a pair of large chortens, a series of extremely long mani walls, and ahead, gleaming with ice, the elegant giant, Gangchempo.

Kyangjin Gompa and the Upper Valley

When Tilman was here Kyangjin Gompa was known as Kyangjin Ghyang; it then consisted of a few stone huts, turnip fields and a small gompa. Three years later the Swiss geologist Toni Hagen surveyed the valley, and his report inspired a visit by Werner Schulthess, an agricultural adviser to the United Nations, who in turn established a cheese factory here in 1955.

Today Kyangjin Gompa is an expanding cluster of trekkers' lodges at about 3860m, and as they're the highest in the valley this is about as far as most trekkers go. It has a splendid location, overlook-ing a broad, open, plain-like section of valley walled by stupendous mountains. Wherever you turn, mountains of savage beauty fill your line of vision. If you were to do no more than sit outside

Naya Kanga and the Ganja La can be seen across the valley from Kyangjin Ri

a lodge in the sunshine absorbing the scene you'd feel justified in coming all the way to Nepal.

But there's much to fill several days based at a Kyangjin lodge. For a start, you could wander up the Lirung Valley behind the gompa to gain close views of Langtang Lirung and Kimshung that form an amphitheatre of towering walls of rock, snow and curtains of ice, dramatically seen from a high pasture known as Tserpochi.

These same mountains present a different perspective when viewed from the prayer-flag-bedecked summit of a minor peak immediately above the Kyangjin lodges, while an even better vantage point is the 4773m Kyangjin Ri – unseen from the village, but easily reached from the previous peak. This summit is marked with cairns, and you really feel on top of the world when standing there.

But to my mind the best way to fully appreciate the wonderland of the Langtang Valley is to take a small tent and enough supplies for a few days and head upvalley beyond the lodges to discover a world of icy streams, glaciers, moraine banks and truly imposing summits. On the way to this wilderness you amble through a soaring avenue of exquisite beauty, passing the *kharkas* (summer grazing huts) of Jatang, Nubamatang and **Langshisha Kharka** (4084m). This is quality mountain scenery. That Pemthang Karpo Ri, Gurkarpo Ri, Dorje Lakpa and Gangchempo will mean nothing in a round of public-bar bragging at home, is neither here nor there. What you see and experience in the upper Langtang Valley is the very stuff of dreams.

Kyangjin Gompa to Gosainkund

There are two main options for trekking out through Helambu to the Kathmandu Valley from Kyangjin Gompa, both of which involve pass crossings – the 5120m Ganja La, or the easier Laurebina La at 4610m. Located to the south of Kyangjin, the steep and exposed **Ganja La** lies below the East Face of shapely Naya Kanga and provides the most direct way out. But this is a

Between Kyangjin Gompa and Langshisha Kharka the valley is wild and uninhabited except for a few yak herders

serious route that often requires fixed ropes and step-cutting on the final slopes leading to the pass, and as there's no accommodation available for several days on the Helambu side, camping equipment and food for at least five days should be taken. A guide who knows the way could also save a lot of route-finding difficulties, and is highly recommended.

The Laurebina La is the preferred choice for most trekkers, and not simply because it is lower and more straightforward than the Ganja La. The Laurebina La is a truly scenic route, with the added incentive of a visit to the sacred lakes of Gosainkund. This is the route described below.

From **Kyangjin Gompa** it will take four days to reach the lodges at Gosainkund, and another four to cross the Laurebina La and descend through Helambu to Sundarijal, a short bus ride from Kathmandu. And with simple lodges all the way, this is a route ideally suited to independent trekkers.

Begin by backtracking for two days to **Syabru**, a gentle walk except for the final steep uphill drag from the Langtang Khola, which makes arrival at the village a source of relief. From Syabru another steeply climbing trail continues the route through broadleaved woods to a ridge on which a couple of lodges are perched with far-reaching views of the Ganesh Himal. Beyond the lodges the trek makes its way through an enchanted forest of mossy trees, pink-barked rhododendron and park-like glades, to the collection of lodges at Sing Gompa (3254m), where there's also a cheese factory, an orchard, and the small monastery after which the place is named. On the hillside nearby the stumps and charred remains of once-graceful trees provide a sad contrast to the delights of the earlier forest.

From Sing Gompa to Gosainkund involves a climb of more than 1100m, beginning with yet another stretch through pine forest, with glorious views between the trees to Langtang Lirung, as well as snowpeaks of Tibet and also the Ganesh Himal. A fine trail now strikes up the ridge of the Chalang Pati Danda to gain the few lodges of Laurebinayak (3930m) whose outstanding panoramic views stretch to Manaslu and (it is claimed) as far as Annapurna. But this is an often cold and windy spot, lacking any protection from the weather, and despite the views it may be better to continue for another two hours or so as far as Gosainkund. The trail is mostly broad and gentle, although there's one place where it's somewhat exposed with a big drop on one side and steep crags on the other.

Perched on an exposed ridge Laurebinayak can be a cold and windy site, but views from its lodges are spectacular

Under heavy skies, with snow dusting the hills and a sheen of ice on the lakes, **Gosainkund** can seem a forbidding place, but on brighter days with sunlight dazzling on the water it produces a charming scene of alpine proportions. Even so, at more than 4380m bathing in the lake must be a supreme test of faith for the crowds of Hindu pilgrims who arrive here during the festival of Janai Purnima that takes place at the August full moon.

Gosainkunda is the largest of several lakes and pools that lie among the hollows of the Gosainkund Lekh; in it, a partly submerged rock is said to be Shiva himself, lying on a bed of serpents. There's a small Hindu shrine on the lakeside, a number of stone shelters used by pilgrims, and a few trekkers' lodges on the north bank.

Helambu is a district of intricate terraces through which trails rise and fall with annoying frequency

Gosainkund to Sundarijal

The hike up to the 4610m Laurebina La is straightforward in good conditions, and may be achieved by fit trekkers in a little over an hour. But in snowy conditions or poor visibility you should seriously reconsider your plans, for descent on the southeast side of the pass is steep and demanding, with potentially dangerous alternatives of which you should be wary. It was down there that Australian trekker James Scott was lost for 43 days in the winter of 1992–93.

Marked by cairns and garlanded with prayer flags, the **Laurebina La** is, however, a stunning viewpoint, and it's worth getting there early in order to absorb its matchless panorama at leisure. With the lakes below, and the mountainside falling away into hinted valleys, the view gathers a long line of Himalayan giants stretching westward way beyond the Langtang, Ganesh and Manaslu ranges to the Annapurnas and Machhapuchhre. It's an immense view: take it all in.

About 45 minutes below the pass the trail forks just beyond the basic lodge of Bhera Goth (c4100m). Avoid the upper trail option, which is a supposedly direct, but very exposed, route to Tharepati that has been problematic ever since it was created. Instead, continue down – steeply

down – for another hour to Phedi (3500m), below which a Thai International airbus crashed in 1992. Crossing the Tadi Khola the way now follows a roller-coaster route along a rough hillside of spooky, mist-wreathed forest and plunging ravines, turning promontories of rock, and almost always demanding attention.

Tharepati is perched on, or a little below, a ridge crest at 3640m. From it the trail strikes southward through Helambu. The big mountains have now been left behind. There are no more snowpeaks, the vegetation changes, villages, the landscape, farming practices – all are different. No less interesting, or less inspiring. Just different. For the remainder of the trek you will follow a series of trails overlooking vast regions of terraced fields, all (it seems) created in artistic orderliness. Thatched houses speckle the landscape; barefooted, doko-carrying farmers pad the trails; goats and hens roam village streets. And as you approach **Sundarijal** and the Kathmandu Valley the air is warmer, more substantial.

At **Chisapani** pause and turn around for a moment. In the early morning and as evening cools, a row of snowbound peaks seems to hang above the northern hills. Not so long ago you were among them. Take the memories home with you. They will guarantee your return.

Everest and Nuptse, the classic view from Kala Pattar ▶

Trek 14

Everest Base Camp

by Kev Reynolds

'B ecause it is there' was good enough for George Leigh Mallory to explain why he wanted to climb Mount Everest in the 1920s, and almost a century on it's a perfectly adequate response to the question as to why thousands of trekkers choose to hike through Solu Khumbu to the base of that same mountain. The world's highest peak is an obvious goal. If that were the only high point at the end of a 10- or 20-day trek, it would still be worth the effort. But it's not. Everest is simply the best known, the loftiest among dozens of bewitchingly beautiful mountains that flank valleys inhabited by people whose hospitality is celebrated worldwide. To trek in this land of superlatives needs no excuse. The name says it all. Mount Everest, Sagarmatha, Chomolungma, the 'Goddess Mother of the World' is the ultimate aim for all who dream of mountains. No wonder this journey through Solu Khumbu has become the most popular trek in all the Himalaya. Because it is there.

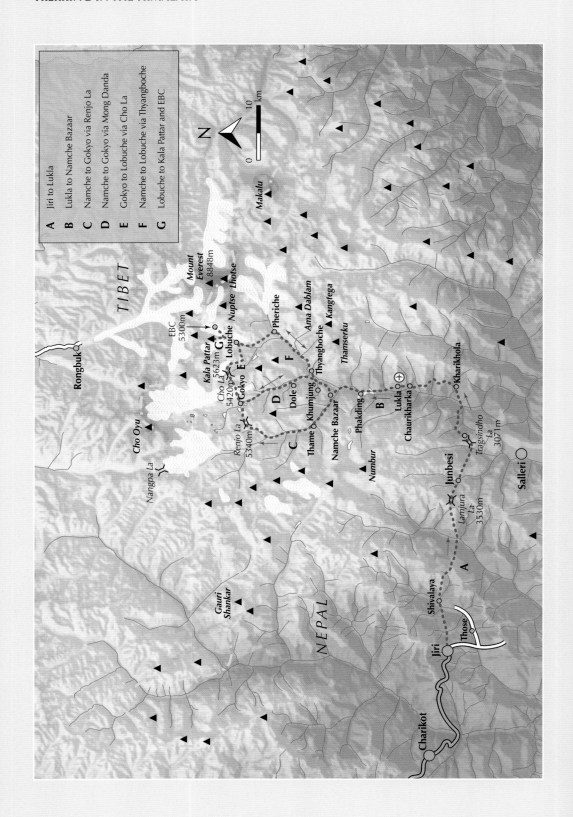

A Jiri to Lukla
B Lukla to Namche Bazaar
C Namche to Gokyo via Renjo La
D Namche to Gokyo via Mong Danda
E Gokyo to Lobuche via Cho La
F Namche to Lobuche via Thyangboche
G Lobuche to Kala Pattar and EBC

Route summary

Location	Eastern Nepal
Start	Jiri or Lukla
Finish	Lukla
Distance	195km (or about 100km from Lukla)
Duration	2–4 weeks, depending on route(s) taken
Maximum altitude	Kala Pattar 5623m
Trek style	Lodges or camping
Restrictions	National Park permits required
Grade	Moderate/Demanding
Guidebook	*Everest: A Trekker's Guide* by Kev Reynolds (Cicerone Press, 2012)

Between Junbesi and Sallung on the long walk in from Jiri, Everest (far left) is seen for the first time

A first view of Mount Everest is always something special. On the ever-popular trek from Lukla to Everest Base Camp you might be lucky to catch a fleeting glimpse of the summit from a bend in the trail below Namche Bazaar. If you miss it, you'll have to wait until you leave Namche's steep-walled bowl and turn a corner near the Sagarmatha National Park headquarters. Everest then displays its summit cone above the long Nuptse–Lhotse ridge, yet its roots are hidden, and you'll need imagination to accept its true stature. But if you walk in from the foothills, along trails used by early expeditions, you'll see some of the mountain's Southwest Face standing proud among a line of peaks from a point between Junbesi and Sallung. Then nothing for several days.

How about Everest Base Camp at the foot of the Khumbu Icefall? Surely Everest will look enormous from there? Well no – you're too close. In

truth you need to stand back, preferably on the summit of Kala Pattar, Gokyo Ri, or one of the lofty passes crossed by experienced trekkers – the Renjo La, for example. Then – oh my! Then you'll have something to tell the folks back home…

Perhaps it's better not to concentrate on Everest at all. Instead, open eyes, mind and heart to the 1001 riches waiting to be gathered along the way – other peaks, glaciers and passes; the villages, manis, gompas and prayer flags; the thunderous rivers, delicate waterfalls; the flowers, rocks and lichens. In short, the whole wondrous environment, natural and man-made, that places the Khumbu region in a category all its own. That's how to maximise the Everest experience.

Jiri to Lukla

The vast majority of visitors fly from Kathmandu to Lukla and trek from there. But my preference is to take the long walk in, to begin among the foothills in order to capture the essence of Nepal, its sheer variety. And as the trek from Jiri is followed by few these days – since the establishment of Lukla's 'airport' in 1965 – the welcome received at lodges and teahouses along the way is both generous and heartfelt.

Local buses make the scenic but bum-numbing 188-kilometre journey from Kathmandu to Jiri in about 12 hours, while a private vehicle takes less time, is more comfortable and gives an opportunity to take photographs along the way. **Jiri** is at the end of a Swiss-built road. Another continues from it, but this is a dirt road like so many others that scar the foothills and quickly become rutted bonebreakers in dry seasons, and impassable quagmires during the monsoon. It's better to walk.

For the first few days the trek heads east across a series of ridges, climbing out of warm river valleys, through terraced fields and strips of forest to gain one high crest after another, before plunging into the next valley with rivers milky blue with glacier-melt. The hills are dotted with farms and villages, and you soon settle into the easy rhythm of the trekking day. This is a time for contemplation, not anticipation. Don't think too far ahead, but absorb and appreciate the timeless nature of the land across which you're wandering.

About five days after setting out you cross the 3530m **Lamjura La**, descend through forest to Tragdobuk, then slant left to **Junbesi**, one of the nicest villages between Jiri and Namche. With several comfortable lodges, a few shops, a school founded by Ed Hillary in 1964, and the fascinating Thubten Chholing Gompa two hours' walk away up a beautiful side-valley, this is a perfect place to spend an extra day.

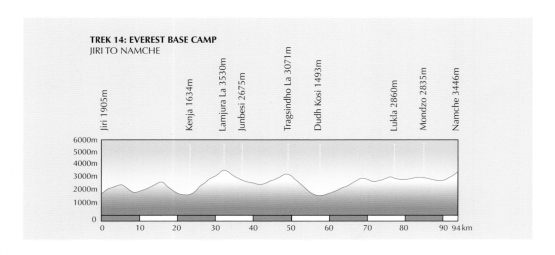

TREK 14: EVEREST BASE CAMP
JIRI TO NAMCHE

Jiri 1905m · Kenja 1634m · Lamjura La 3530m · Junbesi 2675m · Tragsindho La 3071m · Dudh Kosi 1493m · Lukla 2860m · Mondzo 2835m · Namche 3446m

The continuing trail crosses the Junbesi Khola, and an hour and a half after leaving the village turns a spur by a group of buildings, and suddenly there's Everest standing at the left-hand end of a line of big mountains: Thamserku, Lhotse, Nuptse, Kusum Kangguru, Kangtega, Mera Peak and Makalu. It's a view to stop you in your tracks, but it doesn't last long for you're soon swooping down to the Beni Khola, then up to the village of Ringmo among orchards of apple, apricot and peach. And next day, after crossing the 3071m **Tragsindho La**, you descend a veritable stairway of terraced fields to the Dudh Kosi, whose valley leads all the way to Everest.

Now heading north along the east bank of the Dudh Kosi, the trek steadily gains height from one village to the next: **Kharikhola**, Bupsa, Puiyan, Surkhe and **Chaurikharka**, a charming settlement tucked on the hillside below Lukla. The two villages could hardly be more different. Chaurikharka is an attractive collection of Sherpa homes, another Hillary school, and a small gompa. **Lukla**, on the other hand, is a scruffy township at 2860m, dominated by the comings and goings of aircraft from Kathmandu. It has little appeal, and having survived one of Nepal's most celebrated white-knuckle flights, the vast majority of trekkers are anxious to get on the trail. Mountains beckon. Lukla suggests no reason to delay.

Lukla to Namche Bazaar

If you've trekked from Jiri, arrival at the trail junction in Choplung (30mins below Lukla) comes as something of a surprise. For over a week you'll

Between Namche and Thyangboche this large chorten commemorates the 50th anniversary of Hillary and Tenzing's ascent of Everest. Everest itself peers over the Nuptse–Lhotse ridge (photo: Claudia Reynolds)

Less than two hours after leaving Lukla the way passes numerous manis, prayer wheels and a fine chorten in Ghat

have had the trail more or less to yourself. But suddenly the route is busy with groups of crisply attired trekkers smelling of soap and suncream! There are no major peaks in view, but there's an air of excited anticipation among the new arrivals, and from now on lodges will be busy.

Before long you cross a tributary valley with a clutch of lodges at Thadokosi below Kusum Kangguru, a savage-looking 'trekking peak' of 6367m. It's an impressive sight, but as you turn out of the tributary it disappears, and the next notable feature will be Ghat, a strung-out village noted for a group of boulders etched hundreds of times over with the Buddhist rune: *Om Mani Padme Hum*. Ghat also has a small gompa, man-sized prayer wheels and a veritable forest of prayer flags.

Phakding is a two-part village divided by the river where trekkers fresh off the plane from Kathmandu experience their first major

suspension bridge, for the trail crosses the Dudh Kosi to its west bank for the first time. This will probably be far enough for a first day, and there are many large lodges to choose from, as well as decent campgrounds down by the river.

In the garden of a lodge in Benkar upstream from Phakding, hot springs are contained in a shed. There's also a neat waterfall (not in a shed), while a short stroll beyond the village the trail recrosses to the right-hand side of the river and rises through pinewoods and rhododendrons to Chumoa and Mondzo on the edge of the Sagarmatha National Park where you must register your details and obtain an entry permit. Porters and other crew members also provide their details and have loads checked, so bottlenecks often occur.

Through the kani that signifies entry to the park, the trail drops steeply to the houses of Thaog, set among fields of enormous cabbages, and crosses to the west bank of the river once more. But you're on this bank for only a brief spell before recrossing to the east side on yet another suspension bridge, then continuing upvalley towards a major confluence of rivers; the Bhote Kosi emerging from a gorge on the left, to join the Dudh Kosi at the mouth of another gorge directly ahead. Here the trail climbs steeply to gain a long suspension bridge spanning the Dudh Kosi; if you suffer vertigo, crossing will be a major challenge.

There now follows a steady ascent of something like 700m to reach **Namche Bazaar**, the trail winding through forest all the way. Halfway up the slope, at a left-hand bend with the remains of a long-defunct teahouse beside the trail, a brief and distant glimpse may be had of Everest, Nuptse and Lhotse.

Time in Namche

Set in an abrupt, concave scoop of hillside at around 3446m, Namche Bazaar is noted as the Sherpa 'capital' and administrative centre of the Khumbu district. It also houses an army camp and the headquarters of the Sagarmatha National Park; a bustling place and a honeypot for Sherpas, traders from Tibet and porters from distant villages bringing goods for the Saturday market. Not only does Namche boast internet cafés, a bank and an ATM alongside medical supplies and Tibetan souvenirs, it also has a German bakery and dozens of lodges. Should you arrive in town to discover your clothing is inadequate, you can buy everything from socks to down jackets and second-hand equipment left over from expeditions.

It's essential to acclimatise before going higher, and there's no shortage of trails to neighbouring villages and vantage points to help the process. Above the Namche bowl the relatively unspoilt villages of Khunde and **Khumjung** are well worth visiting, and trails leading to them reveal some

Namche Bazaar is built on a steep but shallow cirque above the Bhote Kosi

of the grandeur of the upper valley. Not only does Everest show itself once more across the Nuptse–Lhotse ridge but, even better, graceful Ama Dablam and its neighbours Kangtega and Thamserku flank the valley's right-hand side.

Moving on from Namche takes you into what seems the very heart of the Himalaya, with a bewitching array of options to consider. Do you, for example, take the direct route to Everest via Thyangboche (Tengboche) and the Khumbu Valley? Or perhaps branch first into the Gokyo Valley, cross the Cho La and approach Lobuche by the back door, so to speak? A third option would be to sidetrack into the valley of the Bhote Kosi, visit Thame, where Sherpa Tenzing Norgay spent his formative years, and cross the 5340m Renjo La into Gokyo – this should only be attempted by those who are fully acclimatised and experienced in high-mountain trekking.

Namche to Gokyo via the Renjo La

As yet the Bhote Kosi's valley remains largely unchanged by the influx of trekkers. There are lodges and a few teahouses, but nothing like those of the upper Khumbu, and the short day's hike to Thame is almost reminiscent of Himalayan trekking a few decades ago. At 3820m **Thame** is the

Following a dump of snow trekkers plough their way upvalley towards Gokyo

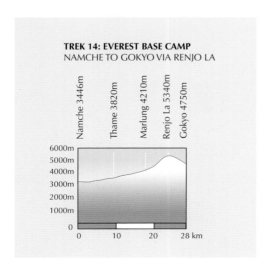

TREK 14: EVEREST BASE CAMP
NAMCHE TO GOKYO VIA RENJO LA

Namche 3446m
Thame 3820m
Marlung 4210m
Renjo La 5340m
Gokyo 4750m

6000m
5000m
4000m
3000m
2000m
1000m
0
0   10   20   28 km

second-most-important Sherpa village, which has produced an impressive number of Everest summiteers, and has a traditional link with Tibetan traders bringing their laden yaks across the glacial Nangpa La at the head of the valley; the same pass used by refugees escaping the Chinese invasion of Tibet in the 1950s.

Upvalley beyond Thame, beyond Marlung and Lungden (lodges in both) a trail rakes up the right-hand side of the valley, passes between two lakes, then steepens towards the 5340m **Renjo La**. A section of stone steps constructed by local people with help from the national park authorities climbs to the pass. Festooned with coloured prayer flags this is gained about three or four hours

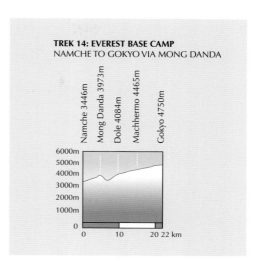

TREK 14: EVEREST BASE CAMP
NAMCHE TO GOKYO VIA MONG DANDA

above Lungden. It's a stunning place with a most magnificent view of Everest and a whole realm of lofty peaks and glaciers. The Gokyo lodges can also be seen beside a turquoise lake some 600m below. As there's no real path for much of the way down, extreme care will need to be taken if visibility is poor, or there's much snow.

Namche to Gokyo via Mong Danda

Gokyo's valley deserves to be savoured. Branching a little west of north outside Namche, and headed by Cho Oyu and Gyachung Kang, it's been carved into a trench by Nepal's longest glacier, the Ngozumpa. Above the east flank Taboche and Cholatse are distinctive 6000m guardians of the valley, while towards its head one sparkling lake after another lies trapped in the ablation trough between glacial moraine and mountain wall.

The valley rises in steps, and it's easy to be seduced into gaining height too quickly. Altitude gain must be taken seriously, so it's imperative to trek to Gokyo in short stages in order to acclimatise. But with stunning scenery virtually every step of the way, going slowly and stopping often should be no hardship. Take at least three days to walk from Namche to Gokyo, and soak in the views.

From Namche either climb directly to **Khumjung**, or take the Thyangboche trail past the national park headquarters on an unforgettable balcony high above the river. It then curves left to a pair of lodges at Kyangjuma, shortly after which it's joined by the Khumjung trail. Shortly after cut away from the Thyangboche route to climb to the tiny ridge settlement of Mong Danda (3973m) with a captivating view of Ama Dablam seen in all its glory from base to lofty summit. You then descend about 300m to Phortse Tenga before continuing on an undulating trail to **Dole** (4084m).

Two days later you'll arrive at the **Gokyo** lodges tucked against a moraine wall on the east bank of a beautiful lake at 4750m. Rising above the north shore the modest-looking hill of Gokyo Ri makes an outstanding 5340m viewpoint, overlooking an immense sea of peaks including four 8000ers – Cho Oyu, Lhotse, Makalu and Everest

itself – plus numerous 6000m and 7000m peaks, glaciers, snowfields, bare rock walls and enticing cols. One of these (the Cho La) takes trekkers across the mountains to Lobuche, Kala Pattar and Everest Base Camp.

Gokyo to Lobuche via the Cho La

Providing a direct route from Gokyo to Lobuche, this is a very fine route. Challenging, yes, and you'll need good visibility and settled weather, and if you have porters they'll need to be properly equipped. But given these things, a rewarding three-day trek begins by crossing the Ngozumpa Glacier to the simple lodges of Dragnag. If you have tents there's a rocky site in which to camp below the Cho La on the far side of a ridge of lateral moraine.

A steep climb over rocks and icy patches leads to the 5420m **Cho La**. Although views may not be as extensive as from the Renjo La, it's still an exciting place to be, and once you've headed down the glacier on the eastern side, you descend steeply into the Chola Valley graced by the jade-green Chola Tscho lake. Simple lodges have been built at Dzonglha (4830m) above the lake at the foot of Cholatse's Northeast Face, and there's a suitable meadow on which to camp a little further

Despite lying at 4750m Gokyo's lake (Dudh Pokhari) is often ice-free, even in November

on with a distant view of Ama Dablam appearing as a graceful pyramid. An easy morning's walk on a good trail leads to **Lobuche**, an expanding group of lodges at 4930m, from where Kala Pattar and Everest Base Camp are but a relatively short walk away.

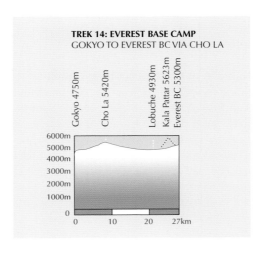

TREK 14: EVEREST BASE CAMP
GOKYO TO EVEREST BC VIA CHO LA

Namche to Lobuche via Thyangboche

If you only make one trek to Everest and are limited for time, fly to Lukla, trek to Namche and continue by way of Thyangboche, Pangboche and Pheriche – the direct route pioneered by all the early climbing expeditions and the first Khumbu trekkers. Without being sidelined by the Thame and Gokyo valleys, without straying east of Dingboche to Chhukhung or making the ascent of Island Peak, this basic there-and-back trek takes you through some of the most exquisite mountain scenery on earth.

From **Namche** a broad, well-worn trail angles along the hillside high above the Dudh Kosi with Everest, Nuptse and Lhotse seeming to block the valley ahead, and Thamserku, Kangtega and Ama Dablam dominating the right-hand wall. After Kyangjuma the trail begins its long descent to the river, which is crossed a few paces from the teahouses and water-driven prayer wheels of Phunki Tenga. Within moments of crossing, you begin a steady climb to the 3867m ridge-top site of the

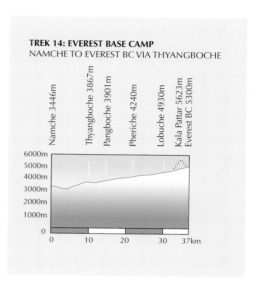

TREK 14: EVEREST BASE CAMP
NAMCHE TO EVEREST BC VIA THYANGBOCHE

Thyangboche: chorten, prayer flags and a view to take your breath away. John Hunt thought it 'one of the most beautiful places in the world' (photo: Claudia Reynolds)

Thyangboche Monastery. On his way to Everest in 1953, John Hunt commented: 'Thyangboche must be one of the most beautiful places in the world.' He could be right.

An hour and a half beyond Thyangboche you pass through Pangboche, a two-tier village whose upper level has the oldest gompa in the district, and outstanding views from a row of chortens and mani walls stretching across the hillside opposite Ama Dablam. Heading through Shomare and Orsho the way then divides. The right fork goes to Dingboche (the trail to Island Peak), while the left branch is the one for Pheriche, Lobuche and Everest Base Camp. Backed by a towering moraine wall, **Pheriche** has a health post supported by the Himalayan Rescue Association and manned by volunteer doctors during the trekking seasons.

A trail from Dingboche keeps to the crest of the moraine wall, while the route from Pheriche stays in the valley bed, here broad and flat-bottomed as it eases between Taboche on the left and Pokalde on the right. Across the Khumbu Khola you mount the terminal moraine of the Khumbu Glacier, pass the teahouses of Duglha and come to a region characterised by numerous memorial cairns, chortens and manis commemorating Sherpas and Westerners who lost their lives in the mountains. Take your eyes off these for a moment, and bask in the glorious panoramic view back the way you've come.

The way now curves into the seemingly barren upper region of the Khumbu Valley headed by Pumori on the Nepal–Tibet border. Cross one last rise and round a bend you arrive at **Lobuche**, which members of the successful 1953 Everest expedition adopted for their rest and recuperation. A mountaineer's holiday camp? Not any more!

Lobuche to Kala Pattar and Everest Base Camp

At 4930m Lobuche is not a restful place. Unless you're adequately acclimatised you should go no further, but all being well, the next stage takes you up the left-hand side of the Khumbu Glacier and over the tongue of the Changri Shar Glacier to Gorak Shep (5140m) in about two hours. Nestling in the lee of an old moraine, the lodges here overlook a basin of glacial sand out of which rises the black cone of Kala Pattar, whose summit offers one of the finest of all close views of Mount Everest.

Decisions need to be made. If you're well acclimatised and have both time and energy, book a bed in one of the Gorak Shep lodges, take the trail to Everest Base Camp and after returning, next day ascend Kala Pattar for an unforgettable view. But if you don't have time or energy for both, choose Kala Pattar. You'll not regret it.

The route to **EBC** passes a small lake and curves round the base of Kala Pattar before getting onto the Khumbu Glacier. There's usually an obvious route along it – make sure you don't stray from the 'trail' – and about two hours from Gorak Shep you should come to the tents of various expeditions based there on the glacier near the foot of the tumultuous Khumbu Icefall. But don't expect a welcome from any mountaineers in camp; respect their privacy and give them space. Take your photographs and return to Gorak Shep, and anticipate a better experience on Kala Pattar.

From Gorak Shep there are two obvious routes to **Kala Pattar**. My preference is to ascend by the left-hand path and descend by the right-hand option. Given good acclimatisation there's nothing difficult; you simply place one foot in front of the other and puff and pant your way to the top. There are in fact two summits with a sort of col between them. Marked with colourful prayer flags the upper summit is at 5623m, from which you can see the South Col between Everest and Lhotse, as well as Everest's immense Southwest Face, a section of the Tibetan flank, the Khumbu Icefall, and (perhaps best of all) the crystal face of Nuptse tapering to a delicate point. But in whichever direction you look, the scene is eye-wateringly lovely.

After this, you can return home contented.

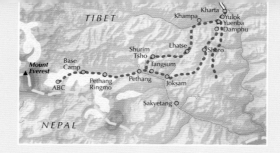

Trek 15
Everest: Kangshung Face
by Bart Jordans

W*hat more can be written about Mount Everest that has not already been put down on paper? Isn't it just a matter of seeing it for yourself? The world's highest mountain can be approached by three possible routes, each one leading to a different face. The most popular is the classic trek through the Khumbu region of Nepal (Trek 14). The others are both located in Tibet: the massive North Face, which can now be approached by road all the way to the Rongbuk Base Camp, and the third option, which heads for the East (or Kangshung) Face. This Kangshung Face trek is the least known and perhaps the most challenging of all, for it spends much of the time above 4000m and has two passes to cross, the highest being over 5300m. Passing through landscapes of unsurpassed grandeur, besides observing Everest and its South Col from a rare perspective it also gives views of two more 8000m giants, Makalu and Lhotse, as well as a host of other significant summits to guarantee an unforgettable experience.*

Plastered with ice and snow, Mount Everest lures trekkers deeper into the Kama Valley

Route summary

Location	Tibet
Start/Finish	Kharta
Distance	80km
Duration	10–11 days (plus a minimum of 2 days' driving)
Maximum altitude	Langma La 5350m
Trek style	Camping
Restrictions	None, but for political reasons entry to Tibet can be cancelled without warning
Grade	Demanding
Guidebook	*Everest: A Trekker's Guide* by Kev Reynolds (Cicerone Press, 2011)

George Leigh Mallory and Guy Bullock were the first Westerners to set eyes on the Kangshung Face during the Everest Reconnaissance of 1921. Seeking a viable route to the summit, the two were camped in the Kama Valley where clouds had hampered any clear sighting of the mountain. But on the morning of 5 August Mallory looked out of his tent to find the weather more hopeful so, deciding to spend the day checking the upper part of the valley, he and Bullock set out as the clouds began to break up. Everest was gradually exposed: '...the great North-east arête came out, cutting the sky to the right; and little by little the whole Eastern face was revealed to us'.

That Mallory later dismissed this vast, complex face as 'impossible' need not concern us here. 'Other men, less wise, might attempt this way if they would, but, emphatically, it was not for us.' Such comments were for climbers to ponder; those of us who wish only to trek to the foot of the mountain, to gaze up at its immense face and experience the wild beauty of this remote region,

Pilgrims make their way to the sacred lake of Tse Chu

will be drawn more by Mallory's description of what he referred to as 'amazing scenery' and the fact that 'three of the five highest summits in the world overlook the Kama Valley'.

In the official expedition book, he went on to confess: 'When all is said about Chomolungma, the Goddess Mother of the World... I come back to the valley...the broad pastures where our tents lay, where cattle grazed and where butter was made, the little stream we followed up to the valley head, wandering along its well-turfed banks under the high moraine, the few rare plants...so well watered there, and a soft, familiar blueness in the air... Though I bow to the goddesses I cannot forget at their feet a gentler spirit than theirs, a little shy perhaps, but constant in the changing winds and variable moods of mountains.'

And at the end of the expedition, Lt-Col Charles Howard Bury, its leader, was moved to recall: 'We had explored many of these Himalayan valleys, but none seemed to me to be comparable with this [the Kama], either for the beauty of its Alpine scenery, or for its wonderful vegetation.'

This then, is one of the highlights of the trek that follows.

Since the starting point is the village of Kharta at about 3750m, it is important to allow plenty of time to acclimatise on the way there. When travelling overland from either Kathmandu or Lhasa, it will easily take four to five days; a spectacular journey crossing just a fraction of the enormous Tibetan plateau with its fabulous mountain views.

Should you fly first to Lhasa across the Himalayan range you will see hundreds of peaks

It may not reach the magical 8000m mark, but Chomolonzo (7790m) is an undeniably dramatic peak

in all directions, while the town itself, though very much modernised, retains many pockets of originality and is, of course, not only the capital of Tibet, but the focal point of Tibetan Buddhism. Make sure you take an early walk through the heart of town to enjoy sunrise on the Potala, and note the pilgrims making their way round it and prostrating at the Jhokhang Temple. Spending time in Lhasa at 3600m is also a useful way to acclimatise before taking a Land Cruiser to the start of the trek.

This journey goes by way of Gyantse, Shigatse and Tingri, in each of which there are impressive monasteries to visit, and – except for the very last section – the road is good. After Shigatse you cross the Lhakpa La at a breathless 5267m, where you can expect to gain a first view of Everest and four more 8000m peaks. Mount Everest – Chomolongma (Qomolangma) to the Tibetans – stands at the heart of the Chomolongma National Nature Reserve, whose southern boundary butts against Nepal's Sagarmatha National Park and the Makalu-Barun National Park, thus forming an extensive area of protected land.

When entering the Chomolongma reserve, the road becomes a dirt track tracing the course of the Pang Qu River through the narrow Yo Ri gorge and into a broader valley where the village of Kharta is located. This is one of the few corners of Tibet to be touched by monsoon rains that travel up the Arun Valley in Nepal and spill over the comparatively low Popti La. As a result vegetation is surprisingly lush with some rare forests to trek through. Rain at altitude can also lead to snowfall, of course, which may result in snowbound passes hampering progress. Another risk here is that of altitude sickness, but if you take time to acclimatise properly, and allow an extra day or two in your itinerary, the trek to the Kangshung Face should create no undue problems.

The cost of the trek is high due to the use of Land Cruisers to reach the start, and because drivers remain in Kharta until your return about 12 days later. Another additional cost factor is that of the Sherpas and kitchen crew who often travel overland from Nepal, because on the whole Tibetan trek crews fail to deliver the same quality of service as do the Nepalese. All should meet at Kharta, along with the yaks and their herders, although the latter do not always show up on time!

Kharta to Joksam via the Shao La

The route described here begins in **Kharta** at about 3750m, and heads south across the Shao La to reach the Kama Valley, which leads to the Kangshung Face. On the return to Kharta the 5350m Langma La is used. Some itineraries tackle

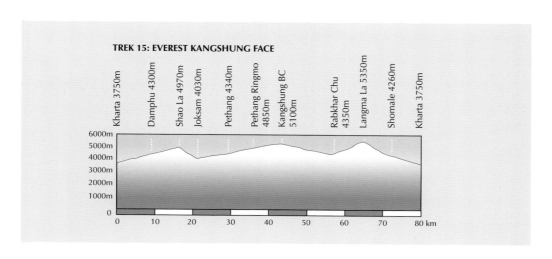

this route in the opposite direction, but I prefer to leave the highest pass until last, to make sure everyone is well acclimatised in order to enjoy the whole experience. Apart from one landslide area, trails are good, but beware of snowfall, which could make the crossing of the Langma La a tricky proposition.

Time permitting, at the start there's a recommended side-trip to be made to the southwest of Kharta, where a long one- or two-day trek leads to the **Samchung La** (4560m) and **Chog La** (4900m), between which lies the beautiful **Valley of Lakes**. From the Chog La the Popti La can be seen on the Tibet–Nepal border. Until the Chinese invasion of Tibet, this was an important trade route between the two countries.

The first day's hike on the main trek is partly on a dirt road through a wide valley next to the Kharta

A lakeside camp below the Shao La – the pass is seen at the far right

Chhu. It was near one of the villages (Mojun) north of the river that the young Tenzing Norgay lived with his parents before moving to Thame in the Khumbu area of Nepal (see Trek 14).

Keep an eye open for a small trail taking off to the south. Climbing steeply to a cairn (a mini chorten) on a ridge, this is a good place to have a rest, enjoy views over the Kharta Valley and eat lunch. The trail now leads into the valley of the **Dambuk Chhu** with the first pass of the trek located at its head. Along the way you might see Tibetans cutting grass and placing it in piles to dry; this will be used to thatch the roofs of their homes. There are two campsites in this valley. Located next to the river **Damphu** is the first, and this should be used in order to acclimatise.

After crossing a boulder field, a good, well-used trail now penetrates deeper into the valley. At its head it should be possible to see the first of the trek's two passes, the 4970m Shao La. Several lakes lie at the head of the valley, and although it will not have taken long to get there,

The Chomolonzo massif is an ever-present giant

a second night's camp is made next to one of these in readiness for crossing the pass next day. The climb to the pass is straightforward, and by now you should be fully acclimatised. An early start is worthwhile since there are rewarding views to enjoy during the climb, as well as from the pass itself and during the descent. Decorated with cairns and prayer flags the **Shao La** offers fine views of Makalu (8485m) and Chomolonzo (7790m). Here you will find a long and impressive stone wall, roughly one metre thick, which is part of an old fortification line used by the Tibetans as protection against invading Gurkha armies from Nepal in the 18th century. A similar wall can be found on the Chog La located further to the east to form a second line of defence, the first of which is on the 4120m Popti La marking the border with Nepal.

The Shao La route is used by Tibetans transporting timber from the forest in the Kama Valley.

Huge logs are carried over the pass by both yaks and locals – an amazing sight with Everest in the background, its Kangshung Face still some distance away becoming evident during the long descent.

The trail winds down through high alpine tundra and meadows, with the landscape changing from barren rocks to the lush vegetation of rhododendron, willow, birch, silver fir and juniper. It is unfortunately a lost Tibetan landscape; not long ago there were many more areas like this before the Chinese invasion and subsequent deforestation. The crossing of the pass is rewarded not only by fine views but also by camping in one of the most beautiful spots throughout the Himalaya. This is the **Joksam** camp, surrounded by thick juniper forest and some very clean water at about 4030m.

You are now in the Kama Valley, where the young Tenzing Norgay would have had his first views of Everest while tending yaks with his family.

Joksam to Pethang Ringmo

Another glorious day starts with a steep climb through thick conifer, hemlock and juniper forests cresting out on a ridge from where a high trail wanders around ridges without gaining or losing any significant amount of altitude. Enjoy the stunning views towards Everest, Lhotse and an occasional glimpse of Makalu. Large alluvial fans cover the base of the mountains while the Kama Chhu slides below; across the river Chomolonzo and Makalu form part of the valley's southern flank.

The trail crosses alpine ridges with summer camps of yak herders everywhere, then descends to a lake called Tsho Nak (the Black Lake). **Tangsum** is one possible campsite; there are several others to be found further on, but it is always a good idea to take it easy with the altitude and enjoy a camp with grand views once more. During the night you may hear avalanches rumbling down from Chomolonzo.

The next stage begins by walking through damp areas with a couple of small streams and a few small lakes. At a major fork in the trail by a large boulder the northern option will be used on the return to Kharta via the Langma La, but for now continue heading west in order to draw

Pethang Ringmo, a sublime site with Lhotse and Everest brushed with cloud across the meadows

closer to Everest's East Face and the Kangshung Glacier.

The way descends steeply for about 200 metres to the campsite meadows of **Pethang** surrounded by rhododendrons more than two metres high, and with the triple summits of Chomolonzo and several unnamed 5500m peaks soaring above the camp.

In a tributary valley nearby lies the sacred lake of **Tse Chu** (meaning Long Life Water). Buddhists believe it has special healing powers, and Tibetans frequently visit the lake and return home with water taken from it. At the base of a cliff on the far side of the lake there's a cave covered with prayer flags, and several small rock buildings below. This cave is where Guru Rinpoche is said to have meditated, and is where Tenzing Norgay was born while his mother was making a pilgrimage to the lake and the nearby Gangla Monastery. Perhaps Mallory and Tenzing saw each other when Mallory visited the valley in 1921 and Tenzing was a small boy herding yaks with his parents…

A large and potentially dangerous landslide area has to be crossed. Taking about an hour, it's a mostly steep climb and not one where you will want to stop for a drink or to take photographs. The site changes from year to year and yak herders have to find a new route through the rubble each summer when they take their animals to graze in the many pastures beyond the landslide. It dates back to the time when the Kang-do-shung Glacier, coming from Chomolonzo, pushed across the valley until it struck rocks on the opposite side to form a moraine dam. The trail goes through the snout of this dam where there are plenty of loose stones, and sometimes the yak herders are reluctant to cross.

After dealing with the landslide there are a few ups and downs to be tackled, but as views become more and more rewarding this part of the trek should cause no problems. The North Face of Chomolonzo is an overwhelming sight, with 3500m-high granite cliffs continuing towards Kangchungtse (7678m) to effectively conceal Makalu.

Finally, the enormous flat meadows of **Pethang Ringmo** at 4850m give exquisite views towards so many famous peaks. This is why you are here! The valley is horseshoe shaped and surrounded by three mountains of 8000m, plus several 7000m and 6000m peaks all crusted with enormous glaciers – it is an incredibly scenic spectacle, and it's easy to understand why this Kangshung Valley has been characterised as 'the valley like no other'. This is where Mallory and his companions camped in 1921, and the site is dotted with several small cylindrical stone huts built by yak herders to shelter yak calves during wild summer storms.

A rest day here is well deserved, for it's possible to get to the East Face of Everest without technical challenges, and to find one of the base camps used by the few expeditions that have attempted to scale the monstrous wall with its cascading curtains of ice, about which some amazing stories have been written.

Return to Kharta

It seems strange now to turn your back on the mountain that has dominated all views for so many days. But even retracing the same trail for the first day and a half will provide ample new vistas to celebrate, and there are two options to consider for the eventual return to Kharta. The easier route, which should be chosen in the event of bad weather, returns by crossing the Shao La and takes four or five days. However, the preferred route, and the shorter option, goes by way of the Langma La (three to four days), a challenging trek due to the height of the pass and the possibilities of getting trapped by snow.

From Pethang Ringmo the landslide area has to be crossed first before reaching camp at a pleasant meadow by the Rabkhar Chu at about 4350m. Next day, after a steep 200m climb, you arrive at the trail division by a huge boulder, last seen a few days earlier. Follow the trail in a northerly direction, crossing some enormous meadows on an easy trail that provides good views of the Rabkhar Glacier coming in from the northwest, and a very steep 6135m peak called Tuolakangboqie. When looking back Makalu, Chomolonzo, Lhotse and Everest create a breathtaking panorama.

The area is covered with trails so keep an eye open for the best direction as you are drawn deeper into the valley, crossing several ridges until you find the outlet of two lakes, Tsho Melongme and **Shurim Tsho**. Camp is usually made beside the first of these at about 4850m before crossing the Langma La. Rise early to enjoy the special dawn light on the lakes and high mountains, and also to cross the pass early in the day.

In good conditions the climb is fairly straightforward and will take up to two hours. Cairns indicate the trail that can be obscured when crossing several big rock slabs, possibly covered with snow. At 5350m the **Langma La** is the final pass of the trek. Remember to add prayer flags to those already fluttering in the wind above the pass. From there you can say farewell to the high mountains, which have provided amazing memories to take

The Shurim Tsho below the Langma La. Chomolonzo gathers clouds

back home: Makalu, Chomolonzo, Pethangtse, Lhotse Shar, Lhotse, the South Col and Everest itself, now some 27 kilometres away.

From this point the Kharta Valley is a good 1500m below, and several steep sections have to be negotiated in order to reach it, passing on the way a lute-shaped lake called Tsho Dramnyen. Walk along the lake's right-hand side, and a view suddenly unfolds down to a meadow called **Lhatse**, a great place to relax.

The trek ends too soon. In less than a day you are down from the pass to motorised transport! It only takes two to three hours to reach the dirt road near the village of Lhundrubling where Land Cruisers are waiting to take you to camp. Or you can walk three to four hours through the valley to **Kharta** where you say goodbye to the yak herders, and start 'trekking' by Land Cruiser out to that other world.

Above base camp, Makalu's South Face is a forbidding wall of tumbling glaciers and steep rock ▶

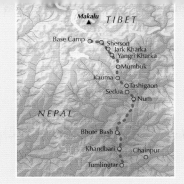

Trek 16

Makalu Base Camp

by Chris Townsend

T he trek to the base of Makalu, at 8485m the fifth-highest mountain in the world, is an adventurous journey from the exuberant richness of a tropical rainforest to the harsh beauty of the alpine zone. Makalu lies 22 kilometres east of Everest at the head of the remote Barun Khola valley, which can only be reached by crossing a high pass. This valley is mostly unspoilt wilderness with little sign of human influence; a spectacular land of subalpine forests, waterfalls, cliffs and meadows, and the trek into it is both tough and committing, but the rewards are incalculable.

Route summary

Location	Eastern Nepal
Start/Finish	Tumlingtar
Distance	about 200km
Duration	18 days (16 days' trekking plus 2 days at Sherson)
Maximum altitude	Makalu Base Camp 4870m
Trek style	Camping (some simple lodges in places)
Restrictions	Special permits required
Grade	Demanding

Makalu Base Camp is remote and little visited, though the journey to get there is magnificent and exhilarating. There are few facilities once the three 4000m cols that lead to the Barun Valley have been crossed, and supplies must be carried. Those high cols have to be re-crossed on the return journey too as there is no way out for the non-mountaineer from the head of this valley. The highest is known as the Shipton La (or Shipton Pass), after the legendary British mountaineer and explorer Eric Shipton, who was the first Westerner to come this way in 1952, but its local name is the Tutu La.

The ascent of Makalu was first attempted by three different expeditions in 1954, but after these all failed an 11-man French team succeeded the following year, putting no fewer than nine climbers on the summit over a three-day period, the first of whom were Lionel Terray and Jean Couzy. However, this high number of first ascentionists does not mean Makalu is easy to climb; quite the opposite. It's regarded as one of the hardest of the 8000m peaks due to its steepness and technical difficulties. Looking at it from below this does not seem surprising, as it's a great rock fang of a peak with fewer snow slopes and icefalls than other giants of the Himalaya.

At over 3000m Kauma makes a fine campsite on a ridge-top kharka on the way to the Shipton La

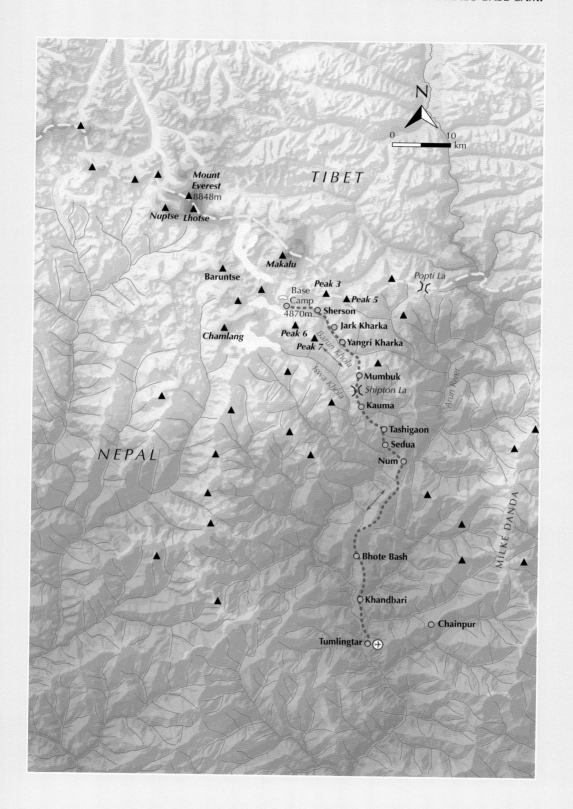

N

0   10
          km

TIBET

Mount
Everest
8848m

Nuptse Lhotse

Makalu

Baruntse

Peak 3

Base
Camp   Peak 5
4870m   Sherson

Chamlang   Jark Kharka

Peak 6   Yangri Kharka
Peak 7

Mumbuk

Shipton La

Kauma

Tashigaon

Sedua

Num

NEPAL

Popti La

Barun Khola

Iswa Khola

Arun River

MILKE DANDA

Bhote Bash

Khandbari

Chainpur

Tumlingtar

But trekking is about the whole journey, not just the final view of the mountain itself. Every step of the way is a joy, as you advance through luxurious rainforest dotted with villages and farms, cross the deep Arun River gorge, climb alpine passes, descend to the coniferous forests of the Barun Valley, and finally reach the glacial moraines at the foot of the mountain.

Much of the route is on rough, narrow trails in uninhabited country, and it feels more like a deep wilderness journey than popular treks such as the Annapurna Circuit or Everest Base Camp. Camping is essential, and once across the Shipton La there are just a few basic campsites and no permanent habitations. By contrast the first part of the trek passes through a succession of small villages along a high forested ridge above the Arun River.

From the Arun River to Makalu the route lies entirely within the Makalu-Barun National Park that was established in 1992 to protect the forests and natural resources, and there's a fee to pay for trekking there. This is the only national park in the world with an elevation gain of 8000m from river to mountain summit.

The trek starts and finishes at Tumlingtar, where there's an airstrip with direct flights to and from Kathmandu. Vehicle transport is available from Tumlingtar up a steep, rugged road to Khandbari, a large village housing the national park head-quarters and a police checkpost plus shops, hotels and other facilities. The drive up is rough and bumpy; walking is far preferable, and from Khandbari you are on foot anyway.

Tumlingtar to Tashigaon

The little town of **Tumlingtar** is set on a dusty plain above which rise steep forested hills. The altitude is only 450m above sea level, so this is tropical. Camping is available, but it's not the quietest or most comfortable place to stay. Nights are hot, jackals howl in the darkness and the first mule trains pass by before dawn, when the many cocks start crowing.

The climb on foot to **Khandbari** takes around three hours, with good views along the Arun and Sabha Khola valleys; the drive may be somewhat faster, but it's far less pleasant. From Khandbari the route rolls north along a wide track on a broad undulating ridge high above the Arun River. This is a land of villages and farms dotted amongst the luxuriant rainforest. There are huge bamboo thick-ets – a major local crop – and big banana trees. Belying what lies ahead the track is likely to be busy with local people, some with mule trains,

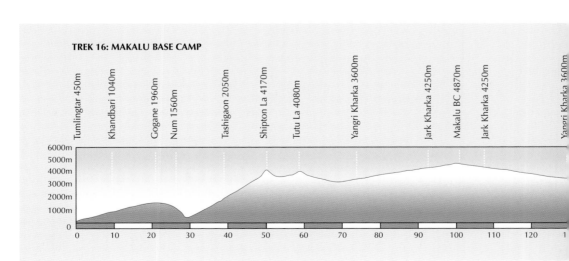

buffalo or goats. Along the ridge there are several possible campsites and a few lodges where food and accommodation are available. I've camped at Bhote Bush, Gogane and Num, from where the route descends to the river. Tumlingtar to Num is

In the early stages of the trek the view north from Gogane shows the long white wall of Chamlang, with Peak 6 and Makalu

about 26 kilometres and this can be walked in two days, and as the elevation is between 1000m and 2000m the nights are much cooler at Num than at Tumlingtar.

Early in the autumn trekking season the end of the monsoon may linger, and heavy rain and dramatic thunderstorms are possible; decent rain gear and waterproof tents are a good idea. Mist rising from the trees and the river valleys is common, but when it sinks or clears, far to the north the high mountains may be seen as a long line of jagged white peaks soaring above the green forested ridges. Dominant are the great white wall of Chamlang, the spire of Peak 6 (called Napo by one of our Sherpas) and the massive wedge of Makalu.

For long sections the route runs through dense forest on the west side of the ridge under big oaks

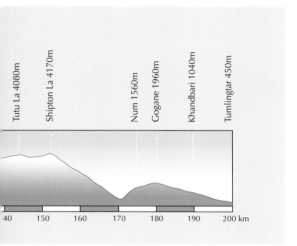

Tutu La 4080m
Shipton La 4170m
Num 1560m
Gogane 1960m
Khandbari 1040m
Tumlingtar 450m

40   150   160   170   180   190   200 km

Two days out of Tumlingtar the thatched houses of Num signal the point where the trail descends abruptly to the Arun River

festooned with moss, ferns and vines. There are more delicate birches too, plus pines and other trees, all rising out of rich thickets of bush and shrub. In places cardamom, a local crop, is grown under the trees. The soil is red and rich here, and very slippery when wet – so watch your footing! The east side of the ridge is drier and more open with smaller trees and more cultivation, including medicinal herb gardens.

The area is rich in birdlife with jays, woodpeckers, magpies and many small birds in the forest, and eagles and hawks high above, circling in the sky. The forest has monkeys too, and large colourful spiders. Less attractive are the leeches that work their way into socks and boots. Oddly, hiking in sandals without socks I had no problems with leeches, while those in boots collected several.

Approaching Num there are views down to the Arun River and up the steep slopes on the far side to Sedua. In a straight line it's only about three kilometres from one to the other. However there's around 850m of descent and reascent on a steep trail as well, so it can take the best part of a day.

With mountains rising on three sides **Num** (1560m) is beautifully situated at the end of the ridge from Khandbari. The descent to the river is on a steep, well-built zigzag path of flattish rocks, mostly in dense wet forest. The lower gorge is steep-sided with many crags and a fine, long, multi-channelled waterfall crashing through the trees. The Arun is a big rushing torrent, grey with glacier-melt and crossed by a long suspension bridge in a dramatic situation. The forest is alive with birds and butterflies, and it feels like a wild and secret place.

However, the steep ascent soon leads to farms with cows and buffaloes, and with terraced rice and barley fields. The path up is stonier but also drier than the descent. The terrain overall is rockier than south of the Arun with many huge boulders and slabs. **Sedua** has campsites, some shops and a national park checkpoint where permits can be obtained, though it's best to get these in advance.

From Sedua the route climbs to **Tashigaon**, the last village on the route. This involves around 600m of ascent, and as it's a climb of another 1400m to the next campsite, Tashigaon is a good place to overnight. On the way there the trek enters Sherpa country and Buddhist mani stones, chortens and prayer flags start to appear. Below the village the Kasuwa River powers down a deep ravine with forested ribs rising from it. A great slice of hillside is green with vegetation but too steep for trees. There's a sense of being on the edge of wilder, higher country, and the nature of the trek is about to change.

Tashigaon to Yangri Kharka

From Tashigaon the route climbs steeply through dense forest, the muddy track eventually becoming a stone staircase up rock outcrops as it climbs above 3000m for the first time to gain a ridge that runs out of the trees to **Kauma**. Here on the steep hillside there's a small stone lodge and terraced tent sites plus superb views over forested ridges fading into the distance. Climb a little way above camp and there are views of the mountains.

Beyond Kauma the trail crosses the three cols of the Shipton La and descends to the Barun Valley. As the only way out is back over the pass, if there's any sign of altitude sickness it would be best to wait a day at Kauma before climbing higher.

The landscape is complex around the Shipton La and different maps and guidebook descriptions don't agree on either the route or the heights, so a guide who knows the way is a big

On the trail from Kauma to the Shipton La the horizon is punctuated with mountains that wall the Barun Valley

Dawn light on Chamlang, a spectacular mountain of 7319m first climbed in 1962 by a Japanese expedition

asset here, especially as the trail may be snow-covered in places.

The crossing of the three cols is one of the most spectacular days on the trek. It begins with a climb through rhododendron forest with views east to distant Kangchenjunga and Jannu, then suddenly arrives at the first pass (sometimes called a false pass as it doesn't cross the main ridge) with a superb view of Chamlang and the summit pyramid of Makalu rising above Peaks 6 and 7, whose slopes plunge into the deep valley of the Isuwa Khola, the west wall covered with huge rock faces topped by two splendid spires. My altimeter made this pass, named Keke La on some maps (Kauma La on others), as 3700m. The rocky path continues to a beautiful mountain lake, Kala Pokhari, and then climbs to the **Shipton La** at 4170m or 4340m, depending on the source of the information. My altimeter made it 4100m. Whatever the height the pass is a dramatic spot with grand views all round. You are above the treeline here and the pass feels wild and remote.

From the Shipton La the final col can be seen across another bowl. Descend into this, pass another little lake, then climb to the Tutu La from where a steep descent leads down into a rhododendron forest and a campsite in a rough clearing at Dobato above **Mumbuk** at around 3500m. Perched on the steep hillside this site gives good views across the Barun Valley to the eastern end of the Makalu range.

The descent into the valley from Mumbuk runs through magnificent fir forest where the ancient-looking gnarled and broken trees are garlanded with moss and lichen. Once down by the raging glacier-fed Barun Khola the trail turns up the valley and climbs steadily through a magnificent ravine with massive cliffs rising above the forest. In places big landslides have to be crossed. There'll be some boulder-hopping too, and the trail may be indistinct or even destroyed. Emerging from the ravine the route reaches broad meadows at **Yangri Kharka** (3600m), where there's a teashop and ample space for camping. Further up the valley rise great cliffs with two shallow caves scooped out high on their faces. Rodra, one of our Sherpas, said they were Lord Vishnu's washing rooms.

Yangri Kharka to Sherson

The two-day walk up the Barun Valley to Sherson is an incomparable trek in a superlative wild landscape with views dominated by the steep pyramid of Peak 6, capped by a snow mushroom, while further away the East Face of Chamlang and the wedge of Hongku Chuli hang white in the sky. All these and other mountains are a soaring complex of rock, ice and snow. Below them vast cliffs replete with caves, overhangs and long thin waterfalls drop into the trees and meadows. Two prominent rock buttresses are in view much of the time and these can be used to mark progress.

Initially you walk through fir forest interspersed with open meadows, entering a sudden calm silence when the trees block the roar of the river. The ancient mossy forest is dark and solemn, a closed-in world contrasting with the immense space of the mountains. The trail crosses many streams, sometimes on single plank bridges. There are numerous birds in the meadows and forest – flocks of snow partridges on the ground, red-billed choughs wheeling in the air and even, if you're lucky, a beautiful hoopoe with its crown of feathers.

Beyond the last trees the teahouse and campsite at **Jark Kharka** is reached, at around 4250m.

Camp at Sherson, with the East Face of Chamlang above a towering wall of moraine

Here in the heart of the mountains you are surrounded by brilliant white snowpeaks.

From Jark Kharka it's only a few hours' walk to **Sherson**, a campsite on big meadows at the base of the Barun Glacier. The route goes through rugged moraines and over glacial rubble through which the Barun Khola meanders, and care needs to be taken that views of the mountains don't distract you from your footing.

Sherson and Makalu Base Camp

Sherson is a comfortable site that makes an excellent base for a couple of days' exploration of the area. After eight or nine days' trekking to reach this place it would be a pity not to linger and absorb the magnificence of this remote and lonely landscape.

Both the original and the current Makalu base camps can be visited from Sherson. The first lies an hour's walk up a moraine and is about 100m

Turning their backs on the high mountains, two trekkers retrace their steps from Sherson to Yangri Kharka

higher than Sherson at 4800m. The ascent is steep, loose and rocky at first, then broad and gentle. It's possible to continue on to around 5100m where a superb view reveals the massive South Face of Makalu towering above you and looking quite forbidding. Makalu probably comes from Maha-kala, meaning 'the great black one', which fits, given its rocky rather than snowy appearance. Also impressive are two satellite summits – Peaks 3 and 5 – the latter seen across a glacial valley filled by a grey silt lake with the spiky ends of glaciers above it. Away to the west a great wedge of pale rock and snow powers into the sky – the

The snow-dusted Shipton La at 4170 metres

Kangshung Face of Everest. This view of Everest is splendid, and better, in my opinion, than the one from Kala Pattar on the Everest Base Camp trek. In front of Everest is the equally impressive pyramid of Lhotse. From the west side of the ridge you can look along the Barun Glacier to the grey waters of Barun Pokhari and the little stone huts at the current Makalu Base Camp. The whole scene is wild and desolate yet starkly beautiful.

In the afternoon avalanches can be seen and heard crashing down the peaks to the south, while cloud plumes develop on Everest and Makalu. I watched as clouds filled the distant lower valleys then rose and spread, pouring like water over the cols.

Down at Sherson the meadows are full of life after the sterility of the rock, snow and ice. There are plants here and birdlife – ravens and yellow-billed choughs and white wagtails. It seems as though you've reached the edge of the habitable world.

The current base camp lies up the Barun Glacier and is too close to Makalu to give a good view. However a walk up the glacier, mostly on rubble rather than snow or ice, is worthwhile for different, closer views of Makalu, and more views of Everest and Lhotse plus a brief immersion into a world of rock and ice. Before the tea-house at the main base camp is reached several other campsites are passed.

Just beyond **Makalu Base Camp** a rickety bridge crosses the swirling grey waters of the infant Barun Khola. By following moraines on the southwest side of the glacier it's possible to progress further up the valley, crossing tongues of shattered ice, to a high point from where you can look down on the glacier and up ahead to icefalls that bar the way for trekkers without mountaineering equipment. Makalu looks tremendous from here, while across the valley the summit of Baruntse appears.

The return

Reluctantly the time comes when **Sherson** must be left to begin the return to Tumlingtar, which now seems a distant place in another world. The walk out takes about a week. Although there is no new country, views are different from this perspective and the landscape is so engrossing that traversing it twice is no hardship. Different campsites can be used in places too, to add some variety. Descending from the subalpine meadows at Sherson into the first bushes, and then rhododendrons followed by silver firs, is a descent into a greener, more colourful and much richer world. Life here is prolific and luxuriant rather than just clinging to the margins of habitability. After the open savagery of the high mountains the forest is a mysterious hidden world.

The final challenge of the trek is the steep climb back up to the **Shipton La**, which was mist-shrouded when I re-crossed it. Then it's down into forest, across the Arun, and through the villages to **Khandbari**, which now seems amazingly large, and then into **Tumlingtar**. The mountains may be far behind by now, but memories of them will remain forever.

Trek 17

Kangchenjunga: North and South Base Camps

by Kev Reynolds

A lthough it had first been climbed in 1955, it was not until the late 1980s that restrictions were lifted to allow trekkers, rather than just mountaineering expeditions, to approach Kangchenjunga from Nepal. When accompanying one of the first trekking groups there in 1989 the words of mountaineer Pete Boardman were soon ringing in my ears. After returning from making the first ascent of its North Ridge with Doug Scott and Joe Tasker 10 years earlier, the experienced Boardman confessed that the walk to the base of the mountain had been the most beautiful he had ever undertaken. Other widely travelled trekkers have since echoed his sentiments, claiming that the route to Kangchenjunga is a strong contender for the title of 'the most beautiful walk in the world'.

Janny and Kangchenjunga drift in evening light when seen from the Milke Danda

Route summary

Location	Northeast Nepal
Start	Basantpur or Taplejung
Finish	Taplejung
Distance	about 210–250km depending on route taken
Duration	20–23 days' trekking (plus 3 days' acclimatisation) depending on route
Maximum altitude	Pangpema 5140m
Trek style	Camping
Restrictions	Kangchenjunga Conservation Area permit required
Grade	Demanding
Guidebook	*Kangchenjunga: A Trekker's Guide* by Kev Reynolds (Cicerone Press, 1999)

Northeast Nepal is dominated by two 8000m mountains, Makalu and Kangchenjunga (8586m), whose snowmelt drains into the Arun and Tamur rivers. These rivers and their tributaries water a fertile land of rice paddies and tea gardens. Banana plantations and straggles of bougainvillea gather around thatched villages. Huge spiders' webs are draped from tree to tree, and in the low-lying valleys semi-tropical forests seethe with humidity while eardrums unaccustomed to the sound of a million cicadas seem close to bursting as you pass by.

But from trails running along the foothill crest between the Arun and Tamur valleys eyes are drawn to a pristine wall of ice and snow. Makalu looks huge. But it's nothing compared with Kangchenjunga whose five lofty summits and bevy of consorts would stand out in any mountain community. Seen from a distance – not of miles or kilometres, but of many days' walking – such visions as these float like galleons on a distant sea; there's little to connect them with the reality of the moment or place from which they're studied, and if there were, they'd be so far off that it would seem an impertinence to imagine that one day they'd be close enough to touch.

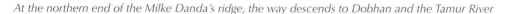

At the northern end of the Milke Danda's ridge, the way descends to Dobhan and the Tamur River

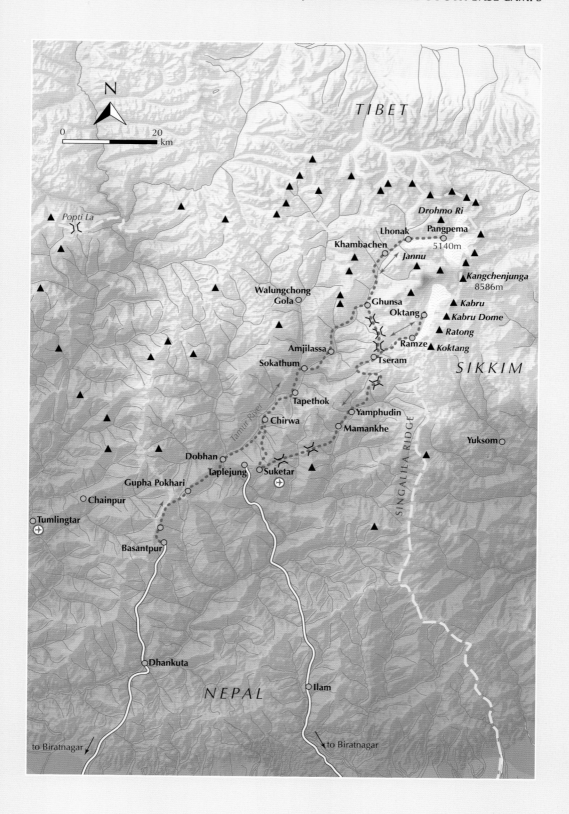

So push anticipation to one side and savour the moment.

There are two main ways to approach Kangchenjunga through northeast Nepal. The most popular focuses on the STOL (Short Take-Off and Landing) airstrip at Suketar above Taplejung, while the other begins at the foothill township of Basantpur on the Tinjure Danda. A third option (rarely taken) uses the STOL airstrip of Tumlingtar beside the Arun, and climbs onto the foothill ridge of the Milke Danda where it joins the Basantpur route shortly before descending to the Tamur at Dobhan. All routes are strenuous and challenging, although the Basantpur approach has the advantage of easing into the trek during the first few days.

The Suketar (Taplejung) approach is the shortest, but not necessarily the best, for it misses the delights of the southern hills and their stunning distant views, which add so much to the trekking experience. Views of the big mountains are there, of course, from Suketar and a few points north, but these are fairly short-lived and only gained by those who take a direct route to Kanch's south side. Those who head first for Pangpema on the northern side of the mountain have no heart-stopping views for several days. They're great treks, no

doubt about it, but my preference is to start low and enjoy a slow build-up, to experience different zones of climate and vegetation, and to meet the various ethnic groups whose homes are passed along the way.

Basantpur to Dobhan

The journey from Kathmandu to Basantpur takes twice as long as the bus ride to Jiri for the foothill trek to Everest (Route 14), and as 24 hours or more on a bus can test one's patience, an alternative option of flying to Biratnagar on the Indian border in the eastern Terai, followed by a shorter bus journey into the foothills via Dhankuta, could be worth considering.

The road through the foothills currently extends to Taplejung, but it has no impact on the route from Basantpur to Dobhan, and the three days spent trekking along the Tinjure and Milke Dandas drift from one small village to the next over meadows and through groves of pink-barked rhododendron with mountains floating among clouds ahead, and the Singalila Ridge running off to your right beyond and above an anonymous rippled farmland.

At 2310m **Basantpur** has little to hold you, so hope your sirdar has arranged for the porters and

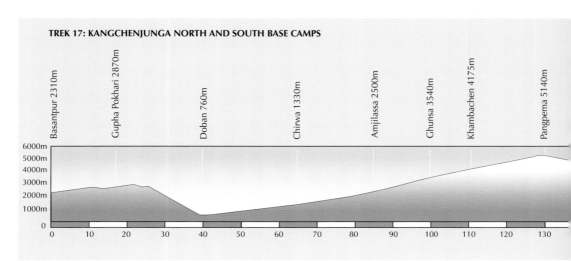

TREK 17: KANGCHENJUNGA NORTH AND SOUTH BASE CAMPS

kitchen crew to meet you there to enable the trek to begin more or less straight away. Some who have written about this little township have commented on its view of the entire Kangchenjunga massif, but such a view has been missing on every one of my visits, and I've had to wait almost until reaching **Chauki** (four hours on) before the Himalayan wall to the west of Kanch has been revealed: Makalu, Lhotse Shar, Everest and Chamlang are all visible – but not Kangchenjunga. For that you must walk a short distance out of Chauki where the trail turns a bend to discover what it was that brought you there. And that's a view worth waiting for.

There's no shortage of places on which to set a night's camp, for the dandas are broad and largely open, the villagers friendly and hospitable. On one occasion, with my tent pitched beside a pool near Manglebari, the surrounding hills were alight with fireflies at midnight, and as dawn broke over

Sitting at his sewing machine in the village street, a tailor in the Tamur Valley pauses in his work to greet passers-by (photo: Linda Reynolds)

Kangchenjunga all the valleys below had been drowned by a cloud-sea. Such moments add to the riches of trekking.

Two-and-a-half hours beyond Manglebari the trail meanders along a narrowing crest, before overlooking the woven bamboo roofs of **Gupha Pokhari** whose houses stand astride a paved street divided by a wall-like chautaara on which porters rest their loads. The blue smoke of cooking fires drifts across the narrow street where hens and their chicks scamper, and behind the settlement in an open meadow lies the tiny lake (*pokhari*) after which the village is named. An alternative trail slopes off the

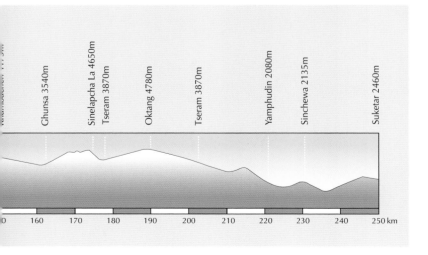

Ghunsa 3540m

Sinelapcha La 4650m
Tseram 3870m

Oktang 4780m

Tseram 3870m

Yamphudin 2080m

Sinchewa 2135m

Suketar 2460m

160 170 180 190 200 210 220 230 240 250 km

ridge to meet with an old trade route between the brass-making village of Chainpur and the Dobhan bazaar.

Before long the way plunges into a forest of rhododendron, the trail twisting, rising and falling with annoying frequency, but almost two hours after leaving Gupha Pokhari you come to a tiny settlement of timber and bamboo houses on a tree-crowded ridge; there's a small meadow and a view guaranteed to pull you up sharp. Directly ahead, but still at least eight days' walk away, Kangchenjunga and Jannu hang in the sky. Twice I've pitched my tent there and been mesmerised by both sunset and sunrise weaving their spell upon those mountains.

The following stage gives one of the loveliest day's trekking I know. With a descent of more than 2000m it's downhill almost every step of the way; at first among rhododendrons and mossy-trunked trees, with straggling cords of clematis and waxy-petalled orchids poking among the branches. The trail then emerges to a magical

land of innumerable terraces of rice and millet stepping all the way down to the Tamur River at a steamy 760m. Thatched farmhouses stand among family-sized banana plantations, orange trees and avenues of poincettia – and all the while Jannu and Kanch, Kabru and Ratong fill the horizon.

Across the Tamur's valley, if you know where to look, the Suketar airstrip can just be seen, with the township of Taplejung below and to its left. But at the foot of terraced hills, at the confluence of the Tamur and the Maiwa Khola, stands **Dobhan**, an important but untidy bazaar and the largest village north of Basantpur on the way to Pangpema. Plant hunter Joseph Dalton Hooker came here in 1848 and commented on the village being 'frequented by Nepalese and Tibetans, who bring salt, wool, gold, musk, and blankets, to exchange for rice, coral, and other commodities'.

Dobhan or Suketar to Ghunsa

The Tamur is followed upstream for three days, but you'll need to check locally to ascertain which bank is to be used for the first two hours out of Dobhan. Some years the east-bank route is almost impassable until you come to a suspension bridge carrying the west-bank trail from Thumma.

It can be desperately hot in the Tamur's valley, vegetation is distinctly tropical and the sound of the river is challenged by the ear-splitting noise coming from insects in the trees and shrubbery overhanging the trail. Several minor tributaries flow out of the hills; some are bridged, but it may be necessary to wade thigh-deep through the rushing water if a bridge has been destroyed.

Approached through an avenue of frangipani, the Chhetri

Making friends along the way is rewarding for both parties, and adds much to the trekker's experience. In Chirwa a local woman offers a welcome smile (photo: Linda Reynolds)

village of Mitlung is a huddle of white and ochre houses, a few simple shops and teahouses, and a pleasant camping area. Beyond it the trail improves, with staircases of rough stone slabs that climb against towering cliffs on the way to Sinwa, one of the busiest villages in this stretch of the valley. Shops and teahouses line the street, and there's a police post where permits need to be checked. Then, between Sinwa and **Chirwa**, a suspension bridge crosses the Thiwa Khola where the trail from Suketar joins the Basantpur route.

It will have taken one-and-a-half days to descend from Suketar's airstrip to the Tamur's valley, much of the way snaking round terraced farmland and through shady woods, losing about 1000m of altitude, and the difference in temperature and humidity will no doubt be felt by new arrivals.

About 10 minutes out of Chirwa a campground above the river is flanked by huge boulders, from one of which Pete Boardman fell and badly damaged an ankle in 1979 when on his way to Kangchenjunga with Doug Scott, Joe Tasker and Georges Bettenbourg. Unable to walk, three tiny Limbu porters carried him in a conical wicker basket all the way to Ghunsa, the last major village on the way to Pangpema. The enormity of this feat becomes evident on the desperately steep and exposed climb from the bed of the gorge-like Ghunsa Khola to the village of Amjilassa; a height difference of more than 900m – a stage tiring enough when carrying just a day-pack, let alone a 12½ stone (80kg) climber!

Since Boardman was carried there a new route to Amjilassa has been made, which begins at **Sokathum** close to where the Ghunsa Khola empties into the Tamur, about four hours beyond Chirwa. Instead of climbing directly above the river, the way now crosses to the south side of the Ghunsa Khola and forges a route through a gorge on an amazing causeway of stone and natural ledges tight against overhanging cliffs. Four times the river is crossed before the trail makes the steep switchback climb to **Amjilassa**, which

consists of a few houses standing on different levels. The former trail went to the 'upper' village, but the present route arrives a little lower down at a farm building, which doubles as a teahouse with a small terraced field that can accommodate a few tents at about 2500m.

Two more stages take the route to Ghunsa. No more the steamy heat of the Tamur's valley: cold afternoon mists and night frosts can be expected now. This is big mountain country. A hint of snow-peaks (the first since the long descent to Dobhan five days before) is gained from Gyapra, the day after leaving Amjilassa. Gyapra, like Phole and Ghunsa, is inhabited by Tibetans; those in Phole are refugees who fled their country in the 1950s. Rosy-cheeked and robust, the children have snotty noses and wide grins; their mothers make handsome rugs, their fathers grow potatoes and tend yaks. Their stone-built houses are roofed with shingles held down with slabs of stone. Prayer flags slap in the wind, and a simple gompa gathers dust in a bare yard.

Go there in the autumn when the larchwoods are gold with the Midas touch, when gentians line the trail and the valley closes in to shut out the sun. Then continue to **Ghunsa** and you know you're on the edge of something special.

Ghunsa to Pangpema

At around 3540m, Ghunsa is high enough to demand attention to the altitude, so it's sensible to spend at least two nights there before continuing upvalley. On arrival it may seem somewhat stark and cold, but after you've been to Pangpema, Ghunsa will feel like the tropics. In *At Grips with Jannu* Frenchman Jean Franco wrote of Ghunsa as being at 'the end of the world… The climate is harsh indeed and life at its most miserable'. Yet in 1930 Frank Smythe had arrived with an international expedition to attempt Kangchenjunga, and he thought the village 'a trim little place, with neatly laid-out fields'.

It's a three-day hike from here to Pangpema. The first ends at **Khambachen**, a summer grazing

On the way from Ghunsa to Khambachen, Jannu's great North Face is seen above the Khumbakarna Glacier

hamlet at the mouth of the Nupchhu Khola's valley at about 4175m. On the way the trail crosses to the west bank of the Ghunsa Khola, climbs above the meadow of Rambuk Kharka and eventually arrives at a huge landslide. This is potentially dangerous for melting night frosts send down a bombardment of loosened stones with little warning. This is no place in which to study the views! For that, wait until you're safely across, then find a rock to sit upon and enjoy the most incredible outlook across the valley to the sheer north wall of Jannu (Khumbakarna, 7710m) soaring above the Khumbakarna Glacier. This is the wild Himalaya at its best; savage, defiant, a face without concession considered unclimbable by Smythe, but won by a Japanese expedition in 1976 who managed to put no fewer than 16 climbers on the summit in three separate teams.

Leaving Khambachen the way crosses another landslide to enter an avenue of lofty peaks where from the yak pasture of Ramtang Kharka a splendid view into a side-valley reveals the ice-sheathed face of Kangbachen (7903m), which forms part of Kangchenjunga's lengthy western ridge. Ahead an impressive finger of rock projects from the lower slopes of Wedge Peak (Chang Himal); opposite this stand the few stone hutments of **Lhonak** where camp is made at a notoriously windy junction at 4815m. Despite this, no matter in which direction you look, there's something magical to focus on.

Pangpema, site of the base camp for attempts on Kangchenjunga's northwest flank, is a morning's walk from Lhonak. And what a walk it is! For most of the way the trail keeps to the ablation trough alongside the Kangchenjunga Glacier, but now and then it climbs onto the moraine wall, and there's one short stretch of boulder-hopping, guided by cairns.

But stop and look around you, for this is the heart of the Himalaya, and the scale of both mountain and valley is difficult to comprehend; trekking doesn't get much better than this. When the highly experienced and widely travelled mountaineer Douglas Freshfield came here on his epic circumnavigation of Kangchenjunga in

1899, he was awe-struck by the sheer scale of it all, which left an impression of 'stupendous vastness'. All around, massive yet elegant peaks thrust up into the Himalayan blue, then suddenly the immense north wall of Kangchenjunga bursts into view, with a shelf of grass spilling down the slope towards its base. This is Pangpema, one of Nepal's most treasured sites.

At 5140m **Pangpema** makes a great, if chilly, campsite for a night or two. If you have the energy and are well acclimatised, you could mount another 1000m to the 6200m summit of **Drohmo Ri** for an even more expansive view, or push further upstream along the moraine bank of the West Langpo Glacier. Or simply sit and gaze in wonder at so much raw beauty. Soak it in, and it will stay with you forever.

Pangpema to Oktang

This north side of Kanch rewards with unforgettable images and (it seems) a lifetime of experience, but there's still the south side of the mountain to visit, so retrace your steps to **Ghunsa** (two days), then make a crossing of the ridge dividing the valleys of the Ghunsa and Simbua Kholas – the latter draining Kangchenjunga's southern flank. There are two options for this: a tough route via the 5160m Lapsang La, or a lower, recommended trail, which crosses no fewer than three connecting passes – the Mirgin La, Sinion La and the Sinelapcha La.

It's a steep haul out of Ghunsa, but the trail is good for most of the way to the grass basin of Selele, reached in about four hours, where tents are pitched at about 4200m in readiness for the long day that follows. With three passes to cross and a steep and lengthy descent to camp at the Tseram meadows, pray for good conditions and clear visibility. In truth, the passes are not difficult, and the highest (the Sinelapcha La) is only about 4650m, but when combined they make a challenging day out. Jannu can be seen from the

Mirgin La, as can Makalu, Lhotse Shar, Everest and Chamlang, while from the Sinelapcha La Ratong, Kabru and the snowbound crest leading to Kangchenjunga make all the effort worthwhile. Descent to **Tseram** takes you past two small tarns, one of which gives exquisite mirror images of mountains at the head of the valley, and once settled in at the Tseram site, sunset has a way of turning its walling mountains to bronze.

A half-day's walk upvalley leads to a pair of shallow lakes trapped in the Yalung Glacier's ablation valley. Ahead, across the unseen glacier, the graceful Ratong and ice-fluted Koktang stand either side of the deep cut of the Ratong La, through which Sikkimese mountains can be seen. Twenty minutes beyond the second lake lies **Ramze** (4580m), the uppermost yak pasture and a fabulous spot for a camp, protected as it is by a curving wall of moraine.

Rise before dawn and hike along the ablation trough as it rounds a bend, then go up onto the moraine crest and keep heading northeast, with Kabru and Talung holding back the sun on the right, and a vast white wall blocking the valley ahead. As light spills into the valley, so the Southwest Face of Kangchenjunga announces its presence. This is a gift of the gods. Sacred to Buddhists, this multi-summited, third highest of all mountains is indeed a sight to behold. Words run out of meaning; the vision becomes an emotion.

Oktang is a pile of rocks on the crest of moraine at 4780m, the simplest of all chortens with a flutter of prayer flags, a stupendous backdrop and an aura all its own. A pile of rocks? Or the ultimate altar at which to worship the mountain gods?

Allow yourself a week to trek out to **Suketar** (Taplejung) for a flight back to Kathmandu, via Lamite Bhanjyang, **Yamphudin**, Sinchewa Bhanjyang and Lal Kharka. The names are easy to list, but challenging to link on foot, for the demands of this trek remain until the very last.

The massive Southeast Face of Kangchenjunga seen from above Tanshing (photo: Steve Razzetti) ▶

Trek 18

Kangchengjunga: Singalila Ridge and Goecha La

by Kev Reynolds

Mention Darjeeling to anyone who has been there, and their eyes will take on a dreamy expression that has nothing to do with either Darjeeling itself or the cascading tea gardens that spill down the slopes ahead. No! What makes this old hill station special is its outlook, described in 1848 by plant hunter Joseph Dalton Hooker as being 'quite unparalleled for the scenery it embraces, commanding…the grandest known landscape of snowy mountains in the Himalaya, and hence in the world'. At the centre of that landscape stands Kangchenjunga, 72 kilometres distant, yet at dawn seeming almost close enough to touch. Of all the great peaks of the Himalaya, 'Kanch' is the most easily visible, and long before the birth of mass tourism it was perfectly feasible to make a week-long excursion from Calcutta to see it. Observation Hill, The Mall and Tiger Hill – each one is a memorable vantage point, but the Singalila Ridge, which leads to Sikkim and the foot of the mountain, proves to be the ultimate temptation.

Route summary

Location	West Bengal and Sikkim, India
Start	Maneybhanjang and Yuksom
Finish	Rimbik and Yuksom
Distance	90km and 80km
Duration	6 days and 7 days (plus 1–2 days' acclimatisation)
Maximum altitude	Sandakphu 3636m and Goecha La 4940m
Trek style	Camping or simple lodges (no food available)
Restrictions	Permits required for the Singalila and Kangchenjunga National Parks, and a special permit for Sikkim
Grade	Gentle, and Moderate +
Guidebook	*Kangchenjunga: A Trekker's Guide* by Kev Reynolds (Cicerone Press, 1999)

Two comparatively short treks are described here. The first traces a route along the Singalila Ridge, which forms a border between eastern Nepal and the Indian states of West Bengal and Sikkim. The other takes place entirely within Sikkim itself, is more challenging than the Singalila trek, but reaches a stunning vantage point to gain a close view of Kangchenjunga's East Face. Kangchenjunga, of course, is the prime objective of both treks, a mighty fortress of rock, ice and snow that dominates the eastern Himalaya like no other. Frank Smythe, who was with an international expedition attempting to climb it in 1930, likened this complex massif to 'a rugged peninsular [jutting] from the main Himalayan coast'. One section of that 'peninsular' pushes north among a knot of peaks that unravels to form the Tibetan border, while another extends southward across the summits of Talung, Kabru, Ratong and Koktang to become the Singalila Ridge, a broad and accessible range of sparsely inhabited hills some 80 kilometres long.

Those who live in the great mountain's shadow hold it in reverence, for this is a sacred peak, the abode of the gods whose Tibetan name, Kang-Chen-Dzonga, is roughly translated as 'The Five Treasures of the Great Snow'. For the people of Sikkim it is their guardian deity.

In the early days of the Raj when Tibet and Nepal were both forbidden lands, Sikkim drew the attention of travellers, explorers and botanists. In the mid-19th century Hooker, one of the greatest of the early plant hunters, spent a considerable amount of time and energy investigating the valley systems of

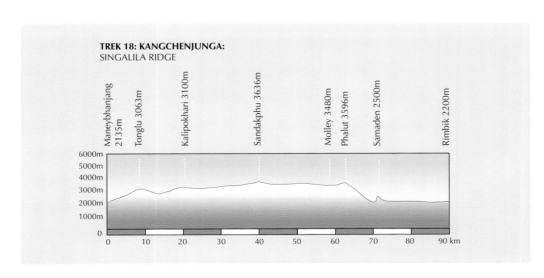

TREK 18: KANGCHENJUNGA: SINGALILA RIDGE

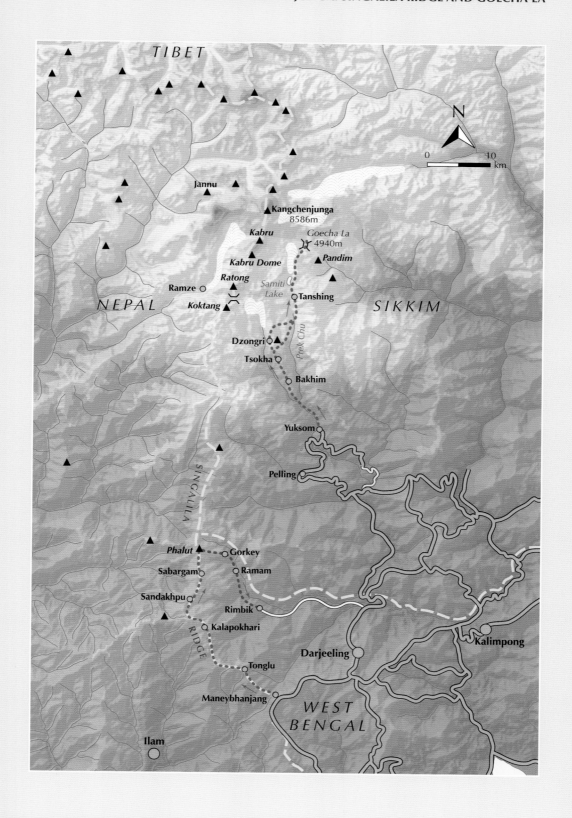

The trek to Dzongri and the Goecha La begins in Yuksom, one-time capital of Sikkim

this (at the time) independent little kingdom, and his *Himalayan Journals* contains descriptions of the mountain scenery there as well as its flora. Thirty years later Captain HJ Harman attempted to climb several peaks while involved in survey work; Major LA Waddell made a few pioneering journeys, and Political Officer Claude White crossed the Goecha La in 1890. In 1899 Douglas Freshfield, the distinguished mountain explorer and one-time President of both the Alpine Club and Royal Geographical Society, made an anticlockwise circumnavigation of Kangchenjunga with an international party that included the geologist EJ Garwood, a young Valtournanche guide Angelo Maquignaz, the pioneering mountain photographer Vittorio Sella and his brother Erminio, and the pundit Rinzin Namgyul. Although it was by far the most important exploration of the Kangchenjunga massif in both Sikkim and Nepal, the Scottish scientist Dr Alexander Kellas did more than anyone to open

Sikkim to mountaineers with several visits to the eastern Himalaya beginning in 1907. During his climbs Kellas made scientific observations of the effects of high altitude on human physiology, becoming perhaps the first real authority on the subject.

In 1903 the Arabian explorer and sometime mountaineer Gertrude Bell made a journey to Sandakphu on the Singalila Ridge (the highest point in West Bengal), from where she studied Kangchenjunga at dawn, climbing a rocky hill above one of the bungalows that had already been built for the use of travellers. 'You see the whole Sikkim chain culminating in Kinchinjunga,' she wrote. 'The enormous mass of the snows is quite overwhelming.'

By the time of her visit the view from Sandakphu was reputed, by those who had seen it, as the most beautiful in the world, and this claim was to be reinforced by the many intrepid tourists who trod in her footsteps during the following decades as the trail along the Singalila Ridge became one of the first of all Himalayan trekking routes. It is indeed, a true classic.

Singalila Ridge: Maneybhanjang to Sandakphu

It's perfectly feasible to hike along the Singalila Ridge as an independent trekker, staying overnight in simple lodges and carrying your own gear. But this is not the same as 'teahouse trekking' in Nepal, for meals are not available here, and accommodation has to be booked in advance; camping is a popular alternative option among both groups and individuals. In the early stages the route passes through or close to Nepalese villages with small shops and teahouses, and as a jeep track runs along the ridge to Sandakphu, with long-established mule trails continuing from it, route-finding is not a major issue.

Traditionally the trek starts at the southern end of the ridge about 30 kilometres southwest of Darjeeling, at the small border settlement of **Maneybhanjang** where there's a police checkpost. As villagers insist on providing the crew for any group treks setting out from here, some continue along the narrow road for another 10 kilometres as far as the one-street village of

Sandakphu is noted for its sunrise view of Kangchenjunga, and the fact that you can see the mountains of four countries

Dotre. Whichever village is used as the start, the trek begins with a sharp climb to gain the ridge proper. At the Maneybhanjang end, rhododendrons flank the trail, while Dotre gives a more open aspect, and the first night is invariably spent at **Tonglu** (3063m) where there's a ridge-top trekker's lodge and a campground by a tiny pool from where it's possible to see the lights of Darjeeling. Best of all, however, is the view to the north where (clouds permitting) the snows of Kangchenjunga are stained by sunset and sunrise.

On many Himalayan treks the best views are only achieved on reaching high altitudes. Not so here: the ridge is broad and mostly open, and there are times when it seems that the whole Himalayan range is spread before you. Sadly the weather is often poor for days at a time, with low cloud and rain from dawn to dusk. When it's

The first night on the Singalila Ridge trek is usually spent at Tonglu, a simple lodge, a campsite and a tiny pool

clear, however, the Singalila Ridge rewards with some of the most extraordinarily wide vistas to be experienced anywhere, with Kangchenjunga at centre stage, its various consorts to either side, and with Makalu, Chamlang, Lhotse and an insignificant looking Everest forming just one portion of a never-ending horizon stretching to the west.

Out of Tonglu the way sneaks alongside the international border and into the Singalila National Park where an entry fee must be paid. After this the track loses height, passing through a forest of rhododendron, bamboo, silver fir and pine, eventually coming to the tiny settlement of Gairibas (2625m), which consists of little more than a few houses, a tree nursery and a red panda breeding centre. Steep forested hills sweep down into valleys carpeted with trees as the track returns to the ridge at **Kalapokhari**. Sandakphu is not far off, but it's just too far away for comfort, so a night is spent here before making a short morning's trek to the high point of 3636m on the India/Nepal border.

The lodges (or bungalows) of **Sandakphu** gather below a small fenced meadow, which makes a fine campsite. Above it a prominent hill, festooned with prayer flags, is an outstanding vantage point from which to enjoy the spectacle of sunrise. The panorama is immense, with the mountains of four countries in view: India, Nepal, Tibet and Bhutan – a vast wall of snow and ice gradually receding from Kangchenjunga's bulky prominence to east and west. Daybreak is unforgettable, for a light show is played out not only on the mountain backdrop, but also in the sky, in the valleys and across the hills that stretch to infinity.

Sandakphu to Rimbik

Sandakphu's viewpoint has a justifiable reputation, but the track that extends beyond the settlement provides one of the most scenic walks I know. For perhaps an hour and a half, practically every step is a celebration of nature's beauty. The way is flanked by rhododendron, berberis and pine. Birds and butterflies flit to and fro; foothills tumble into misted valleys, and a footpath cuts across a glorious alpine meadow punctuated by the blackened fingers of trees struck by lightning. Directly ahead Kangchenjunga entices – as it has done almost all the way since leaving Darjeeling – and to east and west the Himalayan wall shuffles its giants to produce ever-changing vistas.

At **Sabargam** leave the ridge for a short diversion down an easy slope to camp at Molley, which boasts a trekker's lodge and an army camp, and next day return to the ridge where a large cairn and a flutter of prayer flags mark a trail junction. Jannu, one of Kangchenjunga's elegant satellite peaks, looks magnificent from here, but the best is yet to come, for you curve below the ridge-crest for 200 metres or so, then regain the crest to be confronted by the most extensive panoramic view of the whole trek. In truth, it's the most extensive view I have ever witnessed anywhere in the world, for the creamy Himalayan wall stretches in both directions as far as the eye can see; an arc of ever-decreasing summits, contained only by the limitations of sight. One could list recognisable peaks, but it would merely be a string of names; what is seen is beyond words, beyond description. When I was there my group, plus Sherpas and the mules carrying our gear, all stood rooted to the ground. A golden eagle rose out of the landscape, soared on the thermals and hovered above us, displaying its banded underwings. No one spoke. It was one of those moments as big as years.

The trek continues to engage all one's senses as the trail winds along the ridge or a little below it, giving a whole series of eye-watering views. It's an undemanding trail, with no steep ascents or descents until a longish climb brings you to the lodge and army post of **Phalut** (3596m) just short of the Sikkim border. Although the Indian authorities lifted restrictions in 2000 to enable trekkers to continue along the ridge into Sikkim, it's not always possible to get permits for this. So we now turn away and descend southeastwards on an excellent trail that soon enters a light, semi-open forest in which a number of flowering plants add colour and fragrance, among them a vivid blue delphinium and trumpet-flowered clematis, eye-catching amid the mossy-barked trees, giant magnolias and rhododendrons.

There's a lodge at **Gorkey** close to the border with Sikkim, the village houses set among terraces and gardens of pumpkin, beans and bananas. Continue down to a wooden cantilever bridge, which carries the trail across a river 1000m below Phalut, then climb steeply for a wearisome 100m to camp on a meadow belonging to the village of Samaden.

Skeleton trees, singed by lightning, stand above a tiny pool on the way to Molley

The sixth and final stage of the Singalila Ridge trek is largely spent in forest shade, at first with majestic chir pine and huge ferns overhanging the trail with fronds as long as a man is tall. Tiny orchids and stands of Himalayan balsam guard the way, with pink, blue and white forms of clematis straggling among the trees. Cicadas seethe in the post-monsoon heat, spiders' webs lace the vegetation and here and there a conical bees' nest may be seen dangling from a crag.

Out of the forest you pass a school at **Ramam**; above it there's a trekker's lodge within the village proper, while across the valley the houses of a scattered community in Sikkim are dotted over a steep slope, and when you turn to look back upvalley snowpeaks rise above a distant ridge, unrecognisable from this angle. It's all so different from the ridge-crest walk of the previous days, but it's not without its charm. Now there are more villages, hillsides worked into terraces, fields of sweetcorn and sugar cane, great swathes of cardamom, teahouses where you can stop and slake your thirst with mugs of sweet ginger tea. Losing height the atmosphere becomes more humid, but after crossing a suspension bridge over the Shiri Khola you join a road that continues down to the bazaar township of **Rimbik** where the trek ends at 2200m. With a few hotels and no shortage of shops, this is the place to enjoy a long relaxing shower and a good night's sleep before arranging transport to Sikkim and the trek to the Goecha La.

Sikkim: Yuksom to Dzongri

The bureaucracy involved in a visit to Sikkim can seem daunting, so potential trekkers are advised to join a group organised by a reputable trekking agent who will arrange the special permits needed to enter the state and to trek in the Kangchenjunga National Park. Thus freed from bureaucratic hassle, you can enjoy the trek with an easy conscience. It's worth noting, however, that Sikkim receives more than its fair share of the annual monsoon rains, and even out of the monsoon season attracts a lot of

precipitation, with mist hanging in the valleys for days at a time. In the springtime (March until May) rhododendrons and orchids fill the forests with colour, while the post-monsoon period of October until late November is generally reckoned to be the best time for clear mountain views.

This seven-day trek (plus extra days for acclimatisation) begins at **Yuksom** (1780m), once the capital of Sikkim despite being little more than a village. Built on a plateau above the Rathong Chu at the entrance to the Kangchenjunga National Park, about 90 kilometres from Naya Bazaar where you enter the state from West Bengal, it has several hotels and shops, and Sikkim's oldest monastery.

With 7000m snowpeaks seen above the wooded hills, the trek leaves the national park checkpost and almost immediately enters a steamy forest of moss-coated oak, chestnut, pine and giant magnolia. At first narrow, the path is a good one that twists and climbs between the trees, crosses four streams – sometimes by suspension bridge, but once on greasy stepping-stones – and after gaining

For much of the way from Yuksom to Dzongri the trek stays within lush rainforest

through rhododendron forest on a path rutted and muddied by the heavily laden yak cross-breeds and pack ponies that daily ply the route in the trekking seasons. Above Tsokha hundreds of log 'steps' take you up to an open meadow known as Pethang at 3660m, and finally to the famed yak pasture of **Dzongri** (4030m). It's a tiring stage, for the trail is in a poor state, and the altitude will be felt by anyone not yet acclimatised. But sudden views open to reveal Pandim at the head of the Prek Chu Valley, then later on, Kangchenjunga and Kabru. As for Dzongri, Freshfield wrote that to watch sunset from here 'is a thing worth living for'.

Dzongri to the Goecha La

Despite being notoriously cold and windy, Dzongri is a magnificent spot, and it's worth spending at least two days acclimatising here. The scenery is uplifting, and there are side-trips to be made to the 4550m Dzongri La, and the easy 300m ascent of Dzongri Peak above the pasture to capture sunrise on Kangchenjunga, Kabru Dome and other

almost 1000m from Yuksom arrives at **Bakhim**, a tiny settlement with a basic lodge named the Forest Rest House, and a campsite at about 2750m.

Next day a long climb leads to **Tsokha**, a small village of Tibetan refugees, the way mostly

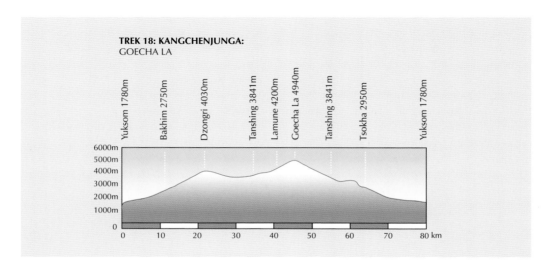

TREK 18: KANGCHENJUNGA:
GOECHA LA

Overlooking the Tanshing pastures, Pandim is a sacred mountain to the Sikkimese people

neighbourhood peaks. For those without tents there's a trekker's hut a little south of the pasture.

Hooker, Freshfield and Smythe were all captivated by the site; Freshfield predicted it would become 'the Riffel Alp of Sikkim' while Smythe thought it should have a proper hut 'run on the same lines as a Swiss Alpine Club hut' as a base for climbs on nearby peaks. In more recent times the Himalayan Mountaineering Institute in Darjeeling chose as a base for their practical climbing operations a site directly accessible from Dzongri.

Leaving Dzongri the trek crosses a moorland-like ridge, then descends into the valley of the Prek Chu, where a three-roomed hut stands just above the river near a trail junction from which a shortcut leads back to Pethang. Boulder-hopping, the way heads upstream to a wooden cantilever bridge that takes you to the east bank. The Prek Chu is a furious river, thundering down from the upper valley dominated by Pandim, a sacred, unclimbed mountain of 6691m. Another basic trekker's hut stands on the edge of the **Tanshing** meadow (3841m) at the southern end of this upper valley, and many trekking groups choose to camp here rather than continue to Samiti Lake.

An easy two-hour walk, crossing streams and weaving among dwarf azaleas, separates Tanshing from Lamune, a yak herder's hut on a rough pasture below **Samiti Lake** where tents may be pitched for a night or two at about 4200m. The lake itself is another sacred place lying directly below Pandim, with fine views from ridges that surround it.

It will take three or four hours to reach the **Goecha La** from here, depending on fitness, acclimatisation and conditions underfoot, and if there's been recent snowfall it can be a tiring ascent through the lateral moraine of the Onglaktang Glacier. In any case you should make an early start for the pass, as clouds often spill over it shortly after dawn, and you'll want to catch the splendour of Kangchenjunga towering over the Talung Glacier. At an altitude of 4940m, with the slapping of prayer flags around you and the world's third-highest mountain directly ahead, you'll perhaps understand why Kangchenjunga means so much to those who live in its shadow.

Goecha La to Yuksom

A return to Yuksom from here can be achieved in two, or two-and-a-half days, using the narrow alternative trail from the **Prek Chu** to Pethang meadow, thus avoiding the climb back to Dzongri. Overnight at **Tanshing** and **Tsokha**.

Day three of the Lunana trek reaches Jangothang below the sacred mountain, Jhomolhari ▶

Trek 19
Lunana Snowman Trek

by Bart Jordans

Hidden in a secluded recess high in the Himalayan mountains of northern Bhutan, Lunana forms the heart of what many experienced trekkers consider to be one of the longest, hardest and most beautiful of all treks. Imposing snow-capped peaks, seemingly impassible river gorges, and mammoth glaciers isolate its villages from the outside world; the only access being via steep and rocky high-altitude trails. With 14 lofty passes to cross and several camps at around 5000m, the four-week long Snowman Trek may be compared to three Everest Base Camp treks in succession. As the weather is generally less stable, and the monsoon rains heavier, than in many other parts of the Himalaya, the time to visit Lunana is limited to May and September–October. However, by adopting a network of trails used for centuries by local people, this magical trek reveals the very best of Bhutan – the country known as the 'Kingdom of the Thunder Dragon' – in a journey of pure meditation.

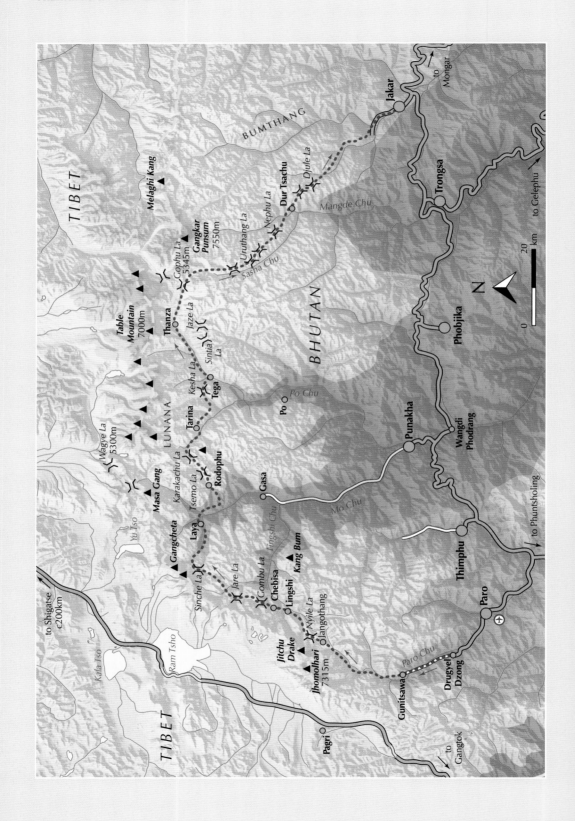

Route summary

Location	Northern Bhutan
Start	Paro/Drugyel Dzong
Finish	Jakar, Bumthang
Distance	about 350km
Duration	about 28 days
Maximum altitude	Gophu La 5345m
Trek style	Camping
Restrictions	Treks to be arranged through an agent approved by the Tourist Authority of Bhutan
Grade	Demanding
Guidebook	*Bhutan: A Trekker's Guide* by Bart Jordans (Cicerone Press, 2012)

Bhutan is different. About the size of Switzerland but with a population of fewer than a million, this is a country steeped in Buddhist tradition and culture. A deeply spiritual land graced by an imposing architectural heritage and the most hospitable of people; a country of which some 80 per cent is covered in forest or shrub and, thanks to abundant rainfall, also boasts an enormously rich flora. In the mountains there are fewer villages than will be found in neighbouring Nepal or Sikkim. There are no teahouses and each trek is led by a qualified Bhutanese guide with a crew to take care of everything in camp. Baggage is carried by mules and/or yaks guided by herders hired locally and exchanged at intervals for a new team, ensuring that each area passed through will benefit from employment. The trails are generally in good condition and while fit, experienced walkers should have no difficulty navigating them, it should be appreciated that the Lunana Snowman route spends many days in remote country with no easy evacuation should anything go wrong. Of my 10 visits to the region, four have been cut short by bad weather.

Trekking in Bhutan is expensive, or appears to be so, as a set fee is charged for each night spent in the country. But this daily tariff is all-inclusive and covers the cost of accommodation, food, transportation and the services of a local guide, so you receive a lot for your money. A portion of the daily rate (about 30 per cent) is a government tax set aside for medical and educational purposes; this makes every visitor an indirect donor to the well-being of the people of this magnificent kingdom. The Lunana trek may be one of the longest and toughest of all; it may also be comparatively expensive, but it can be a life-changing experience – and that experience is priceless!

Paro to Jhomolhari

This epic journey begins with a short drive northwest of **Paro** to **Drugyel Dzong**. Standing on a rocky spur with Jhomolhari as a backdrop, the dzong was built with the dual function of fortress and monastery. Dating from 1647 it is now a ruin following a major fire in 1951, but a visit is still worthwhile. Throughout the country's history, Bhutanese armies have had to defend their land against invasion, and dzongs formed a major part of this defence. Nowadays several military camps have been set up along the route bordering Tibet, partly to control locals smuggling goods.

Recently a dirt road was constructed that could eliminate the first day of the trek. However, it is better to walk in order to acclimatise and to enjoy the upper part of the richly cultivated and prosperous Paro Valley, where red rice is a speciality. Many of the houses have large decorated windows, evidence of the inhabitants' wealth.

The second day is very different. With one exception there is no habitation, but there's plenty of beautiful forest to wander through. The trail is rough and the height gain considerable, so be alert to possible altitude problems. At 4000m on day three, the treeline falls behind to give spectacular views to some of the first high peaks of the trek, while small villages along the way add interest. At the end of the day camp is located at 4044m at the base of **Jhomolhari**, a sacred mountain with an enormous Southeast Face covered by glaciers overlooking the site. A rest day is normally taken

Jhomolhari, sacred to the Bhutanese people, was first climbed from Tibet in 1937

here, with several beautiful side-trips to be made locally.

First climbed in 1937 by Freddie Spencer Chapman and Pasang Dawa Lama, Jhomolhari (7315m) is Bhutan's second-highest peak. Standing astride the border with Tibet, the actual summit was left untrod in recognition of its religious significance. As the Bhutanese believe that climbing defiles the peaks and disturbs the mountain deities who then strike back with numerous, otherwise inexplicable, natural disasters, the king has now banned all mountaineering in Bhutan and the peaks will in future be left untouched.

Jhomolhari to Laya

Before leaving the valley of the Paro Chu savour the views of Jitchu Drake, climbed in 1988 by a team led by Doug Scott before the mountaineering

ban was imposed. The trek then continues with the crossing of the first of the 14 passes, the **Nyile La** at about 4800m. With grand views of nearby 7000m peaks, it is not a difficult pass, but on gaining the summit you should remember to call *'Lha Gey Lo'* ('Praise to the Gods of the pass'). Resounding through the crisp mountain air the cry not only offers thanks to the gods but also celebrates the achievement and ensures luck for the route ahead.

A steep descent is followed by a long flat stretch with stunning vistas along the river valley to the strategically located Lingshi Dzong, backed by huge peaks plastered with glaciers. Badly damaged by an earthquake in 2011, the dzong remains a majestic focal point. It had been more or less deserted until the authorities in Thimphu decided it should have an active monastic presence, for there are between 300 and 400 people living in the Lingshi area who need the services of monks for all manner of ceremonies. Renovation was almost complete when the earthquake struck.

The elegant Jitchu Drake overlooks the Tsho Phu lakes

Below the dzong **Lingshi** village has a boarding school, a Basic Health Unit and a post office; post is delivered and collected once a week by a postman who walks for two to three days from Thimphu.

For me, the next couple of days are always a highlight. The trail is easy and wide, high above the valley floor, and instead of looking where to place your feet you can just enjoy walking. The hillsides are generously covered with medicinal plants and herbs used to make incense. They are collected, dried and transported to Thimphu for the traditional medical hospital and also for the market.

After Lingshi two more villages are followed by several days in remote wilderness without any settlements. This is smugglers' territory, for Tibet is accessible through numerous passes, but if caught by border patrols the smugglers lose their goods and are sent home with a warning. Typical goods are solar panels, transistor radios, rubber boots, Chinese cigarettes (the sale of tobacco being banned in Bhutan), beer, blankets, thermos flasks and Tibetan ponies. Tibetans also like to cross into Bhutan during the summer to collect medicinal plants and more specifically the fungus-infected caterpillar *cordyceps*, which is said to have

aphrodisiac and other medicinal properties. The demand is tremendous and local businessmen pay up to US$12,000 for one kilogram. The Bhutanese government watches for 'poachers' from across the border while at the same time giving local people a licence to collect the cordyceps during a two-month period in summer. This has had a major impact on the economy of many mountain villages, transforming Lunana from a poor hinterland to a growing economic entity.

With three passes to cross in four days before reaching Laya, you will need to be acclimatised by the time the trek leaves **Chebisa**. The 4440m **Gombu La** is gained after a stiff climb from the village, which has a sky burial ground nearby, so watch for eagles and vultures riding the thermals. Views from each pass reveal huge distances. The area is packed with yak herds in the summer, but the valley between the **Jare La** and Sinche La is reserved for the national animal, the strange-looking takin (a member of the goat/antelope family). This is also the realm of the rare snow leopard whose prey, bharal (the Himalayan blue sheep), are seen everywhere.

Sinche La (5000m), the highest of the three passes, is reached after a steep climb. Recently furnished with a huge chorten and a mani wall,

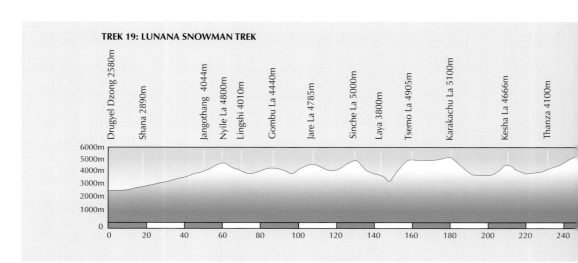

TREK 19: LUNANA SNOWMAN TREK

there are some good views in the distance towards Masa Gang (7194m) and the mountains of Lunana, while nearby Great Tiger Mountain (or Gancheta, 6840m) fills the whole view to the north. To the west you can still see Jitchu Drake and Tsheri Kang.

After an overnight camp at the foot of Great Tiger Mountain, day 10 gives an easy walk through thick forest to the village of **Laya** at 3800m.

Laya to Thanza

Laya marks the end of the first of the three 'Everest treks', and although you may feel you've been on a tough journey by the time you arrive there, there's plenty more to come. Spread over a large area Laya, which lies within the Jigme Dorji National Park, can keep you fully occupied for a rest day. In the autumn locals thresh the buckwheat harvest in preparation for winter, and sometimes in the evenings the women perform traditional dances around a campfire. The women wear clothing seen nowhere else in Bhutan, including long and colourful Tibetan-style aprons, with a black jacket and dresses woven from a mixture of yak hair and sheep's wool. Associated with fertility, a small conical hat with a vertical bamboo spire and a

flat circular disc is a distinctive feature. Attached to it, a 10-centimetre-wide band made of several strands of colourful beads hangs over the back of the head. Necklaces of turquoise, coral and coloured beads are also worn, and often a small silver medallion as well.

With fresh supplies, laundry done and a new team of pack animals, you now descend to 3300m, then start climbing again. A rest day may be good but strangely the day after feels even tougher, especially with almost 1000m to climb through forest before reaching **Rodophu** at 4215m. The trail has recently been improved since the government uses it to get workers and materials into Lunana to lower the glacial lakes that present a constant threat of flooding – a common problem throughout the Himalaya. (In 1994 a moraine dam collapsed in the mountains near Thanza, releasing the contents of a lake that wreaked havoc as far away as Punakha Dzong.)

A steep climb from Rodophu culminates on the **Tsemo La** (4905m) before entering a large barren plateau crowded with yaks in summer. From a point above the pass you can see Kangchenjunga on the borders of Sikkim and Nepal, while somewhat closer Gangla Karchung (6301m) dominates the view ahead. At the end of the valley you make camp at almost 5000m at Narethang, very close to the **Karakachu La** (about 5100m), which leads into the heart of Lunana. The crossing of this pass may be easy, but the views are spectacular and reward all the hard work of the last two days. Ahead and far below three beautiful blue-green lakes are visible, and a long and sometimes steep descent of more than 1000m brings you to the valley bed where there are several campsites next to the Po Chu. Several waterfalls cascade down the hillsides, and these have recently produced some big landslides.

The Po Chu wends its way down to Punakha, northeast of Thimphu, and there are plans to establish a route alongside the river as a year-round gateway to Lunana. At present the area is closed for several months of the year by snow on

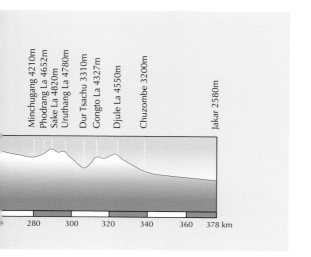

Minchugang 4210m
Phodrang La 4652m
Sake La 4820m
Uruthang La 4780m
Dur Tsachu 3310m
Gongto La 4327m
Djule La 4550m
Chuzombe 3200m
Jakar 2580m

280   300   320   340   360   378 km

Beyond Thanza, more lakes nestle below the Tibetan border. To minimise the risk of further floods, their water level has been lowered

the high passes, so the Lunaps (the inhabitants of Lunana), migrate for the winter months to the lower, warmer areas of Bhutan leaving a few of their elderly folk to tend the cattle. Thanks to the wealth created by the demand for cordyceps, the Lunaps have recently been able to purchase land and property in other parts of the country.

Lunana is remote and sparsely populated with just 13 villages and hamlets. Woche is the first you encounter, a tiny place that shows the recent economic growth with house renovations and extensions. The village is located high in the valley giving good views over the mountains and valleys on the southern side of Lunana. In one of those valleys the Gonju La (5000m) is the fastest

connection with Punakha and central Bhutan, however no pack animals can travel this route.

Before reaching Thanza there is one more pass to cross, the 4666m **Kesha La**. Just before reaching it the trail passes the long and narrow Green Lake, and another smaller, circular, one. A steep descent from the pass leads into a side valley of the eastern Po Chu, towards the end of which there are the two small but prosperous villages of Goptsoe and **Tega** where buckwheat, potatoes, turnips and radishes are grown. From Tega there are excellent views up the valley towards Lhedi and Table Mountain.

After more settlements you cross through a riverbed to reach the small, well-established village of Lhedi (3900m), which has the only school (a boarding school) for the whole of Lunana. Built in the 1960s it is open for only five months each year. Lhedi also has a Basic Health Unit and a radio wireless station, though this has become

Chozo village below Table Mountain has a small ruined dzong

superfluous since the government provided a mobile telephone network here in 2011 – the march of progress makes even the most remote parts of the globe seem close and accessible now.

The 7000m peaks of Jeje Kangphu Kang, Shimokangri, Table Mountain and another couple of high mountains, together with a few settlements and a small ruined dzong at Chozo, are highlights of the trek to **Thanza**.

Thanza to Bumthang

On arrival at Thanza the second 'Everest trek' is finished and another rest day is in order. Built on a moraine below Table Mountain at about 4100m, Thanza is the largest settlement in Lunana, and while there it's worth hiking up a hill to the south to enjoy exceptional views of Gangkar Punsum.

Now another team of pack animals should be waiting to take you to the end of the trek. There are two major exits from here: one uses the Jaze La,

the other is the recommended route to Bumthang over the 5345m Gophu La, the highest pass of the Snowman Trek. It takes two days to reach the pass from Thanza, and of several camping options, the best is located at Tsorim. It's a long day's hike with some steep sections of moraine, but it places you in a good position for the challenging day ahead. In the autumn you may be lucky to travel with large groups of Lunaps and their yaks on their way down to Bumthang to buy provisions for the long winter of isolation in Lunana.

Before reaching the **Gophu La** you walk along the edge of a beautiful glacial lake surrounded by fluted snowpeaks. The pass itself is a big flat area with endless stone cairns and prayer flags. Gangkar Punsum (7550m), can be seen on the

Gangkar Punsum, Bhutan's highest mountain, is seen to the east of the Gophu La

way down from the pass. Although a few expeditions have attempted it in the past, with the ban on climbing now in force throughout the Thunder Dragon Kingdom it may be destined to remain the world's last great unclimbed peak.

From Thanza you walk for several days in a totally remote area, the only sign of habitation being some abandoned yak herders' huts used during the summer months. The trail follows a beautiful valley for one-and-a-half days before a steep climb takes you over two passes to the trek's last high camp. With 14 spectacular passes on this Queen of Treks, these two are among the most dramatic. But there's a great treat in store between them: the **Dur Tsachu** hot springs. Located in thick forest at an altitude of 3310m, this is just what is needed in order to relax after more than 20 days of hard trekking. Bhutan has several hot springs, and locals put great store in their medicinal and restorative qualities. The Dur Tsachu is the finest, especially since the whole place has recently undergone a complete renovation

so that eight of the springs are now covered by small wooden buildings, and a huge guesthouse is being built. Being far from easy to reach Dur Tsachu, it's impressive to note that sick Bhutanese also cross these passes, although most arrive on horseback. The Bhutanese will often stay here for several weeks in order to gain the most benefit from the springs, and it's tempting for weary trekkers to remain with them!

Two passes of around 4500m are crossed on the same day. An enormous climb is made from the hot springs to reach the first of these, from where you can look back on several days' hiking, and ahead to the very last pass. Now there's just 200m of descent and 400m of ascent between you and that final pass.

What a moment – crossing pass number 14! After all that effort it seems like a great victory, but joy is tinged with sadness, for in two days' time **Jakar** will be reached and a 28-day trek through one of the most remote corners of the Himalaya will be over.

A near-perfect site for a base camp with Gangkar Punsum beyond the moraine wall ▶

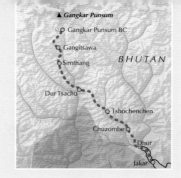

Trek 20

Gangkar Punsum Base Camp

by Steve Berry

A t 7550m Gangkar Punsum is not only the highest peak in the kingdom of Bhutan, it is also claimed to be the world's highest unclimbed summit. Lying some 400 kilometres east of Everest it reigns as lord and master over remote country surrounded by its acolyte peaks. A shy, reclusive mountain, it has largely escaped the attention of man's advances, and even to reach its base is no mean achievement; only a handful of people have ever been there. This trek takes you through jungle inhabited by tigers and bears, past holy lakes, stops at sulphurous hot springs, then on across snow-covered passes until finally you stand on the shores of a lake to gaze upwards at the entity that for locals is a living god.

Route summary

Location	Northern Bhutan
Start	Jakar, Bumthang
Finish	Jakar (or out via Lunana)
Distance	about 160km
Duration	16 days
Maximum altitude	Ridge near base camp c5200m
Trek style	Camping
Restrictions	Treks to be arranged through an agent approved by the Tourist Authority of Bhutan
Grade	Demanding
Guidebook	*Bhutan: A Trekker's Guide* by Bart Jordans (Cicerone Press, 2012)

The Himalayan kingdom of Bhutan had no roads when I was a child. In those days even Indian presidents, if they wanted to visit the king, took seven days on horseback to reach the capital, Thimphu. A land of mediaeval mystery, its interior protected by a ring of mountains, it had seen few explorers. Visited by two Jesuit priests in 1627, it first appeared in 1733 on a map held in Paris entitled *Tibet and Boutan*. The first British visitor was George Bogle on his way to visit the Panchen Lama in Shigatse, Tibet in 1773, but it was not until the 20th century that the *terra incognita* of its remotest region, Lunana, was visited at all. In the days when explorers really were explorers, two British botanists, Frank Ludlow and George Sherriff, made six expeditions in Bhutan between 1933 and 1949. On one of his solo journeys Ludlow, with the aid of occasional nips from his brandy flask, crossed the Gophu La and would have seen Gangkar Punsum from the west. However, the first Westerner to come close to it was Captain MRC Meade who, in 1922, measured the height as 7451m by theodolite and plane table from somewhere near the exceedingly remote Monla

Paro Dzong, the massive fortress/monastery that is one of the most notable features on arrival in Bhutan (photo: Kev Reynolds)

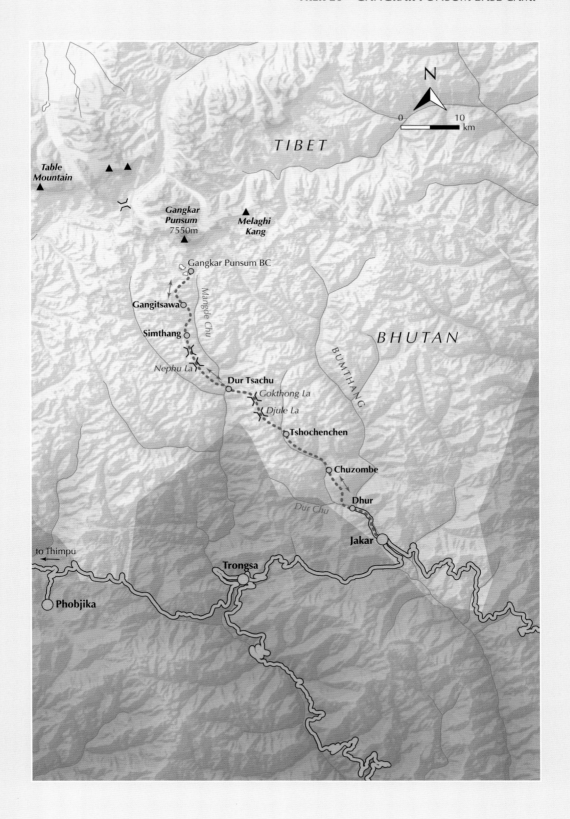

Loading the pack ponies in Jakar at the start of the trek

Karchung La. But the man credited with giving the mountain the name Gangkar Punsum was Swiss geologist Augusto Gansser after his visit in 1965.

It was by a series of lucky coincidences that I first met Colonel Penjor Ongdi in Kathmandu in 1984. For some years I had been scouring maps looking for a special mountaineering objective, and had always wondered about the highest mountain in Bhutan. I mentioned this to Liz Hawley, an extraordinary American woman living in Kathmandu, who practically made it her life's work to meet and record all mountaineering expeditions visiting Nepal. She told me I had to meet the colonel as he was 'Mr Bhutan here in Kathmandu'. The following day I chanced upon his office, and the colonel informed me that he

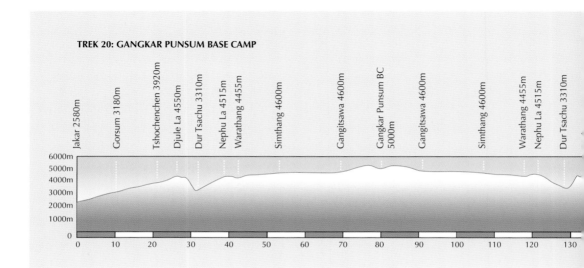

TREK 20: GANGKAR PUNSUM BASE CAMP

was sure that on his next visit to the kingdom he could secure me permission. And so it turned out.

Even today there are still no detailed maps, and all we had at the time was a sketch map and a single photograph of Gangkar Punsum given to me by Dr Michael Ward, which he had taken while exploring neighbouring Lunana in 1965.

The route I describe here is the same one we embarked on in blind ignorance in September 1986. We set off with 22 Europeans, 12 Bhutanese staff, 61 horses and 10 horsemen, not knowing where we were going, which made it all the more exciting! Starting in the Bumthang Valley, after four days we crossed the first major pass, the Djule La, at 4550m, before the path dropped like a stone to the hot springs of Dur Tsachu that bubble in the bottom of the gorge below. On our trek a rest will be needed here to relax muscles in the sulphurous hot tubs before crossing the Mangde Chu and climbing out of its gorge to gain the high valley that leads directly towards Gangkar Punsum. From Dur Tsachu it is still another four days to reach base camp, and the final 5200m pass overlooking the camp affords the most unforgettable views of Gangkar Punsum and the largely unexplored country that stretches tantalisingly to north and west.

Having rested, celebrated, paid homage to Gangkar Punsum – and perhaps even explored a bit to the north – you can then trek back the way you came or, if you have time, energy, and can afford it, you could exit via Lunana (see Trek 19).

Jakar to Dur Tsachu

From the frenetic, hot and dusty streets of Delhi or Kathmandu (your most likely points of entry) you will in all probability fly into Paro on the national airline, Druk Air, having peered out of the Airbus's left-hand windows for mesmerising views of Everest, Lhotse, Makalu and Kangchenjunga. It's surprising that the plane does not veer off course as everyone rushes to the windows – but I suppose the pilots are used to it by now! Finally Bhutan's second-highest mountain, Jhomolhari, looms ahead before the plane makes a series of tight spiralling turns to land at Paro.

The thing you immediately notice is the peace. Bhutan seems bathed in it. The pace of life slows, people smile knowingly, and you share their secret that a fairytale kingdom does exist in reality, and not just in the pages of a fantasy book. Your eyes are now drawn to the massive dzong, the monastery/fortress that broods over the valley. Tibet would have boasted many such dzongs before being destroyed by the Chinese Cultural Revolution, but Bhutan retained its independence, thanks in the main to the actions of its enlightened line of kings, and its unique architecture, national dress, Red Hat Buddhism, legends and customs have all survived.

From Paro the journey now begins by driving across the country soaking up its culture, meeting the people in their traditional costume, and enjoying one beautiful valley after another on the way to the interior. It's basically a three-day drive on twisting mountain roads to reach the region of Bumthang where the trek begins, although you will almost certainly break the drive with a stop in the capital, Thimphu.

The best time to tackle this trek is late September and October. First take a rest day in **Jakar**, the main township of Bumthang, to meet your trek crew who will be busy organising loads for the packhorses – assuming they've arrived on time, that is. Next day, after having had difficulty sleeping with the excitement of it all, you drive for 40 minutes to the roadhead at a place called **Dhur**. The road is pretty rough and you might not make it all the way, in which case walk beside the Dhur Chu before crossing on an old bridge. The way now climbs the east side of a ridge through a straggly village with a nice monastery, then descends to the river.

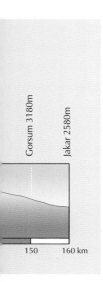

Gorsum 3180m

Jakar 2580m

150   160 km

The first two days heading north are through thick forest. The lower reaches by the river are jungle-like with pine and giant bamboo, while the path is muddy and often covered with gnarled tree roots. Sometimes the undergrowth is so thick you're forced to edge your way beside the rushing river; the Bhutanese warn you to stay at least in pairs as bears are common in their forest. If you see large patches of rotavated forest floor this is certainly the work of wild boar; again confrontation would best be avoided. After six hours and a long climb, you emerge from the forest to discover the large sloping meadow of Gorsum (3180m) – or you could continue for another hour to a forest clearing known as **Chuzombe** where there's a wooden shed and flatter camping.

The second day's trek is a long one – anything from eight to ten hours – but it releases you from

From Chuzombe the route follows the Yoleng Chu through a jungle of giant bamboo

the confines of the forest. From Chuzombe drop a short way down to the Yoleng Chu and follow the river northwards through giant bamboo, crossing at least three bridges. Monsoon rains can sweep these away and even alter the course of the river, and local yak-men often rebuild the bridges in different places, so it's not possible to predict the route accurately. The way goes through fabulous forest with Bhutan's national tree much in evidence. This is a giant form of cedar, liberally festooned with streamers of lime-green Spanish moss. Occasionally there are minor cliff walls where you might spot rock orchids, and for those who are patient there's the chance to spy the small, colourful endemic birds that hide and chatter in the foliage. After three hours of muddy trail you come to a dry area where you can take lunch. A long climb through more forest brings you to the junction of two rivers. This is an important psychological milestone as camp is not so far away. You know when you are getting close to the river junction as the forest thins and is replaced mostly by rhododendron. Pass the junction, cross

the river and make a short steep climb to gain an easy traverse around the mountainside. Before you know it you will enter a valley with no trees but rough yak herder huts, rocky peaks and buttresses, and a broad and shallow river.

In 1986 mist and rain obscured the peaks, lending the valley a foreboding air of mystical quality. Some local barefoot yak herders dressed in black yak hair robes, and with prize-winning weather-beaten grins, gestured for us to join them in their smoke-filled huts at a place called **Tshochenchen** (3920m). We drank salt butter tea and watched two huge male yaks fighting on flat ground in front of us; I'd never seen anything like it before. They repeatedly charged at each other, smashing their heads together, until eventually one staggered groggily away and King Yak huffed and puffed in the middle of the field. From that moment on I understood exactly why all yak-men handle their charges with extreme caution!

Another long day lies ahead, but with the knowledge that at the end of it there will be a rest day, and a soak in the hot springs at Dur Tsachu. Beguilingly the first half hour is a gentle walk past massive cliffs where you can watch black-capped river chats bobbing by the river. At the end of the valley turn left and climb, not too steeply,

Having crossed the Djule La, yaks cool their hooves in the waters of the Djule Tso

past waterfalls and through a band of rock whose stones are peppered with rough garnets, to arrive at a holy lake. Legend has it that a nun threw her red scarf into the lake from a cliff and jumped after it and drowned.

My diary from 1986 reads: 'Very special feeling of peace beyond anything, a place where nothing has changed in millions of years. Something about the place never having been spoilt, a perfect place, where we were allowed to enjoy brief happiness, to enjoy the quiet and the ripples on the lake in a humble way.'

A rising traverse leads to the prayer-flagged **Djule La** (4550m), where you really feel you are in big mountain country. A tangle of peaks stretches before you with tantalising glimpses of snow slopes rising into clouds in the distance. A large lake, the Djule Tso (4125m) lies below, to be gained in less than an hour's descent. Here the shy local people may offer yak curd, or *churpi* – the latter is a Bhutanese favourite 'sweet' and is basically dried yak cheese. It comes in rock-hard squares and is an acquired taste.

An hour's gentle walk from the lake leads to another small pass, the **Gokthong La**. I sat here once enjoying the view and watched a covey of Himalayan pheasant in single file on a narrow rock ledge, when suddenly a huge eagle swooped down and carried one off in its talons. The path now dives headlong through rhododendrons, and once more into forest where there are elusive musk deer, with a knee-crunching muddy descent of just under 1200m from the Djule La. In the bottom of the gorge where it is hot and steamy, **Dur Tsachu** is a couple of timber shacks set amongst lush vegetation 15 minutes above the hot springs at 3310m. On another visit here in 1998 the second king's granddaughter was camped nearby with her entourage, and she invited us to tea.

Traditionally this is the place where you swap horses for yaks, horses being unsuited to the higher altitudes that lie ahead. The yaks are contracted in advance, and the rest day provides a good opportunity for organising the changeover. The primitive wooden tubs at the sulphurous hot springs provide an excellent chance to relax tired muscles, but you have to shout to make yourself heard above the noise of the thundering stream and the incessant high-pitched drone of cicadas. Dur Tsachu itself is also a perfect place for watching exotic birds in the early morning and evening.

Dur Tsachu to Gangkar Punsum Base Camp

Knowing how far down it was from the Djule La makes the thought of ascending that, and more, to the next camp at Warathang, very daunting, but go up you must. It's only half an hour through the forest to a large cantilevered bridge over the Mangde Chu whose sources are the glaciers of Gangkar Punsum herself. To fall into its rapids would spell certain death. Indeed, on our expedition in 1986 we were told that the previous year a Japanese expedition lost most of its cash when one yak barged another off the bridge. When the drowned animal was found days later the cash had disappeared.

Now follows the long haul to the pass, possibly six hours or so from the bridge. After three hours you break through the treeline again; nearby a boulder the size of a house makes for a good lunch stop. Ever onwards to cross the **Nephu La** (4515m), which looks down into a magical valley surrounded by a cirque of often snow-capped rock peaks. Sitting on rocky hillocks in the centre, a few rough stone and wooden shelters belong to yak herders; this is Warathang (4455m).

In the summer men, women, children and their yaks live up here in all weathers. The floors of the huts are bare earth, the walls are of stone, and the roofs are simple rough-hewn planks supported by

At 7550m Gangkar Punsum is Bhutan's highest mountain, unassailably beautiful and forever unclimbed

a log beam. Each hut has one room only; there is no chimney, no draught proofing, no central heating, and cooking is done on an open fire fuelled by dried yak dung. Yet these people laugh, smile and sing far better than we do.

Hopefully you will reach here before it gets dark so you can enjoy sunset over the eastern Himalaya, and I strongly suggest you get up at six o'clock the next morning to enjoy views of the valley.

From Warathang cross the cirque floor and climb steeply to an unnamed pass at 4530m; in

reality this is just a notch on a ridge, and far below you can now see the Mangde Chu making its long journey down a very wide valley. For the next two days at least you thread a way along the left-hand side of this valley, sometimes traversing mountainsides, at others negotiating side-valleys. In places the trail peters out altogether and you have to trust to instinct and the memory of your yak men.

That first day from Warathang to a place called **Simthang** (about 4600m) is relatively easy, and it takes only five or six hours. Simthang is a flat field with two rough huts among rhododendrons where you could camp an army. Route-finding on the second day can be difficult, especially if the cloud comes down. The way contours, crosses a pass and drops into a valley whose floor has been half-covered by a massive rock fall. Pass some huge vertical cliffs, round a corner and tunnel through tall rhododendrons before dropping steeply down to meet the Mangde Chu. Then follow the river for an hour on a rocky path among Himalayan blue poppies, before climbing steeply until the path peters out. It's easy to get lost, so remember to bear right up through some shallow valleys to two more yak huts at **Gangitsawa** (about 4600m). On the morning of leaving in 1986, two of our yak men almost had a knife fight, which was stopped only by rough intervention. Our staff said evil spirits lurked here and I never did find out what the men were arguing about, but we were glad to leave that miserable spot.

Early mornings in the Himalaya are mostly clear of cloud, and this is what you should pray for at Gangitsawa. Just a quick zip up from camp is the edge of a moraine. Below its crest lies the rock-crunching glacier, at the head of which stands

A welcome smile from the caretaker at the Dur Tsachu hot springs

Gangkar Punsum herself. Neighbouring peaks vie for the beauty prize, but none produces the level of sheer awe that she does. Blue sheep might come to investigate before you set off at a leisurely pace – the altitude prevents anything faster. Along the top of the moraine, then over three spur ridges where everything is covered in moss, lichen and beds of gentian. Some of the mosses are so pretty, just like coral, and they come in red, brown and green and are tough enough to support the weight of a man.

The path peters out so you follow your nose to cross the last ridge at about 5200m. Now you can look down at last on the base camp located next to an emerald lake. There are bedazzling peaks on the Tibetan border and wild, wild country to the north.

Base camp is at an altitude of 5000m, and in an ideal world you should build in a few days here to adjust and be the first to explore that wild, wild country so close and yet so far away. You will of course eventually have to leave the way you came, to be left only with a lingering desire to return to see what others have not.

APPENDIX A
Useful contacts

British embassies abroad
www.fco.gov.uk/directory

Map suppliers
Cordee
☎ 01455 611 185
www.cordee.co.uk

Stanfords
12–14 Long Acre
London WC2E 9LP
☎ 020 7836 1321
www.stanfords.co.uk

The Map Shop
15 High Street
Upton-upon-Severn WR8 0HJ
☎ 01684 593146
www.themapshop.co.uk

Omnimap
PO Box 2096
1004 South Mebane Street
Burlington
☎ NC 27216-2096, USA
www.omnimap.com

Medical advice for travellers abroad
www.masta-travel-health.com
MASTA provides health advice for travellers via a network of Travel Health Clinics in the UK, and through an online travel health brief.

www.medex.org.uk
Medex seeks to educate trekkers and mountaineers about altitude-related illness, and have a Travel at High Altitude booklet available free to download from their website.

National mountaineering and expedition bodies
British Mountaineering Council
177–179 Burton Road
Manchester M20 2BB
☎ 0161 445 6111
www.thebmc.co.uk
The BMC can arrange worldwide trekking insurance cover for its members.

Mountaineering Council of Scotland
The Old Granary
West Mill Street
Perth PH1 5QP
☎ 01738 493942
www.mcofs.org.uk

Mountaineering Ireland
13 Joyce Way
Park West Business Park
Dublin 12
Ireland
☎ 353 1 625 1115
www.mountaineering.ie

Royal Geographical Society/Expedition Advisory Centre
1 Kensington Gore
London SW7 2AR
☎ 020 7591 3000
www.rgs.org
The RGS's Expedition Advisory Centre runs training seminars for organisers of expeditions.

Travel advice
Foreign & Commonwealth Office
☎ 0845 850 2829 (travel advice helpline)
www.fco.gov.uk/travel
The Foreign Office provides up-to-date information on circumstances likely to affect travellers to specific countries.

Trekking operators based in the UK
Classic Journeys www.classicjourneys.co.uk
Exodus www.exodus.co.uk
Explore www.explore.co.uk
KE Adventure Travel www.keadventure.com
Mountain Kingdoms www.mountainkingdoms.com
Peregrine Adventures www.peregrineadventures.co.uk
Walks Worldwide www.walksworldwide.com
World Expeditions www.worldexpeditions.co.uk

APPENDIX B

Glossary for trekkers

Note: Bh = Bhutan; Np = Nepal; Pak = Pakistan; Sik = Sikkim; Tib = Tibet

ablation valley	the trough between glacial moraine and mountain
arra	home-made spirit (Bh) – see also rakshi
ba	yak herder's tent (Bh) – see also jha
banchung	small bamboo basket (Bh)
bangchang	local beer (Bh)
bazaar/bazar	trading place or market
beyul	hidden valley (Tib)
bharal	blue sheep
bhat	cooked rice (Np)
bhanjyang	pass – see also deurali and la (Np)
bhatti	teahouse or simple lodge (Np)
Bhotiya	Buddhist people of mountain Nepal
bokkhu	cloak-like garment worn by honey-gatherers in Nepal
Brokpa	mountain people of central and eastern Bhutan
chai	brewed tea, usually with milk and sugar
chaktsel gang	devotional spot (Tib)
chang	fermented beer made from barley or millet (Np)
chapati	flat unleavened bread
charpi	latrine (Np)
chautaara	a resting place beside the trail, usually shaded by a pipal or banyan tree (Np)
chorten	Buddhist memorial, like an elaborate cairn
chhu/chu	river (Bh, Sik, Tib) – see also khola
chuba	traditional dress of Tibet
dal bhat	staple meal of Nepal, rice with lentil sauce
danda	hill, or ridge (Np)
deurali	pass – see also bhanjyang and la (Np)
dharmsala	pilgrims' rest house
doko	conical bamboo basket used for load-carrying (Np)
durbar	palace (Np)
dzong	fortress-monastery (Bh)
gang	hill or mountain (Bh)
gangri	snow mountain (Bh)
gho	national dress for Bhutanese men
gompa	Buddhist monastery
guru	holy man or sage
himal	snow mountain
jha	yak herder's tent (Bh) – see also ba
jhola	'flying-fox' bridge
kani	archway entrance, usually decorated with Buddhist motifs
kata	ceremonial scarf
kharka	a high mountain pasture
khola	river (Np) – see also chhu
kira	national dress of Bhutanese women
kora	circumambulation (Tib)
kund	lake – see also tal, pokhari and tsho
la	pass – see also bhanjyang and deurali
Lhakaps	small group of Bhutanese mountain people
lama	Buddhist teacher or priest
laptse	pile of stones with prayer flags attached to sticks (Bh)
lekh	hill
losar	Bhutanese and Tibetan new year
Lunaps	mountain people of Bhutan living in Lunana region
mandir	Hindu temple
mani	Buddhist prayer, from the mantra: Om Mani Padme Hum
mani wall	stone wall carved with the Buddhist mantra
momo	Tibetan steamed or fried dumplings
Namaste	traditional greeting; 'I salute the god within you' (Np)
namlo	tumpline or sling used to carry loads
nullah	riverbed
pokhari	lake – see also kund, tal and tsho
puja	Buddhist or Hindu prayer ceremony
rakshi	distilled spirit
Shabdrung	title of a spiritual leader (Bh)
shalwar-kameez	baggy trousers and long, loose shirt/tunic (Pak)

Sherpa mountain people of Solu Khumbu, Nepal

sirdar person in charge of a trekking crew

stupa large hemispherical Buddhist chorten

tal lake – see also kund, pokhari and tsho

Tashi delek traditional greeting, also means 'good luck' (Tib, Bh)

tongba fermented millet mixed with boiling water, drunk in Nepal and Sikkim

tsampa roasted barley flour (Tib)

tsho lake – see also kund, pokhari and tal

yak large-haired beast of burden of the ox family

yersa collection of herdsmen's huts (Np)

yeti mythical creature of the Himalaya

zam bridge (Bh)

zopkyo infertile cross between a yak and a cow

Yak trains are sometimes used instead of porters (photo: Kev Reynolds)

APPENDIX C

Further reading

Reading other people's accounts of adventures among mountains you intend to visit can add to the anticipation and help prepare for your own adventures. It's also useful to learn as much as you can about the cultures and the country you'll be travelling in, in advance of a trek. The titles in this bibliography represent but a fraction of the books available about trekking in the Himalaya, many of which should be easy to track down via the internet or libraries, while some of the more esoteric titles may be found in the bookshops of Kathmandu's Thamel district.

General

Barrett, Robert LeMoyne, and Barrett, Katherine. *The Himalayan Letters of Gypsy Davy and Lady Ba* (Heffer & Sons, 1927; Book Faith India, 1994) An unusual but poetic account of a year's travels in Baltistan (the Karakoram) and Ladakh.

Deegan, Paul. *The Mountain Traveller's Handbook* (British Mountaineering Council, 2002) A useful handbook full of good advice for trekkers and mountaineers.

Gilchrist, Thomas R. *The Trekkers' Handbook* (Cicerone Press, 1996) Long out of print but worth hunting for, full of practical advice on all aspects of trekking, and written with a light touch by an experienced trek leader.

Harding, Mike. *Footloose in the Himalaya* (Michael Joseph, 1989) Humorous but thoughtful accounts of trekking in Zanskar and Ladakh, in the Annapurna region and to Kala Pattar in view of Everest.

Kapadia, Harish. *Into the Untravelled Himalaya* (Indus Publishing, 2005) The subtitle says it all: 'Travels, Treks and Climbs across the Himalayan range'. The author is a highly respected mountaineer and editor of the *Himalayan Journal*.

Murray, WH. *The Evidence of Things Not Seen* (Bâton Wicks, 2002) The memoirs of a much-respected climber and author include tales of mountaineering and exploration in the Himalaya.

Schaller, George B. *Stones of Silence* (Viking Press, 1980) The distinguished animal biologist records his journeys among the Hindu Kush, Karakoram and Nepal Himalaya. In his quest to learn more about the snow leopard, Schaller was accompanied in Dolpo by Peter Matthiessen who described the expedition in his classic book (see below).

Shipton, Eric. *The Six Mountain-Travel Books* (Diadem Books, 1985) Five of the six titles in this single-volume collection relate to Shipton's exploits in the Himalaya – a truly inspirational spur to adventure.

Swift, Hugh. *Trekking in Nepal, West Tibet, and Bhutan* (Hodder & Stoughton, 1989) As the title suggests, this book covers a large part of the Himalaya and is packed with anecdotes, advice and suggestions for numerous treks, as is the companion volume *Trekking in Pakistan and India* (Hodder & Stoughton, 1990).

Tilman, HW. *The Seven Mountain-Travel Books* (Diadem Books, 1983) In this prized collection, six of Tilman's idiosyncratic books deal with his climbs and travels in the Himalaya, and along with the Shipton collection (see above) it contains some of the finest travel writing ever published. Both volumes should be treasured by all who go trekking in the mountains.

Bhutan

Berry, Steven K. *The Thunder Dragon Kingdom* (Crowood Press, 1988) Essential reading for anyone planning to trek to the base camp of Gangkar Punsum, this is the story of a British expedition's attempt to climb Bhutan's highest mountain

Grange, Kevin. *Beneath Blossom Rain* (University of Nebraska Press, 2011) A personal account of The Lunana Snowman Trek in Bhutan.

Jordans, Bart. *Bhutan: A Trekker's Guide* (Cicerone Press, 2nd ed. 2012) Packed with information, the author spent four years living in Bhutan, and has trekked almost every route in the country.

India

Freshfield, Douglas W. *Round Kangchenjunga* (Arnold, 1903) In 1899 Freshfield made a complete circumnavigation of Kangchenjunga.

Gibbons, Bob and Pritchard-Jones, Siân. *Ladakh: Land of Magical Monasteries* (Pilgrims Publishing, Varanasi, 2006) A guide to some of the most interesting Buddhist monasteries in Ladakh. It also gives a concise history and brief cultural background to the kingdom.

Hooker, Joseph Dalton. *Himalayan Journals* (John Murray, 1855) A classic account of early exploration in the mountains of Sikkim and eastern Nepal.

Kapadia, Harish. *Trekking and Climbing in the Indian Himalaya* (New Holland, 2001) A selection of 25 treks of varying lengths spread across the Indian Himalaya.

Kucharski, Radek. *Trekking in Ladakh* (Cicerone Press, 2012) In this handy guidebook the author describes eight treks in the trans-Himalayan mountains of Ladakh.

Norberg-Hodge, Helena. *Ancient Futures* (Sierra Club Books, 1991; Rider, 1992) With the subtitle 'Learning from Ladakh', the author describes how the once remote kingdom of Ladakh has been changed by Western consumerism. A passionately argued book, it should be read by all who plan to visit this land on the northern side of the Himalayan Divide.

Sharma, KP. *Garwhal and Kumaon: A Trekker's and Visitor's Guide* (Cicerone Press, 1998) All you need to know about trekking in the mountain regions of Uttar Pradesh.

Nepal

Boustead, Robin. *The Great Himalaya Trail* (Himalayan Map House, Kathmandu, 2009) A pictorial guide to a trekking route that traverses the Nepal Himalaya from east to west.

Douglas, Ed. *Chomolungma Sings the Blues* (Constable, 1997) The well-known mountain journalist produces a thoughtful account of the Everest region and those who live there.

Matthiessen, Peter. *The Snow Leopard* (Chatto & Windus, 1979; Harvill/HarperCollins, 1989) This celebrated book recounts a journey to Shey Gompa in Dolpo in search of the elusive snow leopard. Beautifully written. If you're planning a trek in Dolpo, read this before, during and after.

Razzetti, Steve. *Trekking and Climbing in Nepal* (New Holland, 2000) A beautifully illustrated rundown of 25 treks in the Nepal Himalaya; both authoritative and inspiring.

Pritchard-Jones, Siân and Gibbons, Bob. *Annapurna: A Trekker's Guide* (Cicerone Press, 2012) One of a series of pocket-size guides to major trekking routes in Nepal from Cicerone.

Reynolds, Kev.

Dolpo, a Trekker's Guide (Pilgrims Book House, Kathmandu, 1997) A slim guide to the Juphal to Jumla trek in Lower Dolpo.

Everest: A Trekker's Guide (Cicerone Press, 4th ed. 2011)

Kangchenjunga: A Trekker's Guide (Cicerone Press, 1999)

Langtang, Gosainkund and Helambu: A Trekker's Guide (Cicerone Press, 1996)

Manaslu: A Trekker's Guide (Cicerone Press, 2000)

Snellgrove, David. *Himalayan Pilgrimage* (Shambhala Publications, 1981) In 1956 the author, a scholar in Tibetan Buddhism, made an epic seven-month journey across Dolpo recorded in this book.

Stevenson, Andrew. *Annapurna Circuit* (Constable, 1997) A highly readable travelogue that describes the author's experience of trekking around Annapurna. It also draws attention to the sometimes culturally insensitive behaviour of some of his fellow trekkers.

Pakistan

Buhl, Hermann. *Nanga Parbat: the Lonely Challenge* (Bâton Wicks, 1998) Buhl's climbing autobiography, culminating in his solo summit climb of Nanga Parbat in 1953.

Curran, Jim. *K2: The Story of the Savage Mountain* (Hodder & Stoughton, 1995) All you ever wanted to know about the world's second-highest mountain.

Herrligkoffer, Karl M. *Nanga Parbat: the Killer Mountain* (Elek, 1954) Early attempts to climb the mountain, and the first ascent by Hermann Buhl.

Rowell, Galen. *In the Throne Room of the Mountain Gods* (Sierra Club Books, 1987) Exciting photographs and text that brings the Baltoro Glacier alive.

Tibet

Mallory, George. *Climbing Everest* (Gibson Square, 2010) The complete writings of the man most closely associated with early attempts on Everest, with good descriptions of the northern approaches.

Pritchard-Jones, Siân, and Gibbons, Bob. *The Mount Kailash Trek* (Cicerone Press, 2007) The Kailash kora is described here, as well as information on Lake Manasarovar and the kingdom of Guge.

Thubron, Colin. *To a Mountain in Tibet* (Chatto & Windus, 2011) In this book by an acclaimed travel writer, the author describes his trek to and around Mount Kailash.

INDEX

LISTING OF CICERONE GUIDES

For full information on all our guides, and to order books and eBooks, visit our website: **www.cicerone.co.uk**.

Walking – Trekking – Mountaineering – Climbing – Cycling

Over 40 years, Cicerone have built up an outstanding collection of 300 guides, inspiring all sorts of amazing adventures.

Every guide comes from extensive exploration and research by our expert authors, all with a passion for their subjects. They are frequently praised, endorsed and used by clubs, instructors and outdoor organisations.

All our titles can now be bought as **e-books** and many as iPad and Kindle files and we will continue to make all our guides available for these and many other devices.

Our website shows any **new information** we've received since a book was published. Please do let us know if you find anything has changed, so that we can pass on the latest details. On our **website** you'll also find some great ideas and lots of information, including sample chapters, contents lists, reviews, articles and a photo gallery.

It's easy to keep in touch with what's going on at Cicerone, by getting our monthly **free e-newsletter**, which is full of offers, competitions, up-to-date information and topical articles. You can subscribe on our home page and also follow us on **Facebook** and **Twitter**, as well as our **blog**.

Cicerone – the very best guides for exploring the world.

CICERONE

2 Police Square Milnthorpe Cumbria LA7 7PY
Tel: 015395 62069 info@cicerone.co.uk
www.cicerone.co.uk